MW01002125

# Controversies
## of the
# Music Industry

The Greenwood Press **Contemporary Controversies** series is designed to provide high school and college students with one-volume reference sources that each explore controversies in seven specific areas important to contemporary life: sports, music, entertainment, medicine, education, business, and law. Students will discover that difficult problems occur across disciplines, that they manifest themselves in many different ways, and that not all of these problems have easy answers. The series' unique focus on those in high-profile professions is designed to help readers consider the importance of ethics in all sectors of society. Students will be encouraged to develop their critical thinking by examining the history of these topics, exploring various solutions and drawing their own conclusions.

**Other Titles in Contemporary Controversies**

Controversies of the Sports World
*Douglas Putnam*

Controversies in the Practice of Medicine
*Myrna Chandler Goldstein and Mark A. Goldstein, M.D.*

# Controversies
# of the
# **Music Industry**

## Richard D. Barnet
## and Larry L. Burriss

*Foreword by Paul D. Fischer*

Contemporary Controversies

**GREENWOOD PRESS**
Westport, Connecticut • London

**Library of Congress Cataloging-in-Publication Data**

Barnet, Richard D., 1949–
   Controversies of the music industry   /   Richard D. Barnet and Larry L. Burriss ;
foreword by Paul D. Fischer
       p. cm.—(Contemporary controversies, ISSN 1522–2047)
   Includes bibliographical references and index.
   ISBN 0–313–31094–7 (alk. paper)
   1. Popular music—Social aspects—United States.   2. Popular music—Moral and
ethical aspects—United States.   I. Burriss, Larry L.   II. Title.   III. Series.
ML3918.P67 B37   2001
   780—dc21        00–052432

British Library Cataloguing in Publication Data is available.

Library of Congress Catalog Card Number: 00–052432
ISBN: 0–313–31094–7
ISSN: 1522–2047

First published in 2001

Greenwood Press, 88 Post Road West, Westport, CT 06881
An imprint of Greenwood Publishing Group, Inc.
www.greenwood.com

Printed in the United States of America

The paper used in this book complies with the
Permanent Paper Standard issued by the National
Information Standards Organization (Z39.48–1984).

10 9 8 7 6 5 4 3 2 1

# Contents

# Foreword

Music has been controversial in America since before nationhood. In 1735 New York newspaperman John Peter Zenger was sued for seditious libel for the contents of the paper he published. Part of those contents were lyrics of ballads lampooning the British governor of New York and his cronies. His attorney, Alexander Hamilton, mounted an energetic defense, swaying the colonial jury and winning Zenger's acquittal. The case is most often cited as a precedent for freedom of the press, but it can also be seen as putting song lyrics into the category of "protected speech" long before the Declaration of Independence and the U.S. Constitution were passed. The Zenger case was just the first skirmish in an ongoing struggle.

The United States of America, as a nation, is an experiment in the rule of law. That our Constitution and other governing documents have survived over two hundred years without serious challenge is a political marvel. Culturally, however, two hundred twenty-odd years makes us a toddler. Compared to the cultures of Europe, the Middle East, Africa, and Asia, many of which have thousands of years of continuous history behind them, our creative expressions often seem loud, bawdy, unrefined, and, frankly, unattractive. In time, with greater practice and more refined public taste, the aesthetics of American expression are likely to improve. But the world has acknowledged significant American contributions in the realm of music. The blues, jazz, ragtime, rhythm and blues, country and western, rock 'n' roll, hip-hop, and more have been acknowledged as important forms of indigenous American expression.

As these forms of music have come to mainstream public attention in America, they have often encountered resistance. Part of the originality of many of these forms has been the way they combine varied elements of American culture, often creating hybrids out of African and European styles and traditions. America, having been a legally segregated nation from 1896 through 1954, was not always ready for the new hybrids and the lack of respect they showed for social "norms." This created friction and occasionally opposition to newly popular songs, styles, and artists. Jazz in the 1920s, rhythm and blues in the 1940s and 1950s, rock in the 1950s and 1960s, and hip-hop in the 1980s and 1990s all had social force.

White audiences drawn to jazz and rhythm-and-blues performances in the first half of the century all but demanded renegotiation of the color line. The presence of African American artists and fans on national television, beginning with *American Bandstand* and variety shows like *Ed Sullivan* in the late 1950s, continued the pressure for progress in this area. Gospel and folk music carried the conscience of the civil rights movement to a broad audience using song, and folk's influence on rock added weight to the antiwar movement of the 1960s and 1970s. Rap and hip-hop have done much to raise awareness about ongoing prejudices and inequalities present in America's cities. Rooted in America's dedication to individual liberty and freedom of expression, some popular music has helped this nation develop greater self-awareness and a deeper social conscience. This is often a controversial process.

During this same period popular music has become big business. Since the 1970s the recording industry has contributed at least a billion dollars to America's balance of trade every year. Music is one of our biggest exports because it is valued so highly around the world. But corporate entities that make money from music rarely make decisions based on what's best for the health and evolution of American musical culture. The music must find ways to avoid dangerous collisions at the crossroads of creativity and commerce. Also, opponents to some aspects of musical expression at home have challenged music and musicians in the courts and on Capitol Hill. Popular music in America has become a frequent battleground in the so-called culture wars and requires ongoing vigilance, awareness, and protection if it is going to continue to contribute positively to American culture. Its possible negative effects are being debated publicly too.

If America is to remain a free country, dedicated to freedom of expression and the other principles set forth in its founding documents, its music must remain free as well, so recording artists can continue to "call it as they see it" for the benefit of their audiences. In this book, authors Richard D. Barnet and Larry L. Burriss take up discussion of many of the conflicts and controversies America's popular music has generated. Whether these conflicts are creative, cultural, or commercial in nature, discussion of such controversies is good for American culture. Only in discussing the ongoing impact of popular music in America, from all sides and points of view, will popular music's importance as a unique element of America's culture be driven home to a broader audience. Thank you for joining the discussion.

Paul D. Fischer
Associate Professor, Department of Recording Industry, MTSU
and President, International Association for the Study of
Popular Music, U.S. Branch

# Acknowledgments

I am deeply grateful to my wife, Sarah, for giving me continuous encouragement throughout the writing process. Her proofreading truly helped tremendously and she has been my angel.

I am especially grateful to Middle Tennessee State University for providing me a noninstructional assignment so that I could complete this book. In addition, the Center for Popular Music at Middle Tennessee State University was an invaluable source of information. Both the staff members and the holdings of the center made a positive impact on this work.

Our editor, Debby Adams, has been a patient mentor throughout this entire project. We could not have done this without her.

Thanks to all the persons who shared their insights into the music industry through interviews and correspondence. And, of course, thanks to the music industry for having so much controversy!

—Richard D. Barnet

For Erik—who never really listened to the music at the garden party anyway. For Justin—in those chilly hours and minutes I still can't believe the first time you called the music of Simon and Garfunkel and the Rolling Stones "those old songs." For Kathleen—constructing different meanings from the same old-fashioned love songs.

—Larry L. Burriss

# Methodology

The authors of this work selected twelve controversies related to the music industry that affect consumers as well as industry professionals. The controversies were selected because they have evolved over time and continue to pose questions for our contemporary society to debate. Another criterion for a controversy to be considered was its impact on society. In addition, the level of public misunderstanding of an issue was also considered, because the music industry is plagued by misinformation.

Each chapter presents one controversy and the issues surrounding it. A historical overview offers readers background information necessary to formulate arguments on either side of each controversy and its related issues. A major goal of the authors was to help readers arrive at an informed opinion regarding each controversy by presenting the viewpoints of all sides.

Analysis of each music industry controversy includes possible scenarios for the future. It is likely that some of the issues presented in this book will be the subjects of heated debate at the national level in the first half of the twenty-first century.

This work includes topics for discussion, references, and resources, at the end of each chapter. The topics for discussion will be helpful for teachers, debate teams, and journalists discussing controversies of the music industry. The reference and resource lists include web sites, books, periodicals, interviews, and organizations for those who wish to engage in additional research.

Readers of this work will have the tools to engage in meaningful discourse about the music industry. They will also, hopefully, become more active participants in legal, social, and economic decisions about music in our society.

# 1

# Money, Music, and Marketing: A Few Multinational Companies Dominate the Music Industry

If one company were to dominate an industry, the public would cry "monopoly" and the federal government would take legal action. But when a handful of companies controls an industry, there is rarely a public outcry and the federal government has little power to prevent it from continuing. The term that describes a few companies dominating an industry is "oligopoly." The music industry, much like the soft drink and automobile industries, has seen the emergence of a few multinational corporations that have a strong grip on the industry. These entertainment conglomerates sell the majority of CDs and tapes in the marketplace. The question you might ask is, How does this affect me?

The most immediate impact that the music industry oligopoly has on our lives is the music we hear on the radio and the CDs we buy in record stores. Radio stations play records that are sometimes described as "bland formula music." Radio station music directors typically blame the record companies and say, "We play the best records they send us!" All the free stuff that the stations get from the big record companies—some of which they don't like to discuss—is another reason that radio stations play records from major labels more than records from small labels.

When we visit record stores, we find their bins full of the "Top 40" acts and their accompanying barrage of in-store promotional materials. What is missing, unfortunately, is diversity in the music they offer. Record retail chains are paid millions of dollars by large record companies each year for in-store promotion. A record store owner sees two options: display major label products and receive thousands of dollars for merely advertising them in your store or place numerous high-quality innovative recordings released by independent labels in your racks without much financial support. Obviously, the decision is easy for a store owner.

The largest record companies argue that they are merely practicing good business procedures. But to the smaller companies, it feels like a handful of bullies throwing their weight and money around! Much to the dismay of creative individuals in the industry, especially songwriters and performers, industry executives point out that "show business" is two words. As in most businesses, record company executives must answer to owners or shareholders. Not surprisingly, large record companies are run like any other type of business, and only the strong, aggressive companies survive in the long run.

## A BRIEF HISTORY OF THE MUSIC INDUSTRY IN THE UNITED STATES

Although the music industry in the United States started shortly after the Pilgrims settled on the coast of New England, it did not become a dynamic economic force until the twentieth century. Unlike most other industries, the music industry endured an incubation period of three hundred years. As an art form, music for entertainment has been dependent on the media that deliver it to the public.

If one views the media as "delivery systems" that capture an art form and present it to an audience, then the history of music in America must include the evolution of mass media. The volatile and ever-changing economy has also been a significant factor influencing the development of music and recording. Perhaps most important, the changing values and tastes of our evolving population have affected the music industry. What other nation on the planet could have served as the catalyst for rock 'n' roll, blues, jazz, and country music?

In order to better understand the mindset of our Puritan founders, who unloaded their ships on Plymouth Rock in 1620, one needs to examine their motivation for leaving home to pursue a new lifestyle. The group of English Protestants, soon to be colonial immigrants called Pilgrims, wanted the freedom to practice religious worship ceremonies their own way, not the way dictated by the British monarchy or the Vatican. A terribly important element of that religious celebration was congregational singing. More specifically, they wanted to sing biblical Psalms using simple melodies. These people, the Pilgrims, brought very few musical instruments to America because space on ships like the Mayflower was a precious commodity. Also, they didn't believe in using instruments during worship. The music that these early settlers brought to their new world was transported in two forms: notated and memorized. Some popular songs from Europe were preserved as sheet music called "broadsides" because of their large size. Classical compositions and music for worship services were also notated, but because many of the Pilgrims held in their memories a wealth of popular and folk music from the old country, they passed songs on to their children through the oral tradition.

Books that contained music for church services were called "Psalters." They contained rhythmic settings of biblical text intended for congregational singing in church services. The Pilgrims fled their homeland in pursuit of religious freedom. Therefore, as one might expect, the performance of music in religious ceremonies was of primary importance to the Pilgrims. In fact, the first work published in the colonial United States was the *Bay Psalm Book*, one of the early Psalters used by colonists.

Mention the word "Pilgrim" and most people conjure up images of highly religious people completely preoccupied with the mundane work of subsistence. One would hardly expect the spartan lifestyle of the colonists to give birth to a music industry! Ironically, though, the zealous preoccupation with ensuring a uniform church service gave rise to our music publishing industry. The importance of congregational singing is quite evident, for example, in the following description of the going away party in July 1620 for a group of future Pilgrims: "We refreshed ourselves, after tears, with singing of Psalms, making joyful melody in our hearts as well as with the voice, there being many in our congregation very expert in music" (Winslow, 1646, in Pratt, 1980, p. 6). The allusion to many members of the congregation who were "expert in music" is significant. It was, most likely, a way of describing persons who could read music and sing well. Performing music by reading music notation was later referred to as the "proper way" by church elders in New England. The proper way was encouraged, and the "common way"—learning songs by ear—was discouraged. The proper way of singing Psalms was thought to preserve the consistency of the worship service. The common way, in contrast, was susceptible to variations as the song was passed from one person's memory to another's.

### Music Publishing Is Born

The Psalter the Puritans brought to America was a version created by Henry Ainsworth and published in Amsterdam in 1612. The Ainsworth Psalter was used by the colonists until it was replaced by the *Bay Psalm Book*, created in America around 1692 (Chase, 1994, p. 8). The *Bay Psalm Book*, though printed in Cambridge, England, was published and distributed in the colonies. It is, therefore, considered the first book published in the United States. It also launched our music industry into the first phase of development: music publishing.

Although church leaders urged members of the congregation to preserve the integrity of psalmody, the inevitable secularization of the colonists emerged. Much to the displeasure of the clergy, the public became increasingly interested in popular English ballads and instrumental dance music. One famous religious leader of the colonial era, Cotton Mather, expressed his disdain for popular music in 1713 in a blistering commentary: "I'm informed that the Minds and Manners of many People about the Countrey [sic] are corrupted, by foolish Songs and Ballads which by the Hawkers and Peddlars [sic] carry into all parts of the Countrey" (Colonial Society, 1620–1859).

The hawkers and peddlers Mather referred to were early distributors of sheet music imported from England. As printing technology improved, some of these music distributors evolved into full-service publishers of music. This, the first phase of an emerging music industry, was focused on selling printed copies of sheet music. Performance of the published music took the form of sing-alongs with piano in one's own home or concerts for the general public performed by professional musicians.

Reliance on income from printed music continued until the invention of devices, such as player pianos and phonographs, that relieved consumers from having to perform music themselves. This, the second phase of the music industry, shifted the focus from selling printed music to selling recordings that contained copyright-protected music and, of course, manufacturing and distributing the hardware to play those recordings. The activities of song publishers have, since the invention of the phonograph, gradually become more focused on licensing copyrights of songs and less concerned with creating printed copies of music.

Although publishers were able to sell many copies of popular songs in the form of sheet music well into the twentieth century, increasing manufacturing costs and competition made it difficult to show adequate profit margins. In 1920 a printers' strike increased the labor costs at the same time a shortage of paper jolted the publishing industry. As a result of these two factors, the cost of creating sheet music increased 50 percent while the retail selling price remained constant. During this same period of time, sales of phonograph records that paid royalties to music publishers became increasingly successful in the postwar marketplace. As noted music-publishing scholar Russell Sanjek observed, "Almost overnight, in 1921 the American public turned from sheet-songs to phonograph records for its music" (1983, p. 13).

### Birth of the Recording Industry: The Mechanical Phonograph

Although in 1877 Thomas Edison invented a device he called the "talking machine," the recording phase of the music industry—an industry that today accounts for $38.1 billion per year worldwide—took a great deal of time to become firmly established. From its inception the recorded-music industry has observed a push-pull relationship between its two components: recordings and devices that play recordings. As the hardware to play recordings evolved, the software struggled to catch up.

Thomas Edison made the first known "record" in 1877 when he recorded someone singing "Mary Had a Little Lamb" on his tin-foil cylinder phonograph. He was granted a patent for his crude recording device and, thereby, launched the acoustic phase of the recording industry. The following year he founded the Edison Speaking Phonograph Company. His company did not, as one might expect, move aggressively into the marketplace. Some historians suspect that he devoted most of his time during the next decade to his new invention: the lightbulb.

The first company to compete with Edison's was the American Graphaphone Company created in 1887 by Alexander Graham Bell and his partner, Charles Tainter. The Graphaphone group manufactured and sold a phonograph that played music captured on wax-coated cardboard cylinders. Although Bell's company did not emerge as a dominant company, one of his original investors, Edward D. Easton, was motivated to form his own company in the nation's capital, the District of Columbia, in 1889. He chose the name Columbia Phonograph Company. Even after being acquired by several corporate entities since its inception—CBS and Sony—Columbia remains one of the most respected names in the recording industry today.

One year later, in 1888, German-born Emile Berliner invented the seven-inch disk for recording and a player he called the gramophone. He formed the Gramaphone Company to manufacture and market his new record players and the discs to play on them. Although Berliner's record-playing phonograph was a brilliant concept, the mechanism to power the turntable was quite crude. Another inventor, Eldridge Reeve Johnson, improved the mechanism of the disk player and created a device he called a Victrola. After several years of struggling with patent disputes, lawsuits, and fierce competition, Johnson and Berliner joined forces to form the Victor Talking Machine Company in 1901. The company logo, the famous "Little Nipper" dog looking into a Victrola, went on to be associated with RCA Victor Records. The RCA logo remains one of the most recognizable images in America's recording industry.

By 1889 Edison began to sell recordings to be played on his new line of phonograph machines. In order to produce recordings, he created the first recording studio. At the same time, other companies began to create phonographs and records. Edison, the man who had tried, and failed, to gain a monopoly for his invention, suddenly found himself in an extremely competitive market. Although numerous companies were manufacturing phonographs and records by 1914, three companies emerged as industry leaders.

The three giants of the evolving music industry, Victor, Columbia, and Edison, were dominant for several reasons. Between 1880 and 1910 the

The original Edison Tin-foil Phonograph. West Orange, New Jersey, circa 1877. (U.S. Department of the Interior, National Park Service, Edison National Historic Site)

Thomas Edison with the Cylinder Phonograph. Washington, D.C., April 18, 1878. (U.S. Department of the Interior, National Park Service, Edison National Historic Site)

population of the United States doubled, making the pool of potential customers a continually increasing one. The big three had developed extensive channels of distribution for their respective products, whereas the smaller companies usually had only regional retail outlets to sell their products. In addition, each of the big three had active research and development divisions whose mission it was to continually improve upon the technology of phonograph recordings.

Sales of phonographs and records went hand in hand during the early days of the recording industry. Each of the big three manufacturers worked constantly to develop newer recording and playback technologies in order to have bragging rights to "state-of-the-art" records and phonographs. Retail stores had the burden not only of stocking hardware and software but also of repairing the equipment they sold. Repairs required the store to keep an extensive inventory of parts and a staff of trained repair technicians. As a result, stores tended to sell and service only one brand. As one might expect, the big three were much more effective in gaining exclusive agreements in specialty stores than were the smaller manufacturers.

Soon after Victor, Columbia, and Edison emerged as industry leaders, the music industry was catapulted into a dreadful economic period. Too many companies had entered the marketplace, contributing to a decline in music profits. In 1914 there had been 18 companies in the recording industry, but as the economy rebounded, by 1918 the number had soared to 166. Recording companies proliferated when many of the early patents for phonographs and gramophones expired in 1917, making it even more attractive for entrepreneurs to enter the market. Although Edison's company had its best sales year ever in 1920, the next year's sales were less than 25 percent of the previous year's sales! As they entered the next decade, the recording companies had little to celebrate and could hardly look forward to what came to be called the Roaring Twenties.

To compete, many companies reduced prices for their hardware and software, a business strategy that caused profits to shrink and caused many smaller companies to go out of business or be purchased by stronger companies. The big three saw their sales of disc players decline to unimaginable low points. Columbia was in such bad financial shape that it sought protection in bankruptcy court and creditors eventually took control (Millard, 1995, p. 74). It was clear that the music industry's leading triad needed to change strategies. One change considered was more reliance on sales of recordings and less on sales of phonographs.

The 1920s represented a shake-out period that forced music companies to look at the music preferences of consumers. Until that time recordings had not been thought of in terms of a particular style. Instead, music had been conceived as a generic product that could be recordings of a symphony orchestra, a military band, an opera singer, or a blues singer. The smaller labels were the first to pursue new styles of music in an effort to win customers from different socioeconomic backgrounds and geographic regions. Gradually, styles such as blues, jazz, and "hillbilly music" (the predecessor of country music) were made available to American audiences. But to some industry leaders, the roaring success of radio was threatening the very existence of the music industry.

ALL OF THESE MODELS WILL PLAY THE NEW BLUE AMBEROL RECORDS JUST AS WELL AS OUR AMBEROLA MODELS. SEE THE OTHER SIDE OF THIS PAGE FOR PARTICULARS

A page from a catalog showing the complete line of Edison Disc Phonographs available to consumers in 1913–1914. The advertisement informs buyers that they can play newer "Blue Amberol" as well as older "Amberola" records on these devices, illustrating the importance Edison placed on selling both recordings and the hardware on which to play them. (U.S. Department of the Interior, National Park Service, Edison National Historic Site)

## The Modern Era: Radio and Electronics

Competition from a new entertainment source called radio no doubt chiseled away some of the potential sales of recordings and phonographs in the early part of the Roaring Twenties. And why not? Radios were fairly inexpensive, and the music they brought into one's home was free. Historian Andre Millard summarized the social climate of the 1920s: "Radio captured the imagination of the American public, and in living rooms all over the country, phonographs and gramophones were abandoned for another talking machine" (Millard, 1995, p. 138). To make matters worse, the audio quality of radio, with its greater dynamics and expanded frequency range, was perceived by consumers to be far superior to the anemic sound of acoustic phonographs. It was obvious that the music industry had to improve the technical quality of its recordings and phonographs and to learn to compete in a brutally competitive economy.

The first commercial radio station began regularly scheduled broadcasts in 1919. The station, KDKA in Pittsburgh, was owned by Westinghouse Electric and Manufacturing Company. The advent of commercial radio ushered in the next era of the music industry: the electronic phase (Read and Welch, 1976). Not even broadcasters anticipated how quickly Americans would embrace radio. The amazing popularity of radio developed an audience of millions after only two years!

Record companies initially chose to ignore two important points. First, radio had the potential to present and promote recording artists to a much larger public than live performances. Second, just as the phonograph had replaced the parlor piano as the home entertainment center, the family radio was quickly beginning to nudge the phonograph to a secondary position in America's households. Like ostriches with their heads buried in the sand, music industry executives ignored radio and hoped that it was a passing fad.

It was obvious to radio station programmers that they needed more than news, weather, and agricultural reports to satisfy listeners for long periods of time. In order to create programs that included popular musicians of the day, radio stations approached recording artists. To the amazement of broadcasting executives, most were prevented from performing on radio because they were bound to exclusive contracts with their respective record companies. Only musicians who recorded under nonexclusive contracts (so that they could record for more than one record company) had the legal flexibility to perform radio shows.

Gradually, however, record companies eased into a symbiotic relationship with radio. The Victor company was the first of the big three to allow its recording artists to work with broadcasters. On February 12, 1925, Renee Chemet, a classical violinist signed to an exclusive recording contract with Victor, played on a network radio show (Reed and Welch, 1976, p. 256). Although that feat was noteworthy, the fact that Victor sponsored the show was even more amazing. Other record companies gradually began to view radio as a valuable promotional tool and, therefore, permitted their recording artists to participate in broadcast performances.

Record companies also saw an alliance with radio broadcasters as a mutually beneficial arrangement. A phenomenon emerged that remains unchanged today: If listeners like a performer they hear on the radio, they are inclined to go to the record store to buy a recording by that same artist. The expression "Spins create sales" is still used by record executives. The promotional reach of radio was counted in millions. Therefore, record companies gradually shifted resources from newspaper and magazine advertising to plugging their artists to radio stations.

The other problem the music industry faced—poor audio quality— was solved by a most unlikely inventor: the telephone company. During World War I the need for electronic voice transmission technology spurred the development of microphone and amplifier equipment necessary for wireless telephones. Researchers at AT&T's Bell Labs developed a recording process that used vacuum tubes, like those used in radios at the time, to amplify sounds that were converted to electrical current by their electromagnetic recording head. The electronic signal was later converted back to sound by their reproducing device, the modern phonograph. The electronic record player was thus born, and struggling record companies did not hesitate to license the new technology. The first electrically recorded discs were created in 1925. The Edison company stopped manufacturing acoustic cylinders and discs in 1929, punctuating the end of the acoustic era of the recording industry. (Note: Although the Bell Labs technology is typically referred to as "electronic recording" today, it was initially called an "electrical recording" process.)

From a business perspective, the decade of the 1930s was perhaps the most volatile period that the music industry has ever endured. The stock market crash of 1929 signaled the beginning of the Great Depression in America. Sales of records and record players were ravaged by the obvious lack of spendable income that descended on the population like a plague. Some large companies, however, were able to capitalize on the economic climate by acquiring troubled music companies.

### The Corporate Chess Board

During the turbulent 1930s, the Victor company became a part of the Recording Corporation of America (RCA); Columbia recording company merged with the American Recording Company and became a part of Columbia Broadcasting System (CBS); the Edison Company had lost its dominant position in the industry and was replaced in the powerful triad by Decca Records. It seemed as if recording companies were being brokered according to some grand scheme. The message was loud and clear: The recording industry is no longer an autonomous enterprise; it is part of a larger, more complex entertainment industry.

Almost overnight, the recording industry emerged from its sales slump. In 1935 sales of records and players accounted for a paltry $9 million. One year later, in 1936, sales had blossomed to an unexpected $31 million. As far as the record companies were concerned, the Great Depression was over. By 1940 the major record companies were no longer concerned only with music. They were parts of larger organizations that included divisions that created films and manufactured a wide range of electronics, including combination radio–record players and automobile radios. Two of the big three, RCA/Victor and Columbia/American Recording Company, were also kindred divisions to powerful broadcasting operations. One fact remained constant: Although the names of companies changed, three record companies still dominated the music industry.

If the 1930s represented a period of transformation for the business structures in the industry, the decade of the 1940s was a time of emerging music styles. Changes in American culture included a migration of African Americans to urban business centers. Both radio programming and recordings reflected the changing demographics of the country. Blues, jazz, black gospel, and other music previously referred to as "race music" by record companies began to rise in popularity but remained stigmatized by an overtly racist industry and society.

The white analog of "race music" was big band dance music. Radio, film, and jukeboxes launched the careers of jazz band leaders and helped create the jazz era. Names like Benny Goodman, Tommy Dorsey, and Glenn Miller became household names. A vibrant postwar economy and a national mood to celebrate added momentum to the rise of danceable big band jazz. Big bands tended to be segregated as did radio formats.

Although the big three record companies continued to focus their attention on recording big bands, classical music, and crooners like Bing Crosby, new entrepreneurial record labels began to emerge. Many of the new start-up labels identified a particular market niche in which to specialize. Two styles that proved profitable were rhythm and blues (R&B) (new terminology to describe race music) and country and western (country). As the big three naively ignored emerging styles, country and R&B not only developed but also contributed to a new genre of music: rock 'n' roll.

As the 1940s came to an end, two important technological innovations were developed. Columbia Records introduced the first twelve-inch 33-1/3-rpm long-playing (LP) album to the world on June 21, 1948. The following year, RCA Victor released its first seven-inch 45-rpm record. From then on, the public would refer to these configurations as "album" and "single."

By 1950 the number of large labels dominating the industry increased to six, including Columbia, RCA Victor, Decca, Capitol, MGM, and Mercury. The term "major label" was coined to refer to the six companies and their affiliated record divisions. Unfortunately for the majors, the growing number of teenagers, eager to buy music distinctly different from the music their parents listened to, tended not to buy the music of the major labels. The growing number of smaller, more specialized record companies were referred to as "independent" labels, or indies. Some indies realized the potential of the teenage demographic and quickly moved to record the type of music teenagers preferred. Meanwhile, the big six moved at glacial speed toward the new youth-oriented music.

In an effort to determine why the new independent labels were becoming so successful at marketing nontraditional music, the majors took a closer look at consumer preferences. The most significant revelation was that white listeners accounted for about 40 percent of the listenership for R&B radio stations (Sanjek, 1996, p. 241). Majors, mimicking the marketing strategies of the independent labels, began attempting to influence disc jockeys (DJs) at radio stations in key cities. Thus, the recording industry's love affair with radio promotion was elevated to a new high.

According to Recording Industry Association of America (RIAA) data, sales of records increased each year throughout the 1950s, with the exception of 1954. Although historians differ on who first coined the phrase "rock 'n' roll," the person typically given credit is Alan Freed, a Cleveland disc jockey whose show, *Moondog's Rock and Roll Party*, became immensely popular. Freed's format included dance-oriented music, especially R&B, and his target audience was teenagers (Millard, 1995, p. 233).

Much to the dismay of many "old guard" industry executives, rock 'n' roll was here to stay! Once again, the independents moved more quickly and more aggressively to sign the new breed of recording artists. Frank Sinatra, who had created his own record label, Reprise, reflected the attitude of most conservative label executives: rock 'n' roll was a "passing fad" (Stokes, 1977, p. 150).

Although the major labels were maintaining their historical oligopoly, the success and proliferation of the indies, the independent labels, was shaking up the corporate ivory tower. The indies experienced a 44 percent increase in sales from 1955 to 1956. From 1954 to 1958, four majors, Columbia, RCA Victor, Decca and Capitol, accounted for 75 percent of all hit records listed in *Billboard*, an industry trade publication. In 1958–1959, the same four were responsible for only 36 percent of all hits (Millard, 1995, p. 229). In 1962 forty-two labels had at least one charted album in *Billboard* (Hull, 1998, p. 29). Clearly, indies were on the cutting edge.

The major labels assumed a new business strategy to deal with the indies: "If you can't beat 'em, buy 'em." Majors began to devour the most successful indies through distribution deals, major stock purchases, and outright buyouts. Of the 3,000 record labels in the United States in 1960, 500 were under the corporate umbrella of one of the majors. The concept of a single-purpose major record company had gone by the wayside. A major record company had become a "family" of owned or controlled "labels" under a corporate umbrella. One thing that helped the majors remain competitive against the hordes of aggressive indies was a unified national distribution system. The indies quickly learned that it was great to get a song played on radio, but they could not benefit from the airplay unless copies were available for sale in the record stores. National distribution was, and remains, another trump card of major labels.

The next two decades saw a consistent pattern of indies carving out a market niche, becoming successful, and then being acquired by one of the majors. Occasionally, the indie-major mergers seemed like logical symbiotic relationships. In the best situations the indies were permitted to operate autonomously and do what made them successful in the first place, that is, scout and develop new talent. The major organization, in contrast, assumed the national distribution and sales function of the new label. Perhaps the most famous, and most "American," indie was Motown Records, the brainchild of music industry mogul Berry Gordy, Jr., who seemed to have found the formula for successful hit records. When Gordy announced in 1983 that Motown would become a part of a major label, MCA, the industry was reminded that the handful of labels that formed the oligopoly were clearly back in control.

## A GLOBAL BUSINESS IN THE DIGITAL AGE

The first digital recordings directed at mass consumers arrived at record stores in 1982. This, the beginning of the digital era of the music industry, also confirmed the end of U.S. control of record companies. Digital technologies, developed initially by Sony music of Japan and the Phillips Corporation of the Netherlands, were no longer wed to American patents. Digital technology forced the music industry to embrace the computer industry and the concept of global economics. The corporate chess board became the globe, not just the United States.

As we entered the final decade of the millennium, six companies controlled the overwhelming majority of records sold in the music industry. Only one of those companies, AOL/Time Warner, remains a U.S.-based company. Sony (Japan) had acquired the Columbia/CBS music legacy;

Capitol Records became a part of EMI (England); Mercury Records was under Polygram (Dutch); MCA was purchased by Seagrams (Canada); and RCA was a division of the Bertellsman/BMG company (Germany).

In 1999 two of the most powerful major label groups merged into a multinational company that has sent shockwaves throughout the industry. MCA, which is owned by Seagrams of Canada, purchased Polygram, one of the most dominant forces in the European music scene. Soon after, Vivendi (France) acquired MCA/Polygram. As of 1996, the combined sales of Polygram and MCA accounted for approximately 25 percent of all recordings sold worldwide (Wacholz, 1996, p. 3). Some industry analysts are asking, Can any indie compete with MCA/Polygram and the four other multinational giants in the next millennium?

## HOW A RECORD TRAVELS FROM SONGWRITER TO LISTENER

The process through which a song becomes a record, and perhaps a lucrative hit, is conceptually somewhat simple. Like most things, though, the process is more complicated in real life. The recording industry, like the medical profession, has become more specialized. At one time someone with a health problem needed to see only the family doctor. Today one must engage a repertoire of physicians who treat only ailments within their specialty. Similarly, record executives no longer scout an act, take them into the studio, and then promote their record. In order to survive in the contemporary music business, one must learn who does what.

Fortunately, one thing has never changed: It all starts with a song. A song is generally viewed as the melody and the lyrics. The harmonies of songs are typically uncomplicated. In fact, it would not be difficult to find a few hundred hit songs that have an identical harmonic progression or chord structure. The arrangement, typically guitar, bass, drums, and back-up singers, is considered part of production, not the song. Therefore, one might find numerous different productions of the same song.

A song is created by someone called a songwriter. (The term "composer" is more appropriately used to describe someone who creates a notated score for symphonic or other fine art music.) As soon as songwriters put the melody and lyrics into a fixed form, such as a cassette recording, federal law recognizes their exclusive rights to that particular work of art. Exclusive rights are referred to as "copyright" and are controlled by the creator of the music and lyrics. In order to further ensure protection of the song, the songwriter registers the song with the federal copyright office housed in the Library of Congress.

Most songwriters want to earn money from the songs they write. Therefore, their next step is to find a publisher for the song. A publisher assumes control of the copyrighted song in exchange for a percentage, typically 50 percent, of the income derived from the song. From that point on, it is the job of the publisher to aggressively attempt to have the song recorded and performed. Any record company that uses the song must pay a few cents per CD manufactured. That money, called "royalties," is split by the publisher and songwriter. Other users of music, such as radio broadcasters, clubs, television broadcasters, and film producers, must also pay royalties to the songwriter and publisher if they use the song's melody or lyrics.

Radio stations are rarely interested in songs that are not recorded and released by reputable record labels. Therefore, getting a recording artist on a label to record the song is an important step for publishers and songwriters. The division of a record label responsible for signing new acts and helping them select songs for their album is the artist and repertoire (A&R) department. Once a recording artist is signed to a label deal, the A&R department assigns a producer to the project. Publishers have staff persons, called song pluggers, who spend many hours pitching the songs of their songwriters to producers and A&R executives. Occasionally, songwriters themselves pitch a song to anyone who might affect the final decision on song selection for an album. The most famous song pitch was by songwriter and actor Kris Kristofferson. It is rumored that he wanted Johnny Cash to hear a song he had written; but even after Kristofferson made numerous attempts to contact him, the man in black wouldn't listen to the song. So Kristofferson rented a helicopter and flew it to Cash's house. After the aircraft landed safely on the lawn, an amazed Johnny Cash said, "If you want it that bad, I guess I better listen to your song!"

After the songs are recorded and made into CDs and cassettes, the label works vigorously to promote the album while shipping copies to retail stores through a distribution system. The primary means for promoting the album is through radio and video. The promotion division of a label is a blend of science, interpersonal communication skills, and voodoo. Label executives basically do anything legal to get metropolitan radio stations to play the record. Indeed, a few promoters have been accused of going beyond legal tactics to get a song on radio!

Major labels have an advantage over indie labels when it comes to radio promotion. Radio station programmers, the people who decide which songs are added to a playlist, become familiar with major label promotion personnel, but not necessarily with the indie representatives. If a radio station program director receives fifty calls in one day, he or she will likely return the call of a familiar promoter first and then the others if time permits. Also, the calls of a major label promoter representing superstars and established artists like Whitney Houston or Garth Brooks will be answered, even if the promoter is calling about an unknown "baby act" album.

If all goes well, radio stations will play the album, listeners will like it, and lots of people will go to a record store to buy the album. A well-coordinated album release plan will also include a tour by the recording artist to "work" the album around the country or even the world. Because new artists typically aren't known well enough to sell large numbers of tickets at concerts, they are often billed as an opening act for an established artist. Again, a major label with an extensive roster of successful acts is better able to promote new artists to concert audiences.

The release of an album is, at best, a dice roll. To improve the odds of success, a label needs to commit a large amount of money for production, manufacturing, and promotion of a new release. A small indie label might be able to invest only $50,000 for an album release. A major label, in contrast, might commit $250,000 or more per album. If releasing an album is a dice roll, then larger promotional budgets have the effect of improving the odds.

## IT'S A MONEY GAME: RECORD COMPANIES TODAY

Labels under the corporate umbrella of one of the five multinational entertainment corporations get their recordings to the public through a complex global distribution system. The parent company owns and controls the branch distribution system. Each of these five enormous entertainment corporations has one organized system for distributing recordings. Each also has numerous labels that feed recorded products to the corporate-owned distributor.

A more accurate term for all the labels under a major entertainment corporation is "major distributed labels" rather than major labels. The mergers that have put numerous record labels under one company have also changed the way we describe the five largest companies, more accurately described as "major label groups" that share a common distribution system. Also, most major label groups are currently owned by multinational entertainment conglomerates that include other media holdings.

The hundreds of smaller record labels—indies—are those that are not owned or controlled by one of the multinational entertainment conglomerates. Most small labels are finding it increasingly difficult to compete in a marketplace controlled by the "big five" majors. Indies often try to avoid going head-to-head with the majors by selling to niche markets rather than to mass markets. Thus, they tend to specialize in a particular style of music. An independent label might, for example, specialize in punk music and release no other styles of music. Other independents focus on trance, ambient, punk, vintage jazz, or dozens of other esoteric styles of music. In other words, independent labels try to carve out a niche that represents a small percentage of the record-buying public but has little competition. In contrast, the majors often release records that represent several different styles, but only styles that have a large percentage of the total market.

## OLIGOPOLY AND NEW MUSIC

A rock band typically pursues a recording contract in order to launch the band's career. If, however, the band performs a cutting edge style of music, it is unlikely that the band will be able to obtain an offer from one of the majors. A large record label that thinks a band's music is not mainstream enough to appeal to a large number of potential buyers will avoid signing the act, no matter how talented the musicians. The band's alternatives are to seek a deal with an independent label or to modify the music to make it sound more marketable. As one might expect, most musicians refuse to compromise their musical integrity by changing their songs or sound. Hence, for their first recording contracts the most innovative bands are usually signed to independent labels rather than to major labels.

Make no mistake about it, the majors would love to sign lots of new cutting edge bands. Unfortunately, the cost of releasing a record through a major label is astronomical. The large distribution system is wonderful, but it comes with a hefty price tag. It is not unusual for a major to spend a half-million dollars on a record release. An independent label, in contrast, can launch a recording into the marketplace at a fraction of that cost. Therefore, it is not possible for a major to sign great numbers of bands. It comes down to basic economics.

You might think, "Wow! This less-expensive album release scenario is great for the independent labels and the artists signed to them!" The sad truth is they rarely see the tremendous sales figures that majors and their acts do. Success generates more publicity, which in turn stimulates more sales. The public usually hears about the success stories: Records that sell 500,000 units are awarded a "Gold Record"; records that sell 1,000,000 units are awarded a "Platinum Album." These awards, presented by the RIAA, are used by the labels as fodder for even more publicity. Unfortunately, the public never hears about the other side of the coin: Of over 17,000 records released to the public, only 9.5 percent sell more than 5,000 units (Silverman, 1996).

Recording artists are paid a percentage of the retail or wholesale price from each record sold. This income, called "artist royalties," is tied to the total number of CDs and tapes sold, much like songwriter royalties. Therefore, artists earn big bucks only if their recordings sell well above that meager 5,000-unit level. It is not unusual for major labels to drop a band from their roster even if they sell 200,000 copies of an album. Again, major labels are most interested in recording artists and styles of music that sell substantial numbers of units.

An ugly catch-22 emerges: A band that hopes to reach superstar status, with its associated six-figure income, must have the distribution and promotional clout of a major label. But in order to sign to a major, all too often the band must modify its art form and image. The most disappointing result of oligopoly in the music industry is the possibility that some great music may never reach the marketplace in its unaltered form. Too often independent releases aren't promoted as vigorously as major releases, and therefore potential buyers never know they exist. Some critics of the music scene in the United States believe that we have, as a result, "homogenized" our music as well as our milk!

Another way oligopoly has affected the music industry is through the disappearance of many independent labels. Some indies cannot compete because they don't have enough capital to weather the inevitable economic downturns. Majors, financed by multinational corporations, are able to loose millions on some bands yet persevere long enough to earn millions on others. An indie label, in contrast, cannot survive too long unless each of its releases at least breaks even. Moreover, the profits from one indie album often subsidize the marketing expenses for the next release on that label. In a viciously competitive market, many indies do not survive.

It is possible, though, to justify the current music industry business system from a Darwinian viewpoint. Perhaps new bands should start out in the indie label environment as a recording industry minor league or apprenticeship. As they hone their craft and learn the ropes of the business, they will begin to attract the attention of major labels. Some "one hit wonders" who released one successful album and then disappeared into the discount bins of record stores might have had longer careers had they first signed with an indie rather than a major.

## SELLING—OR SELLING OUT—AMERICA'S CULTURE?

In looking at the music of the twentieth century as a chronicle of popular culture, one should not overlook the impact of independent labels. One might even speculate that popular music around the world has followed the lead of the United States ever since the development of rock 'n' roll in the 1950s. The many and varied forms of popular music that were developed in the United States, such as R&B, rap, and country, are part of our cultural fabric.

The most significant documentation of our popular music is in the original recordings by the innovators of our indigenous styles. Those original recordings, called "masters," are owned by the record label. If a major label buys an independent label, the masters become property of the new label. This raises concern that some of the independent labels responsible for developing American art forms have been purchased by majors. Moreover, because all but one of the majors are headquartered outside the United States, many masters of indigenous American music are now owned by foreign companies. Whatever opinion one has about multinational labels, this reality must be faced: Three of the most uniquely American indies to succeed in the United States—Geffen Records, A&M and Motown—are currently owned by foreign labels.

Yet, a multinational major label has the ability to present America's music to every corner of the globe. The export of American music cannot be overlooked as an asset to our national economy. In addition, our music also serves as an unofficial diplomat to foreign populations. It is likely that more Europeans know the names Bruce Springsteen and Michael Jackson better than the name John F. Kennedy. Export of American music will likely increase in the future as a result of the efforts of multinational major labels.

## NEW MEDIA AND THE MUSIC INDUSTRY

To say digital transmission of music evolved faster than record labels ever imagined is probably an understatement. Perhaps label executives were lulled into a feeling of security after the federal government amended our copyright laws to protect digital transmission of music via the Internet. The "Digital Performance Rights in Sound Recordings Act," enacted in 1996, did offer some protection of music used on the Internet. But labels quickly learned that enforcement of laws is not as easy as creating laws when it comes to the Internet. Record labels and publishing companies want the means to prevent anyone from making unauthorized copies of music. Furthermore, they want anyone who downloads music from the Internet to pay for it.

One creation the music industry never anticipated was MP3, an acronym for MPEG Audio Layer-3. In layperson's terms, MP3 is a digital compression method that reduces a piece of recorded music to one tenth of its original size so it can be transmitted more quickly over the Internet. After users download the MP3 file to their computer hard drive, they have a high-quality digital recording. More important, they can share the file with friends without losing audio quality as one would when copying cassette recordings to share with friends. Most major labels and music publishers worry that the ease of trading songs using the MP3 format will discourage consumers from buying legal copies of albums and songs.

As more and more Internet users aquire high-speed modems in the twenty-first century, MP3 downloading has become more extensive. In addition, MP3 has made it quick and easy for consumers to download their favorite music. In the year 2000 one MP3 website had 45,000 CD recordings accessible to users. Although the RIAA took legal action against the San Diego–based MP3, piracy of music continues to grow. College students have been identified as a group that frequently downloads music illegally. One university has estimated that 28 percent of its students have copyrighted music on their hard drives. The fears of major labels and publishers seem to have been confirmed: Large numbers of consumers, especially high school and college students, are illegally copying music that has copyright protection.

## NAPSTER TRAUMATIZES THE INDUSTRY

In 1999 Shawn Fanning, a freshman at Northeastern University in Boston, decided to help solve a problem his roommate had complained about: Locating MP3 files on the Internet. Shawn created a software program that provides users a simple way to index and catalogue their music files. In addition to providing the automated system of organizing songs, the system offered a centralized directory that facilitated efficient searches for songs, albums, and artists, thereby making the "borrowing" or "trading" of music easier than ever before (Harmon, 2000).

Shawn Fanning named his system Napster, after the nickname his friends had given him in middle school because of his hair. He allowed users to download Napster software for free, and its use spread quickly, especially among high school and college students. Because college and high school students represent a large number of record buyers, the industry reacted to Napster by filing a lawsuit against the company on May 7, 1999.

The National Music Publishers Association (NMPA) and the RIAA, representing publishers and major labels respectively, sought a preliminary injunction from the U.S. District Court in San Francisco. The lawsuit alleged that Napster contributed to widespread and continued violation of federal copyrights guaranteed the music that was being downloaded freely on Napster. Among the information presented to a federal judge was a study of 2,555 college students conducted by Field Research Corporation and presented by E. Deborah Jay, Ph.D. The field study revealed disturbing information. Every user in the sample was engaged in at least one instance of copyright infringement while using Napster. In addition, the study indicates that at least 87 percent of the songs being copied and downloaded on Napster are infringing copyright laws (Field Research Corporation, cited in Business News Service, 2000).

On July 26, 2000, Chief Judge Marilyn Patel ruled in favor of the music industry and ordered Napster to discontinue operations (Richtel, 2000). However, litigation continues as both sides try to prevail in the courts as well as in the media. Napster Chairman Hank Barry revealed one important fact after Patel's decision was announced: Over 20 million people have downloaded Napster software. One might assume that the practice of downloading music from the Internet without paying for it is now a part of our culture. As Napster battles RIAA and NMPA in the courtroom, other systems for trading music on the Internet have appeared: Freenet, Gnutella, Gnarly!, and Wired Planet. One thing is certain, Napster and MP3 have changed the way all record labels will operate in the future.

## MAJOR LABELS REACT TO E-COMMERCE

In a move that may become a model for media and entertainment enterprises of the future, Internet service provider America Online, Inc. (AOL), acquired Time Warner in 2000. The various AOL/Time Warner divisions will provide music, film, and print media content distributed by traditional means as well as through the Internet. To music analysts, this strategic alliance will offer AOL access to music transmitted over the Internet. More important, music copyrights will likely be more secure because income generated from Warner Brothers music publishing is now part of the corporate bottom line. However, some skeptics worry that AOL will be more concerned with advertising income generated from the Internet sites and less concerned about the royalty income for music used on those sites, even if the music is that of Warner Brothers.

Shortly after employees of the newly merged MCA and Polygram labels adjusted to living under one corporate roof, their parent company, Seagrams, announced their intent to sell all entertainment holdings to Vivendi, a French conglomerate. To visualize the size and reach of Vivendi's holdings, one need only consider that they have operations in ninety different countries and employ 275,000 employees. Vivendi holdings include long-distance and cellular telephone service, satellite television operations, cable television stations, and, more important, a 50 percent share in a European Internet service provider (Schiesel, 2000).

It seems that Seagrams of Canada was merely following the AOL/Time Warner model of having media, entertainment, and Internet portals under one roof. How will the other three major label groups respond to their competition? Capitol/EMI has indicated an interest in merging with AOL/Time Warner rather than trying to compete. German-owned BMG/RCA has forged a corporate alliance with Lycos, an Internet service company. Sony/CBS, the only remaining entertainment conglomerate not to have a major Internet business under its corporate umbrella, will likely merge with one in the future.

## THE FUTURE OF THE MUSIC INDUSTRY

Major labels gained market dominance over independent labels because of several factors. Large multinational labels have the capital to manufacture larger inventories of CDs than do indies. With their company-owned international distribution systems, majors can quickly move many recordings from their CD manufacturing plants and warehouses to retail stores if a song suddenly gets radio airplay. Indeed, it is more likely that radio stations will play songs promoted by major labels. It is quite possible, however, that some of these advantages may crumble as we enter the new millennium.

If consumers of the future ignore retail record stores and turn instead to Internet "stores" for record purchases, traditional distribution channels will be less significant. Another possibility is the replacement of radio with other music delivery systems such as web radio and satellite-to-automobile radio, both of which have quietly entered the marketplace. In addition, "buying a record" may be replaced with "downloading a record" off the web. Downloading eliminates the need for labels to manufacture, warehouse, and ship tangible products. This will have the effect of leveling the playing field for indies as they compete with the major label groups.

If the delivery system changes this radically, the industry will, in all likelihood, affect what music the public listens to and how they listen to it. A "digital label," compared to a traditional recording company, will be fairly inexpensive to start. In the new web-based music industry, new and innovative record labels, many of which are owned and operated by the artists themselves, will likely be created with the click of a mouse.

One recording artist, Ani DiFranco, seems to have her finger on the pulse of the industry and has already created what some people call the "label of the future." Ani started her label, Righteous Babe Records, from her apartment in New York. She did so initially as a way to make her own marketing and creative decisions rather than letting an executive in an office building make them. She moved aggressively toward promoting her records over the Internet and soon became so successful that she began signing other recording artists to her label. Her formula appears to work because Righteous Babe Records has been recognized as one of the most successful independent labels in the world.

Another innovator in the indie music scene, singer-songwriter Mike Rayburn, has broken the mold as far as music careers go. He literally takes his recordings to his customers. Rayburn's touring includes as many as two hundred college campus shows a year. His dedication to college audiences has generated numerous awards, including "America's

Campus Entertainer of the Year" for 1998 and 1999, an honor bestowed upon him by *Campus Activities Today* magazine's readers' poll.

Although Mike Rayburn sells more CDs and cassettes at his shows than do most artists signed to labels, he is not satisfied with that market alone. Therefore, in addition to promoting and selling his albums at his live performances, Rayburn has licensed some of his songs to Songs.com, an innovator in music e-commerce. Songs.com, which was acquired by Gaylord Corporation in 2000, charges music consumers per song rather than per album. This concept seems to be popular for two reasons: Customers don't have to buy the entire album if they only want one or two songs; neither do customers have to pay shipping costs or wait for the music to arrive—it is downloaded immediately.

Although embracing new marketing techniques offered by the digital era, Mike Rayburn believes major labels will continue to steer the industry. He points out that the web offers the same technological tools to majors as it does to indie labels and self-promoted artists. "Therefore, though there will always be a few exceptions to this rule, I believe the major labels will retain their place as leaders in the recording industry," says Rayburn (Rayburn, 1999). He points out a basic fact of life in the industry: "Majors have the cash necessary to get a song on radio, and airplay sells records."

It is logical to assume that because it is becoming easier to establish a label, more indie labels will spring up in the next few years. This proliferation of labels will likely lead to a subsequent shake-out period much like those of earlier decades. It is also possible that many of the new indies will become as successful as other digital age phenomena such as Yahoo, Microsoft, and Amazon.com have become in a relatively short time. If enough indies are truly successful, the system of oligopoly that has hovered over the recording industry since its inception will give way to a more dynamic free market. Perhaps the next stage of the music industry will be called the "Entrepreneurial Era."

## TOPICS FOR DISCUSSION

1. How will small independent labels compete with the major distributed labels in the future?

2. Companies like the Edison Speaking Phonograph Company sold recordings and the devices to play them. How likely is it that major labels will return to that same strategy and merge with companies that manufacture playback equipment?

3. Will major labels still dominate the industry as we move away from manufacturing CDs and begin delivering music over the Internet?

4. The Pilgrims who settled the United States performed music by reading notation from sheet music or from memory. Do musicians today use these methods? Do different musical genre typically depend on one method to the exclusion of the other?

5. How has the income publishers receive from music changed over the years? How will publishers generate income in the future if music is distributed over the Internet?

6. Is "trading" music over the Internet the same as stealing? If Internet users continue to download music for free, will songwriters no longer make a living from music? Will record labels no longer stay in business?

## REFERENCES AND RESOURCES

### Interview

Rayburn, Mike (1999, July 9). Rayburn is an award-winning performer who specializes in campus entertainment.

### Books

Barnet, Richard J., and John Cavanagh (1984). *Global Dreams*. New York: Simon & Schuster. (Part One, "Global Images, Global Beat," provides an excellent comparison of Sony Music and BMG/RCA.)

Chase, Gilbert (1994). *America's Music: From the Pilgrims to the Present*, Rev. 3rd ed. Ann Arbor, MI: Books on Demand. (Part One, "From Colony to Republic," provides a thorough overview of the music during our colonial period.)

Colonial Society of Massachusetts (1620–1859). *Publications of the Colonial Society of Massachusetts*, vol. 22. Plymouth, MA: Plymouth Church Records, 1620–1859. Part I, p. 160.

Frith, Simon. The Industrialization of Popular Music. In James Lull, ed., *Popular Music and Communication*, 2nd ed. Newbury Park, CA: Sage Publications, 1992.

Hall, Charles W., and Frederick J. Taylor (1998). *Marketing in the Music Industry*, 2nd ed. New York: Simon & Schuster. (Hall and Taylor have created a how-to book for anyone interested in marketing a recording, from manufacturing through the channels of distribution.)

Haring, Bruce (1996). *Off the Charts*. New York: Birch Lane Press, a division of Carol Publishing Company. (This is a wonderful book based on numerous interviews with recording industry executives. It provides an in-depth look at the politics and strategies typical of a major record company.)

Hull, Geoffrey P. (1998). *The Recording Industry*. Needham Heights, MA: Allyn & Bacon. (Chapter 2, "Recordings: The Main Stream," presents the evolution of record companies from the beginning of the industry to the present.)

Knoedelseder, William (1993). *Stiffed: A True Story of MCA, the Music Business and the Mafia*. New York: HarperCollins. (The author presents the darker side of the music business through his profile of a major record company.)

Millard, Andre (1995). *America on Record: A History of Recorded Sound*. New York: Cambridge University Press. (An extremely thorough history of music and technology from the invention of the phonograph to the introduction of the compact disc.)

Negus, Keith (1992). *Producing Pop: Culture and Conflict in the Popular Music Business*. New York: Routledge, Chapman and Hall. (Negus describes the people who work for record companies and analyzes the influence they have on music and culture. It is interesting to read an Englishman's diagnosis of the U.S. music industry.)

Pratt, Waldo Selden (1980). *The Music of the Pilgrims: A Description of the Psalmbook Brought to Plymouth in 1620*. New York: Gordon Printers Publishing. (This is a fascinating book that offers a brief discussion of the earliest music performed in this country. The discussion is followed by excerpts from the actual Pilgrim Psalter used in the first colonial church services.)

Read, Oliver, and Walter L. Welch (1976). *From Tin Foil to Stereo: Evolution of the Phonograph*. Indianapolis: Howard W. Sams & Co. (This is probably the best chronology of recording technology in print. Chapter 27, "Corporate Genealogy," is a comprehensive list of the companies that manufactured and distributed phonograph records until the point when the "profusion of labels got too complex.")

Sanjek, Russell (1983). *From Print to Plastic: Publishing and Promoting America's Popular Music (1900–1980)*. Brooklyn: Institute for Studies in American Music, Conservatory of Music, Brooklyn College of the City University of New York. (A brief overview of the publishing industry in the United States during the twentieth century.)

Sanjek, Russell; updated by David Sanjek (1996). *Pennies from Heaven: The American Popular Music Business in the Twentieth Century*. New York: Da Capo Press. (Sanjek and Sanjek offer a historical survey of the recording industry with more attention on the business and legal aspects than other history books.)

Stokes, Geoffrey (1977). *Starmaking Machinery*. New York: Random House. (Stokes chronicles the careers of musicians in the band Commander Cody and the Lost Planet Airmen. The band's ephemeral success in the music industry is well documented and includes much background history on the industry as a whole.)

Vogel, Harold L. (1986). *Entertainment Industry Economics*. New York: Cambridge University Press. (Vogel examines the music industry from the viewpoint of financial analysts on Wall Street.)

Wacholtz, Larry E. (1996). *Star Tracks*. Nashville: Thumbs Up Publishing. (Chapter 6, "Mega Entertainment Corporations," and Chapter 7, "Record Labels," describe in detail the differences between major and independent labels. Wacholtz also illustrates the relationship between labels and distribution arms of affiliated corporations.)

Winslow, Edward (1646). *Hypocrisie Unmasked*. London, England. As cited in Pratt (1980).

## Magazines, Journals, and Newspapers

Business News Service (2000, June 14). Music Industry Files Motion for Preliminary Injunction against Napster. *mi2n Music Industry News Network*.

Harmon, Amy (2000, March 7). Powerful Music Software Has Industry Worried. *New York Times*.

Labaton, Stephen (2000, May 11). 5 Biggest Music Companies Settle Federal Case on CD Price-Fixing. *New York Times*, p. 1.

McCampbell, Candy (2000, August 9). Record Companies Sued for CD Pricing. *The Tennessean*, p. 3E.

Richtel, Matt (2000, July 21). Judge Issues Injunction against Napster's Main Music Activity. *New York Times*, Business Day, p. C1.

Schiesel, Seth (2000, June 21). Vivendi vis-à-vis the Internet. *New York Times*, p. C8.

Silverman, Tom (1996, May 18). Preserving Diversity in the Music Biz. *Billboard*, p. 6.

Strauss, Neil (1995, July 5). Pennies That Add Up to $16.98: Why CDs Cost So Much. *New York Times*, Final Edition, p. C11 (LEXIS).

## Organizations to Contact

Association for Independent Music (AFIM)
www.afim.org
This organization was formerly known as the National Association of Independent Record Distributors (NAIRD). AFIM represents independent labels, distributors, retailers, and other professionals who work in the indie side of the industry.

Edison National Historic Site
Main Street and Lakeside Avenue
West Orange, NJ 97052
Phone: (201) 736-0550
The historic archives of Thomas Edison are documented in the holdings of this organization. They include 5,000 publications from 1869 to 1931. Edison's lab notes, business records, photographs of his inventions, and motion pictures are housed at this site.

National Association of Record Merchandisers (NARM)
www.narm.com
NARM is the organization that represents major distributors, retailers, labels, and support service companies. They conduct research, offer workshops, and support college internship programs at universities that have recording industry degree programs.

## Web Sites

http://ac.acusd.edu/History/recording/notes.html
Recording Technology History (Dr. Steve Schoenherr)

A remarkable web site to accompany a course in history of recording technology taught by Dr. Steve Schoenherr, History Department, University of San Diego.

www.riaa.com

The Recording Industry Association of America, Inc.

This site is the definitive source for recording industry statistics. One can find sales figures broken down by gender, style of music, and configuration (i.e., cassette, CD, or vinyl LP). The RIAA awards Gold Records and Platinum Records; statistics on records that reached these sales levels are archived here, too.

www.rronline.com/reclabel.htm

Radio and Records Passport

*Radio and Records* (R&R) is one of the trade publications widely read by program directors at radio stations and executives at record labels. This particular site lists many record labels' web sites. Merely find the name of the label and click on the name to go directly to the web site.

www.taxi.com/insider.html

The A&R Insider

This is the site of A&R Taxi. For a fee, the company will help bands find recording contracts by submitting demo recordings of their clients to A&R representatives at selected record labels. The site publishes many interviews and articles about various facets of the industry. For example, the "Industry Advice" section of the archives has advice on making demos and selling indie records.

www.themusiczone.com/chart.html

SoundScan Charts

SoundScan is the company that monitors over-the-counter record sales and tabulates these data for the industry. SoundScan "charts" indicate top-selling albums, in rank order, for a particular week.

**2**

# From Hendrix to Cobain: The Drug Culture of Music

Many of the controversies in the media come down to issues of perception and reality. There is the behavior of those involved in the media—the actors, singers, and other performers who engage in real-life activities—and there is the behavior they *pretend* to do or the activities they *appear* to promote. This distinction between the pretend world and the mediated world is particularly vexing when we discuss the nature of drugs in the recording industry. Are we talking about the actual use, and sometimes promotion, of drugs by singers? Are we talking about the glorification and promotion of drug use in lyrics? Or are we talking about music that happens to deal with drug abuse? And what about anti-drug messages that may be present in music?

It is also important that we separate the drug use (and deaths) of rock stars from the songs they are singing. This issue is particularly acute in the music industry, where creative license and the First Amendment often run straight up against societal norms, religious fundamentalists, teachers, parents, and civic leaders.

## DRUG CASUALTIES

One doesn't have to look very far or very long to see the deadly effects of drug usage in the music world, as a simple Internet search reveals:

- Jimi Hendrix (age 27), barbiturate overdose, 1970
- Janis Joplin (age 27), heroin overdose, 1970
- Jim Morrison (age 27), heart attack brought on by alcohol abuse, 1971
- Sid Vicious (age 21), heroin overdose, 1979

- Kurt Cobain (age 27), suicide during heroin overdose, 1994
- Jerry Garcia (age 53), heart attack possibly brought on by long-term heroin addiction, 1995
- Dwayne Goettel (age 31), heroin overdose, 1995
- Shannon Hoon (age 28), cocaine overdose, 1995
- Jonathan Melvoin (age 34), heroin overdose, 1996

And if you can't think of names, you can go to any of numerous web sites devoted simply to lists of dead rock stars (Dead Musician Directory, 1999; Dead Rock Stars Club, 1999; Covault, S., 1999; Premature Death, 1999; Woodall, 1999).

More speculative, but still tragic, are those whose deaths, though not caused by drug overdose, nevertheless followed lives shortened by previous drug abuse. The name of Jerry Garcia, of the Grateful Dead, comes immediately to mind. Another name is that of Elvis Presley. Depending on whom you ask, drugs either ended Elvis's life or were a significant contribution to his death. Ironically, Elvis had been appointed to a federal drug task force prior to his death.

It has also been suggested that the rock music lifestyle is itself a contributing factor to drug abuse:

- The very nature of travel and performing can be debilitating. Top artists may give fifty or more concerts a year and still continue to produce studio work. There is, as a result, a dangerous disruption of normal sleep-wake patterns. A performer may be exhausted, yet he or she still has to be "up" for the show and may thus be tempted to use stimulants. After the performance, in order to get some sleep, the star may have to take depressants or sleeping pills. As the body becomes conditioned to these drugs, increasingly larger doses have to be taken to achieve the desired effect.
- Part of the rock mystique is the use of drugs: "It's just what singers do" is a common misconception. In reality, some or the most energetic and animated performers never use stimulants.
- The notion of rebellion against authority is also a factor. After all, ever since the beginning of rock 'n' roll, the top artists have not been part of the American mainstream, and part of being "outside" has sometimes included drug use.

Dick Hamilton, a substance abuse counselor in Wilmington, North Carolina, said, "Certainly, professions like being a rock 'n' roll musician lend themselves more to chemical dependency. If you're in rock 'n' roll, chances are greater that you're using chemicals than you're not. The

Elvis Presley's untimely death as the result of a drug overdose was a sad reminder that rock music is too often associated with drugs. The expression "sex, drugs, and rock 'n' roll" is not as humorous when an artist loved by millions suffers so tragic a death. (Photofest)

lifestyle and the environment certainly contribute to much of it" (quoted in Irwin, 1999).

Tony Sanchez, in his book about life with the Rolling Stones, describes the early rockers' behavior thus: "Drugs were everywhere on this tour—jars of cocaine, uppers and downers. [Mick] Jagger snorted quantities of coke before every show; he felt he couldn't get up there to dance and scream without the high of the drug. . . . Keith [Richards] fixed so much heroin that on stage he was an eerie, shambling wreck" (Sanchez, 1979, p. 257).

## THEORIES REGARDING THE EFFECTS OF MUSIC ON BEHAVIOR

It could be argued that most kids don't have any direct contact with lifestyles of famous rock stars. After all, the lifestyle of a rock star is far removed from the world most people inhabit. In fact, though, by listening to music that may contain drug-related lyrics, kids come into direct contact with the music lifestyle and all that this lifestyle represents. Thus, in dealing with drug-related lyrics in popular music, we must consider the psychosocial "projective-reflective theory of media." This theory asks, "Do the media *project* a certain viewpoint (i.e., taking drugs is okay) onto society, or do the media merely *reflect* what society is already doing (e.g., kids are already abusing drugs and don't need the influence of music to do so)"?

How you answer these questions depends upon your particular viewpoint. For example, if you believe the "projective" part of the theory, then you probably feel drug-related music exerts an influence on young people that can lead them to drug abuse. You probably also feel there should be controls on music in order to restrict these lyrics. Such controls might include an outright ban, labels on CDs and tapes, or inserting printed lyrics with the recording. If, however, you believe the medium, in this case the music industry, is *reflecting* what is going on in society, then you probably favor more drug education programs. In addition, you also support programs aimed at preventing drug abuse in the first place, perhaps by harsher penalties for drug dealers. In either case, you probably feel that drug-related lyrics have no real impact on youth and that controls are tantamount to censorship and a violation of the First Amendment guarantee of freedom of expression.

Dr. Herbert Kleber, medical director of Columbia University's Center on Addiction and Substance Abuse, speculates:

> Is popular culture leading or following? That's a difficult issue to disentangle. I think it's a little bit of both. . . .
> You can't lay all the blame on popular culture, just as you can't lay all the blame on President Bill Clinton or his parents. . . . But when you have all those entities going against you, then you've got problems. (quoted in Tayler, 1996)

In statements directly related to the content of music, Hillary Rosen, president of the RIAA, has said:

> There is an element of this in the creation of music and in the mirror which recording artists must and do hold to society. Not everything they see and, therefore, not everything we hear in their music is

pretty. But ultimately songs are depictions. They are descriptions and not prescriptions for living. We have to look far deeper than the mere depiction of the problem to find the true root of it. (Rosen, 1996)

Another conflict concerning the effects of music is illustrated by the dispute between the "magic bullet" or "hypodermic" theory of the media and the "agenda-setting function" theory of the media. The magic bullet and hypodermic theories—really the same theory with different metaphors—propose that media messages act something like a bullet or hypodermic syringe, and "inject" messages into listeners and viewers. People who believe this theory contend that lyrics *make* listeners do something. Since the media supposedly exert powerful, yet subtle, influences, there need to be more controls over the message and the messenger (Orman, 1984). Those who believe in the agenda-setting function, however, contend that the media don't so much tell us what to think as they tell us what to think *about*. Proponents tend to believe the media identify the issues in society but leave the solutions to society itself. Thus, the media act as messengers, merely relaying information to anyone who wants to receive it. Drug-related lyrics are therefore merely a manifestation of what is happening in society, and it is society that is driving the lyrics, not the other way around.

We are concerned in this chapter primarily with drug-related song lyrics, not with issues related to drug use in society. First, we assume drug use is bad both for the individual and for society. Second, we need not take up issues such as whether alcohol is a drug, whether marijuana should be legalized, or whether illicit drugs critically affect society. Rather, we are concerned with overt and covert drug-related messages in music. Finally, we must accept the unfortunate assumption that drugs play a role in the lives of many performers and that many performers have died from drug abuse.

## DO WE REALLY UNDERSTAND THE LYRICS?

Another contentious debate revolves around whether listeners actually understand, at a cognitive rather than a physiological level, what lyrics mean. A 1972 study by Serge Denisoff, using the song "Eve of Destruction," found that approximately 33 percent of the listeners said the song meant to them the same thing it meant to the songwriter. Perhaps more significantly, slightly less than 25 percent interpreted the song "wrong"; that is, their interpretation had nothing to do with what the song's composer intended (Denisoff, 1972). Even if music consumers think a song contains drug-related lyrics, we cannot always assume the listeners are accurately interpreting the lyrics. We need to ask ourselves, Are the lyrics in a particular song really about drugs? To answer this question, we must once again delve into the realm of social psychology.

There are two famous sayings in media studies: "Perceived reality *is* reality," and "When perception becomes reality, reality becomes irrelevant." Both statements have a direct bearing on our perception of drug-related lyrics. The first, "Perceived reality is reality," posits that we each carry around in our head various perceptions or ideas based on feelings and attitudes, not on objective facts. For example, if I am from North Dakota, then I will consider (perceive) a temperature in mid-January of thirty degrees to be "warm." Someone from Florida, in contrast, will consider thirty degrees to be "cold." Which is it? Is there an objective truth that defines "warm" and "cold"? If one believes that perceived reality is indeed reality, then there is no totally objective truth in this example. Likewise, if in listening to music you perceive or *think* lyrics are drug-related, then for you they *are* drug-related.

The second statement—"When perception becomes reality, reality becomes irrelevant"—goes along with the first. It doesn't matter what the objective truth is; what matters to you is what you perceive the truth to be. In our later discussion of controversial rock songs that may or may not have drug-related lyrics, you may think the lyrics have a drug message. If you do, probably no amount of evidence will convince you otherwise.

Yet another psychosocial aspect of music controversies involves the "deconstruction" of lyrics. Deconstruction is the notion that what the creator—author, singer, painter, and so on—produced has meaning beyond the mere words, music, or visual art form. Thus, in deconstructing a song, we take the lyrics, not as the writer says they are, but as we interpret them to be. Suppose, for example, a writer has a lyric that says, "I'm going to pot." This is an expression that for years has meant, "I'm getting tired; I'm falling apart; I hurt all over." Further suppose that in the rest of the song the writer tells us about being tired. The pretend lyric in our pretend song goes something like this: "I've been working all day, I haven't rested a lot. I feel so old, I'm going to pot." In deconstructing this song, someone could say, "Ah ha. This person feels so bad, they are going to find some marijuana. That's what the lyric *really* means." Even if the writer explicitly says, "No, the song is about being tired and feeling bad," the deconstructionist will not accept that meaning and will continue to believe firmly (perceived reality is reality, remember) that the song is drug-related. Thus, as we proceed through this chapter, we will continue to question, "What did the artist *really* mean?" and "Even if the artist says the song is not drug-related, we could disagree, couldn't we?" How we answer those questions will reveal as much about the answerer as it does about the song.

## A HISTORICAL PERSPECTIVE

Concerned citizens who discuss drugs in the music industry may well believe our nation's drug problem sprang full grown, like Athena from the head of Zeus, from rock 'n' roll in the 1950s. Another common misconception is that hippies, with their notion of "Tune in, turn on, drop out," were the first music consumers to eagerly pursue music with drug-related lyrics. A closer examination of the history of American music reveals, however, that early in our history there were concerns about explicit drug lyrics. For example, in the 1930s, Cole Porter, in the hit musical *Anything Goes*, mentioned getting a "Kick from Cocaine." Public sentiment was such that he had to change the lyric (Plant, 1999). Some writers even contend that Sigmund Freud, the father of psychoanalysis and an enthusiastic proponent of cocaine use, wrote "a song of praise to this magical substance," which was published in 1884 (Plant, 1999).

So, most types of music, including jazz, rhythm and blues, folk, and rock 'n' roll, have come under criticism for promoting drug use: "American radio kept busy trying to keep its turntable clean of records that dealt with . . . drugs, [and] American songwriters kept busy outwitting the censors with lyrics that had . . . multiple meanings" (Block, 1990). Indeed, in sharp contrast with today's efforts to have record labels provide printed lyrics with CDs in order to warn parents about what their children were listening to, there were early prohibitions *against* putting lyrics on record jackets.

Here is one person's list of the "Top 10" songs most associated with drug use (Violanti, 1993):

1. "Cocaine," Eric Clapton
2. "Purple Haze," Jimi Hendrix
3. "White Rabbit," Jefferson Airplane
4. "The Pusher," Steppenwolf
5. "Mother's Little Helper," The Rolling Stones
6. "Heroin," Lou Reed
7. "Cloud Nine," The Temptations
8. "Casey Jones," The Grateful Dead
9. "Panama Red," New Riders of the Purple Sage
10. "I Want to Be Sedated," Ramones

Interestingly, this list, created by a writer for the *Buffalo News*, illustrates the problem with trying to decide just what is a drug-related song and whether such songs are, in fact, promoting drug use. Eric Clapton's "Cocaine" and the Temptations' "Cloud Nine" certainly seem to be pro-

As far back as the 1930s, musicians such as Cab Calloway used drug-related lyrics in songs. (Photofest)

moting drug use, whereas Jefferson Airplane's "White Rabbit" takes a more fanciful (drug-inspired?) view, obviously based on the Lewis Carroll stories about Alice. At the opposite extreme, Steppenwolf's "The Pusher" seems to be a warning about the dangers of using drugs.

A more "official" list—and thus one more threatening to artists—was created by the Department of Defense (Block, 1990). The list consisted of twenty-two songs considered drug-related, among them

"Acid Queen," The Who

"Along Comes Mary," The Association

"Cloud Nine," The Temptations

"Eight Miles High," The Byrds

"Happiness Is a Warm Gun," The Beatles

"I Get By with a Little Help from My Friends," The Beatles

"Lucy in the Sky with Diamonds," The Beatles

"Mellow Yellow," Donovan

"Puff, the Magic Dragon," various artists

"[Mr.] Tambourine Man," The Byrds

"White Rabbit," Jefferson Airplane

Other songs have been accused of containing drug-related lyrics, though some people contend that those same songs have a more benign interpretation:

"Along Comes Mary" (The Association): Is this a song about a girl-friend named "Mary," who helps the singer get "kicks" and "set them free" to "see reality," or is it about marijuana?

"Bridge over Troubled Waters" (Simon and Garfunkle): Is this a song about taking drugs to escape troubles, or is it a song about a friend who helps us "over troubled waters"?

"Eight Miles High" (The Byrds): The Byrds say it is about an airplane ride, but critics contend commercial planes don't fly that high (42,240 feet) and that the song is about being on a drug-induced high. Is it valid to assume the songwriters knew how high airplanes fly or how many feet are in a mile?

"Honky Tonk Woman" (The Rolling Stones): The song contains an alleged reference to snorting cocaine. Or perhaps it really is simply about a woman in a bar (Ross, 1998).

"I Am the Walrus" (The Beatles): "[This is] one of the most important and studied songs he [John Lennon] ever wrote. 'I am the Walrus,' from the Beatles' *Magical Mystery Tour* album, has been studied since its release for symbolism, drug references and hints about the death of Paul McCartney. . . . [A]t the time of its release many believed the song related to the 'Paul is dead' rumour that was circulating. The lines 'stupid bloody Tuesday' and 'waiting for the van to come' were interpreted by many to refer to McCartney's death" (McCann, 1999).

"Light My Fire" (The Doors): When the Doors were scheduled to sing the song on the *Ed Sullivan Show*, Sullivan, some sources say, insisted that one of the lines in the song was about drugs. Other authorities contend that Sullivan thought the line obscene. In any event, he insisted that lead singer Jim Morrison not sing the lines. Morrison agreed, but then he sang them anyway. The story goes that a furious producer caught up to the group in the dressing room after the segment and said they would never sing on Sullivan's show again. Morrison, so the story goes, said it didn't matter because they needed to be on the show only one time (Barber, 1999; Giegerich, 1998; Prescott, 1997; Walker, 1994).

"Lucy in the Sky with Diamonds" (The Beatles): Writer John Lennon said the initials LSD are not making a reference to the hallucinogen, but are nonsense words about a picture drawn by his infant son. However, reporter Rob Thomas said in late 1999, "From the bizarre imagery to the 'LSD' acronym, it's difficult to buy the Beatles' insistence that the lyrics are a description of a drawing by George Harrison's daughter" (Thomas, 1999). The album cover only adds to the mystery, with marijuana plants prominently displayed in the lower center of the cover.

"One Toke over the Line" (Brewer and Shipley): The title to this catchy little song just about says it all, although the singers insisted the song was about troubles in general, and not particularly about marijuana (Morthland, 1990).

"Puff, the Magic Dragon" (Peter, Paul and Mary): Some have claimed the story is about Jackie Paper smoking marijuana. Peter Yarrow says it is a children's story and not about drugs.

"Rocky Mountain High" (John Denver). Is the song about a drug-induced high, or is it, as Denver insisted, about a natural high from seeing the mountains? Despite Denver's protests to the contrary, several radio stations refused to play the song because of its supposed drug-related lyrics (McDougal, 1985).

"With a Little Help from My Friends" (The Beatles): "[S]ome interpret Ringo's 'friends' to be drugs, an analysis that seems based solely on the line that refers to getting 'high' with the help of friends. [But] I'm pretty sure the song is as obvious as it appears to be, an ode from a lovelorn guy to his friends" (Thomas, 1999).

## RECORD LABELS AND DRUGS

The most blatant pro-drug effort has been the production of the *Hempilation* albums, the first in 1995 and the second in 1998. These compilations of pro-marijuana songs, the first of which sold more than 110,000 copies (Bloom, 2000; Vote for Hempilation 2!, 2000), contain efforts by such diverse groups as Black Crowes, Ziggy Marley, Willie Nelson, and Sacred Reich, which reportedly sent out 5,000 red bongs to radio stations and music critics to promote a new album (Violanti, 1993). Phil Walden, president of Capricorn Records, the company that released the albums, said the records do not "advocate the use or legalization of marijuana," although the royalties from the work went to the National Organization for the Reform of Marijuana Laws (NORML) (quoted in Tayler, 1996). Walden, by the way, is a former board member of NORML.

None of this is to say that the industry is not cognizant of the problem of drug abuse. According to Hillary Rosen, president of the RIAA, a trade association that represents the interests of the largest record labels, the industry has taken action against drug abuse by artists. In addition, Rosen has noted that a number of artists have either taken anti-drug stands or recorded anti-drug songs:

> Artists such as Janet Jackson, Chuck D., Ted Nugent, Steven Tyler, and Little Richard have all publicly criticized drug use. Groups such as Fugazi, Cranberry [sic], the Indigo Girls, Natalie Merchant, Neal Young, the Eagles, de la Soul, TLC, Micalico [sic], Public Enemy, just to mention a few, all have songs on the charts today which discourage and negatively depict drug use. (Rosen, 1996)

However, Rosen has also asserted that the industry would not make any effort to control drug-related lyrics.

On the use of drug-related lyrics on MTV, in testimony before a congressional committee, Rosen was even more emphatic. She said that other industry witnesses had to fabricate a song with drug-related lyrics in order to produce an anti-drug jingle. Rosen noted that criticism of drugs on MTV is part of a conservative anti-media agenda: "I actually defy you to find a video on MTV that glorifies drugs. . . . But the jingle about heroin was a made-up jingle about heroin in a studio. They didn't find a song that said how great heroin was" (Rosen, 1996). Indeed, in a collection of humorous MTV public service announcements, *I Want My MTV*, the only references to drugs were in the anti-drug segments.

As might be expected, others were not convinced of the industry's view of drug-related lyrics. For example, Robert Bonner, former head of the U.S. Drug Enforcement Administration, said: "The record industry in this country has been incredibly irresponsible in terms of the messages that are being put out in lyrics. And have been . . . I think in a very unrepentant way for at least the last 20 or 25 years" (Bonner, 1996).

## DO LYRICS CHANGE BEHAVIOR?

Even if songs are full of drug lyrics, there is still the question of cause and effect: Does listening to such lyrics make kids take up illegal drugs? Unfortunately, all the data, such as they are, reflect simple speculation or word of mouth. For example, Mark Silva, who spent time in a rehabilitation facility for using marijuana, LSD, cocaine, Ecstasy, and a cat tranquilizer, said, "I know individuals who are drug-free who listen to the same music . . . as kids who do drugs. I believe it's the environment you're in and where you're at with your families and how you view yourself" (quoted in Tayler, 1996).

In addition, Dr. Harolyn M. E. Belcher of the Kennedy Krieger Institute and Dr. Harold E. Shinitzky of the Johns Hopkins School of Medicine, writing in the October 1998 issue of the *Archives of Pediatrics and Adolescent Medicine,* have identified a number of factors that can contribute to the use of drugs by children: low self-esteem, abuse or neglect, association with others who use or tolerate drugs, and lack of self control. Overall, they note, "Genetics, personality traits and family, peer group, and community influences all affect the likelihood that a child or adolescent will use drugs" (Belcher, 1998).

## DRUG LYRICS AND THE GOVERNMENT

Because drug use constitutes a "clear and present danger to society," the federal government has made several attempts to work with the entertainment industry, in particular the music industry, to "denormalize" drug use. But such efforts have, in many cases, led only to confusion and bewilderment. On March 5, 1971, for example, the Federal Communications Commission (FCC) issued a notice that said it was up to the licensee, not the government, to regulate drug-related lyrics. Furthermore, according to the FCC, playing such songs may be permissible if station management is aware of the lyrics. "The thrust of this notice is simply that the licensee must make that judgement and cannot properly follow a policy of playing such records without someone in a responsible position (i.e., a management level executive at the station) knowing the content of the lyrics" (Licensee Responsibility, 1971). On the surface, the notice seems clear-cut: The licensee has to be aware of the content of records it plays. However, public outcry against the measure was immediate, with several newspapers claiming that the notice was an order from the FCC not to play certain records (Stations Told to Halt, 1971; FCC Bars, 1971).

As a result of this confusion, which seems to plague much of the debate about drug lyrics in music, barely six weeks later, on April 19, 1971, the FCC was forced to issue another statement to clarify the first: "We stress that such an evaluation process is one solely for the licensee. The FCC cannot properly make or review such individual licensee judgments" (In the Matter of Licensee Responsibility, 1971, p. 378).

In regard to a list of songs circulated by the Department of Defense, the FCC noted it had no part in creating the list and would have no part in using it to enforce actions against stations (p. 379). However, in what was apparently another about-face, the FCC later said that playing such records might not be "responsible" (p. 379). To add to the confusion, although the FCC may have been saying a station could be penalized for playing drug-related lyrics, a federal appeals court in *Yale Broadcasting* (1973) seemed to say otherwise, noting that what some listeners may perceive as "music," others perceive as simply noise, making effective regulation meaningless. Thus, "No radio licensee faces any realistic possibility of a penalty for misinterpreting the lyrics it has chosen or permitted to be broadcast (*Yale Broadcasting*, p. 598).

## INDUSTRY SELF-HELP PROGRAMS

As noted earlier, like most media industries, the recording industry is split on the effect song lyrics have on listeners. But if Congress, the courts, artists, and public interest groups seem ambivalent about how, or even if, drug lyrics and drug use in the music industry should be controlled, the industry itself is coming to grips with the problem of drug use by artists.

After Shannon Hoon of Blind Melon died of a cocaine overdose in 1995, music industry executives formed the Industry Substance Abuse Intervention Program. The organization is concerned more with intervention and treatment than with taking action against artists who abuse drugs. In fact, the president of the National Academy of Recording Arts and Sciences (NARAS), Michael Greene, said he was "not a proponent of drug testing, censorship or imposed royalty restrictions" as means of controlling artists' use of drugs (quoted in Smashing Pumpkins, 1998). Others, including Ginna Martson of the Partnership for a Drug-Free America, are not impressed. Martson speculates, "All of pop culture in the '90s has really contributed to sending a message to kids that heroin is cool and glamorous" (quoted in Smashing Pumpkins, 1998). Obviously, there are disparate views regarding industry intervention programs. Should the industry do more to persuade artists to avoid destructive drug use, or should industry executives stick to business relationships and stay out of artists' personal affairs?

## CONCLUSION

Despite all the attempts to link drug-related lyrics and artists' behavior with drug use, one overriding theme remains: We simply are not sure what effects music has on people. We have seen that listeners may interpret lyrics differently than the songwriter.

It appears that industry programs will continue to avoid sanctions against musicians who develop drug dependency problems. In all likelihood, the music industry will continue to support substance abuse awareness and recovery programs. Some critics believe the music industry should implement a unified program to eliminate drug abuse and glorification of the drug culture by musicians. Arguments for that plan of attack appear to be moot: The industry is, apparently, unwilling to support any type of "drug-free industry" tactics.

The federal government has been ambivalent about drug-related music, whether sold in record stores or broadcast on radio. Lawmakers try to balance First Amendment rights of freedom of expression with social responsibility to prevent dangers to society in addressing drugs and music.

Having examined the list of musicians whose lives were brought to a halt because of drugs, one must ask, "Are rock performers the victims or the villains?" Although there are no easy answers, parents, government leaders, industry executives, artists, and fans of rock music need to address the drug problem as it relates to the music industry. One thing is clear: There is a drug problem in the United States, and the music industry is dramatically affected by it.

## TOPICS FOR DISCUSSION

1. Should the government pay recording artists to produce anti-drug songs? Why or why not?

2. Who is your favorite recording star? Suppose this person decides to record a song with a subtle anti-drug message. Do you think the song would be effective in preventing someone from using drugs?

3. Is there a difference between a song that glorifies cocaine use and a song that glorifies marijuana? How are they different or alike? What about a song that glorifies drug use as opposed to a song that glorifies cigarette smoking? Alcohol use?

## REFERENCES

### Books

Denisoff, R. S. (1972). *Sing a Song of Social Significance*. Bowling Green, OH: Bowling Green University Popular Press.

Orman, J. M. (1984). *The Politics of Rock Music*. Chicago: Nelson-Hall.

Sanchez, T. (1979). *Up and Down with the Rolling Stones*. New York: Morrow.

### Legislative and Judicial Proceedings

Bonner, R. (1996, September 26). The Epidemic of Teenage Drug Use. Statement before the Joint Hearing of the National Security, International Affairs and Criminal Justice Subcommittee of the House Government Reform and Oversight Committee and Early Childhood, Youth and Families Subcommittee of the House Economic and Educational Opportunities Committee.

In the Matter of Licensee Responsibility to Review Records before Their Broadcast, 31 F.C.C.2d 377; 21 Rad. Reg. 2d (P&F) 1698 (1971).

Licensee Responsibility to Review Records before Their Broadcast, 28 F.C.C.2d 409; FCC 71–205 (March 5, 1971).

McCaffrey, B. R. (1999, October 21). The National Youth Anti-drug Media Campaign and Entertainment Industry Outreach. Statement before the House Committee on Appropriations, Subcommittee on Treasury, Postal Service and General Government.

Portman, R. (1996, September 26). The Epidemic of Teenage Drug Use. Testimony before the Joint Hearing of the National Security, International Affairs and Criminal Justice Subcommittee of the House Government Reform and Oversight Committee and Early Childhood, Youth and Families Subcommittee of the House Economic and Educational Opportunities Committee.

Rosen, H. (1996, September 19). The Reemergence of Heroin. Testimony before the National Security, International Affairs and Criminal Justice Subcommittee of the House Government Reform and Oversight Committee.

*Yale Broadcasting Co. v. Federal Communications Commission*, 478 F.2d (D.C. cir.) 594, 598–599 (1973); cert. den., 414 U.S. 914 (1973).

*Yale Broadcasting Co. v. Federal Communications Commission*, 414 U.S. 914 (1973) cert. den.

### Magazines, Journals, and Newspapers

Barber, N. (1999, February 20). The Map: New York State of Mind; The Map Beats a Path to Manhattan's Music Landmarks. *The (London) Independent*, Features, p. 54.

Belcher, H.M.E., and H. E. Shinitzky (1998, October). Substance Abuse in Children: Prediction, Protection, and Prevention. *Archives of Pediatrics and Adolescent Medicine*, pp. 952–60.

Block, P. A. (1990, March). Modern-day Sirens: Rock Lyrics and the First Amendment. *Southern California Law Review* 63:781. Legislative and Judicial Proceedings.

FCC Bars Broadcasting of Drug-linked Lyrics (1971, March 7). *Washington Post*.

Giegerich, S. (1998, April 26). Steve Giegerich Column. *Asbury (N.J.) Park Press*, AA:1.

Glasser, I. (1987, December 5). Keeping the Censor out of Rock. *New York Times*, p. 26.

Irwin, S. (1999, November 14). Drug Overdoses Continue to Plague Rock Music. *Wilmington Star-News*, Lifestyle, p. 1D.

McCann, P. (1999, October 1). Lennon's I Am the Walrus Lyric Sold for Nearly 80,000 Pounds. *The (London) Independent*, p. 11.

McDougal, D. (1985, September 20). Zapping the Threat of Censorship. *Los Angeles Times*, Calendar, p. 5.

Morthland, J. (1990). *AM Gold—1971* (Liner Notes). Time-Life Music.

Plant, S. (1999, September 12). The Coke Connection. *(London) Daily Mail on Sunday*, pp. 42–43.

Prescott, J. (1997, April 28). The Lineup for "TV Land's Really Big Shows." *Knight Ridder/Tribune News Service*.

Rock Does Have a Conscience (1986, October 21). *(Arkansas) Democrat-Gazette*.

Ross, D. (1998, October 5). Dissecting Rolf; The Deborah Ross Interview. *(London) Independent*, Features, p. 1.

Stations Told to Halt Drug-oriented Music (1971, March 6). *Washington Evening Star*.

Tayler, L. (1996, September 17). Pop Culture and Drugs. *Newsday*, p. B4.

Thomas, R. (1999, September 2). Beatles Did More Than Get By on "Sgt. Pepper." *Wisconsin State Journal*, p. 22.

Violanti, A. (1993, May 7). Going to Pot: A New Generation of Musicians Is Slipping into the Drug Abuse of Rock's Past. *Buffalo News*, Gusto, p. 1.

Walker, D. (1994, August 13). Sullivan Opened Doors, and More Moments with the Late Rock King. *Arizona Republic*, p. D6.

Warning: 'Love' for Sale (1985, November 11). *Newsweek*, p. 39.

## Web Sites

Bloom, S. (2000, December 7). http://www.hightimes.com/Magazine/1995/9512/hempila.tpl.

Covault, S. (1999, December 2). Dead Rock Stars. http://home.san.rr.com/sgc/deadstars.html.

Dead Musician Directory (1999). http://elvispelvis.com/fullerup.htm.

Dead Rock Stars Club. (1999, December 2). http://users.efortress.com/doc-rock/deadrock.html.

Premature Death of Rock Stars. (1999, December 2). *Dial-the-Truth Ministries*. http://www.av1611.org/rockdead.html.

Shales, T. (1985, September 29). Commentary, *Los Angeles Times*, TV Times, p. 2.

Smashing Pumpkins' Keyboardist Dies of Heroin Overdose in New York amid Music Industry's Anti-drug Drive. (1998, November 22). http://www.ndsn/org/SUMMER96/MUSICARE.html.

Vote for Hempilation 2! (2000, December 7). http://www.hightimes.com/Lounge/HighMusic/hempilation2.tpl.

Woodall, M. (1999, December 2). Death Rock: Rock's Greatest Deaths and Personal Tragedies. http://www.vti.com/deathrock/.

# 3

# Music and Social Issues: Art Form or Soapbox?

Of all forms of media, none is so personal, so personalized, or so pervasive as music. Personal, in that everyone finds his or her own meaning for the words and melody. Personalized, in that we all use music for different things. Pervasive, in that music is used by all other media as a means of expression, as a means of setting a mood, or as a means of communicating feelings, attitudes, and beliefs. In short, music is an almost transnational form of communication that can both bridge gaps and build walls. Yet, for all of that, or perhaps because of that, music has been one of the most consistently criticized forms of media expression. To be sure, some forms of criticism seem warranted. After all, songs that glorify drug use, that promote violence, that degrade women, are songs that seem to be at odds with social values everywhere. Can one really argue that a song promoting violence against women is serving any social function?

What about songs that seem to promote generally recognized social values or political viewpoints? Can they be controversial as well? Of course they can. After all, one person's social cause is another person's social criticism. A song that speaks out against the government is certainly a message followed by thousands of people. At the same time, a song that stresses following government rules and "my country right or wrong" can be appreciated by a specific group of people. And, though there are those who would ban drug-related music, no one has proposed banning socially conscious music, even if the lyrics speak out against commonly held values and beliefs. Indeed, most music listeners assume artists are sincerely dedicated to the causes they promote, but nonetheless, critics have speculated that some performers use well-known causes merely to help promote themselves. After all, a benefit concert may sell thousands of tickets and be broadcast to millions of viewers. Could it be, then, that some music celebrities don't really care about the cause—starving children, a political movement, or an environmental issue—associated with a concert in which they perform?

In some ways controversies surrounding socially aware music are the same controversies that confront society; the controversy is related not only to the music itself but also to the social issue addressed by the music. Although there may be only two sides to a particular controversy, the music may address innumerable issues. Thus, in many cases an issue involves not simply the music itself but also the social cause addressed by the music. This linkage, of course, illustrates the connection between music and society and explains why all forms of music are subject to criticism and controversy. Said syndicated columnist Molly Ivins in 1992, "Good Lord, the zeal put into denouncing rock, sneering at opera, finding classical [music] a bore, jazz passe, bluegrass fit only for snuff-dippers—why, it's stupefying. It's incomprehensible." And nowhere are these contradictory functions and uses so evident as when music is used by conservatives and liberals alike to express ideas about social problems, to promote one particular point of view over another or to support social causes. Everyone has a favorite kind of music, and one person's "good" music is sometimes another person's trash. Music is part of our social fabric, however, and in many ways it becomes a metaphor for the controversial events themselves: If you favor a particular social issue, then you tend to like the music that supports that issue. Those on the other side of the issue, of course, tend to listen to and enjoy music that supports *their* viewpoint. Thus the study of social controversy is, by its very nature, also a study of music controversy.

If music is an art form in which aesthetic ideas are created, one might believe that causes or political viewpoints do not belong in a musical creation. Yet one might believe that music, or any art form, is by nature a platform for social causes. Through this musical art form the performers are generally provided a pulpit from which to preach their social views. Is it fair or appropriate that the performer's views should hold higher value in the eyes of the public than the views of any other citizen simply because the performer has star status? Do rock performers have insights the rest of us don't? Or does celebrity status elevate the views of otherwise ill-informed people to an undeserved level of importance?

In this chapter, we will look at how rock, folk, and country music have been used to support various political and social points of view and causes. In particular, we will consider how differently rock music treated the Vietnam War and the Gulf War and examine why. We will also examine the current trend in rock music called "cause rock," wherein rock musicians support farmers, starving children, and rain forests, among other concerns. In doing so, we consider whether celebrities should interject social causes into their recordings, concerts, and public statements.

Despite current concern about rock music and its effect on society, the role of music in the political life of the community is nothing new. As far back as 400 B.C., Plato wrote, "The introduction of novel fashions in music is a thing to beware of as endangering the whole fabric of society, whose most important conventions are unsettled by any revolution in that quarter." Even more strongly, Plato said that "musical innovation is full of danger to the whole State and ought to be prohibited" (quoted in Denisoff, 1972, p. 19) and that musicians should be exiled because they might influence others to a "luxurious effeminacy or corrupting aspiration" (quoted in Harrington, 1985). In his *Politics*, Aristotle said, "Music has the power of producing a certain effect on the moral character of the soul, and if it has the power to do this, it is clear that the young must be directed to music and must be educated in it" (quoted in Dimmock, 1998). Totalitarian regimes have, of course, kept a close rein on music. In Iran, for example, the Ayatollah Khomeini said music is "no different from opium," and "music stupefies persons listening to it and makes their brain inactive and frivolous" (Anderson, 1989).

## THE SOCIAL ROLE OF MUSIC IN THE UNITED STATES

Going all the way back to the time of Cotton Mather and the Puritans, music has played a role in the life of the community. In fact, the first complaints about the harmful effects of music were expressed in the earliest colonial times when church leaders banned Christmas celebrations because carols were deemed irreverent. Since then, every social upheaval and change has been accompanied by its own message, sometimes presented through music.

Indeed, music has often paralleled the issues and concerns of the society in ways that are nearly impossible to express through any other medium. Until fairly recently, however, music was seen primarily as another form of cultural art or popular entertainment. Thus the notion of music as message is of fairly recent origin and can be traced back to the 1930s and 1940s, when artists such as Woody Guthrie, "arguably, the greatest American songwriter" (Dominic and Moorhead, 1999), were performing songs like "This Land Is Your Land" and singing about the plight of the homeless and the farmers.

Still other songs have dealt directly with current events in a way that has personalized tragedy as only music can. For example, on October 31, 1941, the U.S. Navy destroyer *Reuben James* was torpedoed by a German U-boat off Iceland, even though the United States had not yet entered World War II. One hundred fifteen people died, and the event was memorialized in a song written and recorded by Woody Guthrie, "Reuben James," immediately after the sinking. The song was recorded in the late 1950s by the Kingston Trio, and still later by numerous other groups. Was the song merely a musical version of journalism, or was it an early form of using music for a social or political agenda?

Despite, or perhaps because of, its social relevance, rock 'n' roll has always generated some degree of dislike, if not fear, on the part of "the establishment." As far back as the 1950s, parents were being warned by the Ku Klux Klan (Harrington, 1985), "Help save youth of America. Don't buy negro records. The screaming, idiotic words and savage music of these records are undermining the morals of our white youth in America. Call the advertisers of the radio stations that play this type of music and complain to them" (quoted in Finn, 1999). In 1954, a songwriter's association passed a resolution saying, "It is in the best interest of the music industry voluntarily to curb the publication, recording and public performance of material offensive to the public taste" (Harrington, 1985).

At least one writer has linked political songs of two centuries ago with events in the 1940s and on to the Beatles and the turmoil of the 1960s:

> The French Revolution had the "Marseillaise," the Nazis the Horst Wessel song. The [Nineteen] Sixties was the first decade in which the power of music and words was communicated to a mass culture through electronic amplification. . . .
>
> For the first time, the musician became the focus for the sort of mass hysteria which until then had been confined to the political revolutionary and the religious revivalist. Pop music was in itself the real political philosophy of the Sixties. In that decade the Beatles were every bit as effective as say, the great 18th-century radical political propagandist Tom Paine was in his. (Clark, 1995)

Other writers, however, see music as a minor force when compared to all the other factors at work in society: "Elvis and the Beatles didn't unleash the youth rebellions of the 1960's, except maybe for a few short-term disturbances. They were more like Hegelian Silver Surfers, riding the wave of historical destiny" (Rockwell, 1990). It is thus apparent that the role of music in society is bewildering and confusing at best. Says Serge Denisoff, who has written extensively on the relationship between music and society:

> Music is unquestionably a form of communication, but what is it saying and to whom? High school kids Bugaloo and Frug to the civil rights anthem "We Shall Overcome" while Southern share-croppers sing the song to reaffirm their courage to go down and face *the man*. Merle Haggard's "Okie from Muskogee" receives a

thunderous ovation from an audience of Southern supporters of Governor George Wallace. Meanwhile Arlo Guthrie's rendition of the same song generates an equally positive response from the very people Haggard was condemning. . . . Such a bizarre and schizoid collection of attitudes has rarely been encountered by either social scientists or psychiatrists. (Denisoff, 1972)

More recently, regarding the music of the 1999 war in Kosovo, both Bill Clinton and Slobodan Milosevic could have been the targets of Nirvana's version of David Bowie's "The Man Who Sold the World."

Music as a medium of communication does not necessarily support just the conservative or just the liberal point of view. In fact, the opposite is true. Various kinds of music, particularly rock 'n' roll and country music, have come to be identified with different political points of view.

Unlike many of their country music brethren, rock 'n' rollers usually are ambivalent about these United States and what it means to be an American.

Country music's nature is tradition, of family, of flag. Merle Haggard's "Okie From Muskogee" is more famous, but his "Fightin' Side of Me" better unfurls his unabashed patriotism: You got a problem with my country, you got a problem with me.

It's a sentiment prevalent among country music's singers and players, from Johnny Cash's "The Ragged Old Flag" to Aaron Tippin's "You've Gotta Stand for Something." (Mayhew, 1994)

Generally speaking, both folk and rock have been linked to a liberal, "things have got to change," perspective, whereas country is seen as taking a more conservative, "my country right or wrong," perspective.

However, socially relevant songs were certainly not the mainstay of popular songs or of the omnipotent Top 40. "The interim between Elvis Presley's reign and the emergence of the Beatles in popular music was, according to most social historians of 'Rock 'n' Roll,' a period of uncertain drift, with novelty teenage death songs predominating" (Denisoff, 1972, p. 33). Interestingly, what little social protest there was in rock music was likely to be performed by lesser-known artists such as the Kingston Trio, who didn't become famous until they had a hit with Pete Seeger's "Where Have All the Flowers Gone," which reached the Number 21 position in the *Billboard*'s Top 40 in March 1962. The group, however, softened the lyrics when they changed the last line from "when will *you* ever learn" to "when will *they* ever learn," thus impersonalizing Seeger's message.

## MUSIC AND VIETNAM

Music as protest seems to have reached its peak in the 1960s and 1970s, when the confluence of the women's movement, black power, concern for the environment, and the war in Vietnam galvanized the youth of America, and songs moved away from the typical rock 'n' roll boy-meets-girl to protest and agitation. Research, for instance, shows that in 1955, 83 percent of popular songs dealt with boy-girl relationships (Horton, 1969) but by 1966, that number had dropped to 65 percent (Carey, 1969). Said Paul Hersch about the remaining 35 percent, "Many of these hit songs contained lyrics which condemned war, acknowledged drug use, or otherwise challenged the status quo." We can see these conflicts and confusions by examining several songs that took opposite views of the war in Vietnam and then looking at songs relevant to the Gulf War.

The first commercially successful song dealing directly with the war in Vietnam was Barry McGuire's "Eve of Destruction," a "pessimistic, nihilistic warning . . . sung and shouted by Barry McGuire, a former member of the New Christy Minstrels" (Orman, 1984, p. 62). Although a shorter, more mellow version was recorded by the Turtles in 1970, it is McGuire's hard-edged version that still captures most of the attention. "Eve of Destruction" entered the Top 40 on August 28, 1965, stayed in the Top 40 for ten weeks, and was the Number 1 song for one week. Despite, or perhaps because of, its high ranking, the song was, without a doubt, the most controversial of the antiwar era, as evidenced by its being banned by a number of Top 40 radio stations (Anderson, 1986).

Said John Morthland, a freelance writer who has contributed to both *Rolling Stone* and *Creem*, "With 'Eve of Destruction,' [nineteen-year-old] songwriter P. F. Sloan took on . . . war, racism, the space race, religion, the bomb . . . in just over three minutes. . . . 'Eve of Destruction' is easily the most dissenting record to hit the pop charts up to that time" (Morthland, 1993). However, if conservatives were convinced the song, or any antiwar song for that matter, was influencing the youth of America, the research data suggested that music was, in fact, having almost no impact: "A cursory examination of these discussions finds much disagreement upon the sociopolitical effect of popular music. One interpretation sees popular songs as a form of 'background noise' which has little meaning when examined as a total entity" (Denisoff and Levine, 1971).

To test whether or not the song was understood, researchers asked 400 San Francisco State College students who believed in what the song stood for what the song meant. Out of the 400 students, only 56 (14 percent) said the song meant what the writer himself said it meant (that the world was living under a cloud all the time and that we have to change the hate to love). More than two-thirds of the respondents either completely missed the meaning Sloan intended or only partially understood what he was trying to say. The authors of the study conclude that the song, like many other protest songs through the ages, was intended not to convert people but, rather, to reinforce listeners' existing beliefs (Denisoff and Levine, 1971).

Another antiwar song that ran into trouble was "Waist Deep in the Big Muddy," written by Pete Seeger, of whom it has been said, "No musician had greater impact on the social conscience of the 1960s than Pete Seeger" (Peter Seeger, 1996). He was also "perhaps the most picketed, boycotted performer in American history" (Vranish, 1995). "[Seeger] recalls fondly, for example, the colonel who followed his various Connecticut appearances like a die-hard fan, so he could hold up his protest sign: 'Seeger: Khrushchev's Songbird' " (Catlin, 1995). "Big Muddy" was originally written about the plight of a group of World War II foot soldiers who had been ordered to march through a deadly river by their overly gung-ho sergeant. Although written about foot soldiers in World War II, the song was adopted by anti-war movement activists in the 1960s and became a euphemism for Vietnam.

Suffering through years of unofficial but nevertheless very real blacklisting during the McCarthy era and facing a 1955 contempt citation issued by the House Un-American Activities Committee (Catlin, 1995), Seeger was booked onto the CBS hit show *The Smothers Brothers Comedy Hour*. The appearance was to be Seeger's return to television. When the Smothers Brothers had Seeger sing "Big Muddy" on their top-rated program, however, the network cut that portion of the tape. That network action caused the Smothers Brothers to begin an anticensorship campaign in the media, and CBS finally relented and allowed Seeger to sing the song. The fact that public opinion had begun to turn against the war probably also contributed to CBS relenting and allowing Seeger to sing his song.

There were, of course, dozens of Top 40 songs protesting the war in Vietnam, many of which were banned by radio stations around the country. Many antiwar songs also dealt with other social ills, as well as songs decrying the general state of the world. Some of the more popular antiwar songs, as opposed to antiestablishment songs, were the following:

- "Alice's Restaurant Massacree," Arlo Guthrie
- "Blowin' in the Wind," Peter, Paul and Mary
- "Bring the Boys Home," Freda Payne
- "Draft Dodger Rag," Chad Mitchell Trio and Phil Ochs
- "Feel Like I'm Fixin' to Die Rag," Country Joe (McDonald) and the Fish
- "Fortunate Son," Creedence Clearwater Revival

- "Give Peace a Chance," John Lennon and the Plastic Ono Band
- *I Ain't Marching Anymore* (album), Phil Ochs
- "Imagine," John Lennon
- "Last Train to Nuremberg," Pete Seeger
- "Lyndon Johnson Told the Nation," Tom Paxton
- "Masters of War," Bob Dylan
- "Ohio," Crosby, Stills, Nash and Young
- "Sky Pilot," The Animals
- "Street Fighting Man," The Rolling Stones
- "Talking Vietnam Potluck Blues," Tom Paxton
- "Unknown Soldier," The Doors
- "War," Edwin Starr
- "The War Is Over" Phil Ochs
- "White Boots Marching in a Yellow Land," Phil Ochs
- "Where Have All the Flowers Gone," Pete Seeger, The Kingston Trio, and numerous others
- "With God on Our Side," Bob Dylan

One song, "Give Peace a Chance," was reprised more than twenty years later by Lennon's son, Sean, during the Gulf War in 1991. The later version was updated, though, to include references to AIDS and pollution.

As noted above, there were numerous antiwar and antiestablishment songs during this period. Yet, there seems to be only one song directly supporting the war in Vietnam, and that was "The Ballad of the Green Berets," written by Army Special Forces medic S.Sgt. Barry Sadler while he was recuperating from wounds he received in Vietnam. The song, which entered the Top 40 on February 19, 1966, spent eleven weeks in *Billboard's* Top 40, with five weeks at Number 1 on the pop charts, and it reached Number 2 on the country chart. It eventually sold more than 9 million copies. The song, said *Soldier of Fortune* in 1992, "stirred a nation's soul in the early days of the Vietnam War" (Pate, 1992).

A few months after "Ballad," Sadler released "The 'A' Team," about the basic twelve-man special forces unit. Although *Bachelor Magazine* described the song as "another sensational single," it reached only Number 28 and remained in the Top 40 for only four weeks.

Still another song that captured the hearts of the silent majority and the anti-antiwar elements of society, although it had only one line directly related to the war, was "Okie from Muskogee," by Merle Haggard, who has been called one of "the most bellicose and prolific defenders of rural folkways and national traditions" (Peyton, 1999) and "the poet of the common man" (Nominees, 1993). With lines condemning those who burn draft cards and take drugs, the song came to represent everything the anti-war movement was not: a return to traditional American values. Ironically, "Haggard always said the hoopla was overplayed, claiming he intended the song as a kind of jest" (Morse, 1999), a statement that does not, as we will see later, accurately reflect what Haggard himself thought about the song. This could be the first example of a misinterpreted song that accidentally became part of a social cause.

The song reached the Number 1 spot on the country charts, was named the top song and top album by the Country Music Association (CMA) in 1970 (the same year Haggard was named "Entertainer of the Year" by the CMA), and was Number 41 on the pop charts. Yet the song is a prime example of the dangers of deconstruction we discussed in Chapter 2, and if any song of the era illustrates the split personality of music and its relationship to society, it was "Okie from Muskogee." Said Philip van Vleck, writing a review in the *Herald-Sun* in Durham, North Carolina, of the 1999 release of a new compilation of Haggard songs, "The dumbest song Haggard ever recorded, 'Okie from Muskogee,' is also here. This 1969 redneck rant against hippies and war protesters was quite the joke among Okies who knew Muskogee County as a prime locale of marijuana cultivation." However, said Randy Rodda (1999), writing in the *Buffalo News*, " 'Okie from Muskogee' and 'The Fightin' Side of Me' are lyrical pile-drivers of the wedge that split generations back in the Vietnam War era."

Haggard was subsequently invited a number of times to the White House, and the impact the song had on the silent majority is perhaps best illustrated by a quote from H. R. Haldeman, White House chief of staff, who wrote in his diary in 1973: "Tonight was the Merle Haggard 'Evening at the White House. . . . ' The 'Evening' was pretty much a flop because the audience had no appreciation for country/western music and there wasn't much rapport, except when Haggard did his 'Okie from Muskogee' . . . which everybody responded to very favorably, of course" (quoted in Berlau, 1996).

Although Richard Nixon said "Okie" was one of his favorite songs (Peyton, 1999), its origins can hardly be said to be that of middle America, as this dialogue on National Public Radio (NPR) vividly shows:

> [Host Scott] Simon: [L]et me point out, as Merle Haggard has said in any number of interviews over the years, he and his crew were stoned out of their minds on marijuana when they wrote this song. They were philandering on the road. This was written ironically, archly.
>
> [Historian Bill] Malone: They drove by the—a sign that said "Muskogee," and somebody in the group said, "Boy, I bet they

don't smoke marijuana in Muskogee. . . . And they said, "Wow! What a great idea for a song!" And so he turned that into a sort of an anthem against hippies and softies and anti-war people. (Simon, 1998)

It is without a doubt that the song delivered a clear message supporting traditional American values, something anathema to the liberal side of the political spectrum. For example, said Paul Kantner, cofounder of the Jefferson Airplane, an antiestablishment group if there ever was one, "Okie from Muskogee" "was the typical redneck reaction, the 'send 'em back to Russia,' the 'America, love it or leave it' mentality. . . . It was amusing in the sense that Barry Sadler's 'The Ballad of the Green Berets' was amusing" (quoted in Boehm, 1989).

Other comments were equally biting:

- "The two most famous patriotic songs are both by Merle Haggard: "The Fightin' Side of Me," which speaks of squirrelly draft-dodgers who don't believe in fighting, and "Okie from Muskogee," which commends leather boots instead of Roman sandals for manly footwear (King, 1974).

- "There is something utterly sinister about the image of Richard Nixon inviting Merle Haggard to sing at the White House." (Goldstein, 1973)

But now, with the passage of time, liberals, despite clear evidence to the contrary, have given the song new meanings:

- "While the song represents a very conservative point of view, with a speaker who is proud of Muskogee, it is supposed to be a wry and ironic commentary on the nature of these conservative people in this small town who are unthinkingly jingoistic" (Lawler, quoted in Berlau, 1996).

- "He wrote a song ["Okie"] as a lark, kind of a gentle joke, and he became the biggest star in country music" (Kingsbury, 1995, p. 139).

Was the song written merely as a joke? Not according to Haggard, and he should know. Although the song "started as a joke, . . . it only lasted about three seconds before we realized the importance of it" (Haggard, quoted in Berlau, 1996). Depending on whom you ask, he said the song took between ten minutes (Boehm, 1989) and twenty minutes (Kingsbury, 1995, p. 139) to write. He also told Tom Roland, author of the *Billboard Book of Number One Country Hits*, "The main message in Muskogee was pride, and the patriotism was evident" (quoted in Berlau,

1996). Earlier still, Haggard had said: "I was trying to say something about being proud to be an American in spite of the conditions [in America at the time]. . . . There's something to be said for the person in the middle of America who likes things the way they are" (Haggard, quoted in Boehm, 1993).

Haggard's follow-up song, "The Fightin' Side of Me," made his views crystal clear as he sang about the dangers of running the country down. Critics said Haggard wrote the song only because he was forced to by record executives, but Haggard himself said that although he believed in freedom of expression, he was also concerned that someone needed to defend the traditional (i.e., middle-class) American way of life (Roland, quoted in Berlau, 1996). Even today the song seems to resonate with fans who attend Haggard concerts: "A great many ticket buyers want to hear it, and you offend them if you don't do their song. . . . Somebody has to sing it, and I guess I'm the likely guy, since I wrote it," Haggard said (Boehm, 1993). Of course, the song may be the target of criticism simply because it is country. Said Molly Ivins in a tongue-in-cheek look at country music:

> Country music is easily parodied and much despised by intellectuals, but like soap operas, it is much more like real life than your elitists will admit. What do most people truly care about? International arms control? Monetary policy? Deconstructive criticism? Hell, no. What they care about most is Love. . . . Betrayal. . . . Revenge. . . . Death. . . . Booze. . . . Money. . . . Loneliness. . . . Tragedy-love songs. . . . Now here we're talking major themes. (Ivins, 1992)

In still another Vietnam-era song written by Haggard, "I Wonder If They Ever Think of Me," a prisoner of war blames the North Vietnamese for his troubles, and says he's glad to be part of "Uncle Sam."

Another successful country song of the time was Johnny Wright's "Hello Vietnam," which reached Number 1 in October 1965. The only other successful song of the era that even hinted at a pro–Vietnam War stance was "Ruby, Don't Take Your Love to Town," by Kenny Rogers. Although the 1969 song had a Vietnam theme, the song's storyline had its base in a different era, again showing how historical facts set to music can have multiple meanings: As originally written by Mel Tillis, the song was about a neighbor who had been wounded in Germany during World War II. Although Tillis changed the ending in the song, in real life the veteran killed both himself and his wife (Morthland, 1992). "Ruby" reached Number 29 on the country charts and Number 6 on the pop charts.

Other pro-Vietnam songs in country music were two by Ernest Tubbs, "Love It or Leave It" and "It's for God and Country and You, Mom

(That's Why I'm Fighting in Vietnam)" in early 1966, and "The Fightin' Side of Me," Haggard's follow-up to "Okie." What makes these songs interesting is that country music has always championed both traditional values and populism and protest. Noted music historian Bill Malone, author of *Country Music USA*, has pointed out that the roots of country music in fact go back to the protest songs of Woody Guthrie (Simon, 1998).

One last group of songs from the Vietnam era must be mentioned, and these are songs that are apparently pro-military, or at least have a military theme. We need to remember that during the initial phases of conflict, the public was solidly behind President John F. Kennedy's and then President Lyndon Johnson's efforts to win the war. Thus two songs in particular come to mind: the Shirelles' 1962 hit, "Soldier Boy," which reached Number 1 on the pop charts, where it stayed for three weeks; and "Navy Blue" by Diane Renay, which reached Number 6 in 1964. Renay also had another Top 40 song favorable to the military, the Number 29 "Kiss Me Sailor." "Soldier Boy" has been described by Morthland (1991) as "a tribute to every working-class teenage girl whose sweetie would not be going to college (in those days, there was only one alternative to college, and that was the military)," and it was the group's biggest hit, which says just as much about the audience as it does about the song itself.

## DESERT SHIELD/DESERT STORM (THE GULF WAR)

In 1991, during the Gulf War, popular music seemed to embrace the war, although few of the songs are remembered today. David Menconi of the *News and Observer* in Raleigh, North Carolina, pointed out that although the war sparked several songs ("From a Distance" by Bette Midler, "Get Here" by Oleta Adams, "Desert Angel" by Stevie Nicks, "Lines in the Sand" by Randy Newman, and "Bombs over Baghdad" by John Trudell), "none . . . have survived in the popular memory" (Menconi, 1999).

Other writers have despaired over the lack of musical history associated with the Gulf War: "Years from now, will some delicate strain of guitar or soaring vocal remind us of the 40 days and nights that shook the world? . . . Will any song sparked by the Persian Gulf conflict make us stop in our tracks, stare dreamily into space and remember when? Probably not" (Smith, 1991). Part of the reason may be that the songs inspired by the war were, like the war itself, simply quick hits with little depth of feeling or passion. Who, for example, can get terribly excited by lyrics such as those in the rap song "Saddam Hussein" by the group

Endorsed by the President, which talk about Saddam Hussein as "insane" and "deranged."

Other songs seem to have been forgotten since the end of the war:

- "Don't Give Us a Reason," Hank Williams, Jr.
- "The Eagle," Waylon Jennings
- "Going by the Book," Johnny Cash
- "Headin' for Armageddon," Joey Welz
- "Highwire," The Rolling Stones
- "Iraq and a Hard Place," Tommy Vale and the Torpedoes
- "Just You and Me Now Mommy," Karen Jeglum Kennedy
- "Letter to Saddam Hussein," Jerry Martin
- "Military Wives," Donna Mason
- "Shiftin' Sands," Bob Ellis
- "Soldier's Eyes," Joseph Nicoletti
- "When Duty Calls," Biggy Smallz

One of the differences between music produced during the Vietnam era and the numbers composed during the Gulf War is the advent of music videos. In this category we have "The Voices That Care" project, which included nearly one hundred singers, actors, and actresses. Although the video won something less than critical acclaim, the lyricist for the song, Linda Thompson Jenner, said she believes the work actually contributed to the end of the war, something that was never said about music from the Vietnam era: "I . . . think the video caused the end of the war. . . . I think it intimidated Hussein to see all those powerful faces. The timing . . . was impeccable (quoted in Smith, 1991).

Interestingly, the songs that seem to have been remembered were older ballads and popular tunes from years before. These include the following numbers:

- "Deck of Cards," Bill Anderson
- "From a Distance," Julie Gold
- "Get Here," Oleta Adams
- "Give Peace a Chance," Sean Lennon
- "Mother's Pride," George Michael
- "Show Me the Way," Styx

• "Soldier Boy," two different versions, one by Donna Fargo and the other by Boston Dawn (also a Number 1 hit for the Shirelles in 1962)

Perhaps the best remembered of the Gulf War songs will be Lee Greenwood's "God Bless the U.S.A.," a song that was seven years old when Greenwood revived it. In fact, so popular was the song, that the 118th Airlift Wing of the Tennessee Air National Guard had the first few notes painted on the nose of one of its C-130H Hercules aircraft, the *Spirit of Music City*. Another song that enjoyed something of a reprise was Tony Orlando and Dawn's 1973 Number 1 hit, "Tie a Yellow Ribbon Round the Ole Oak Tree," the song that inspired the entire colored-ribbon phenomenon. In this case, the resurrection was done by Sonny James and Karla Taylor. And what music were the troops listening to in the desert? Why, the music of the antiwar 1960s and 1970s! "Today's GIs may listen to rap and speed metal at home, but they associate the Doors, Bob Dylan and Jimi Hendrix with fatigues" (Pisik and Hewitt, 1991).

Because the Vietnam War and the Gulf War engendered distinctly different feelings in the national psyche, the musical results from each are not the same. Even songs with no particular connection to war seem to have become known as "antiwar songs": "And back then, too, songs with no direct relevance to the [Vietnam] war resonated with one side or the other of our national division—and are still remembered as 'Vietnam songs' as a result (Creedence's 'Who'll Stop the Rain?' for example). But we probably won't recall the 'Voices That Care' theme long enough for the returning troops to unpack their duffels" (Smith, 1991).

Perhaps there is a more basic reason for the difference between Vietnam era songs and those of the Gulf War: We noted, remember, how folk music and rock music were more antiestablishment and thus antiwar than was country music, whose artists tended to favor traditional American values. "Rock-and-roll may have provided the soundtrack for Vietnam in much the way big bands did for World War II, but country music is (for now) first to the turntable with musical takes on the Persian Gulf War" (Harrington, 1991). A look at the lists of Gulf War–related songs does indeed show a preponderance of country artists.

Other views explain the contrast in musical results. One reason for the difference, said Studs Terkel, chronicler of American life in the last half of the century, was technology.

How can you make music about missiles? The central figures in the Persian Gulf weren't humans, they were inanimate objects—Patriots, Scuds. It was as if we were looking at a video screen the whole time.

During Vietnam, we saw real blood and heard real screaming. It was a war of body bags and small white crosses. When Country Joe sang, "Be the first one on your block to have your boy come home in a box," it shook a lot of kids. You can't sing about, or against, a war if it looks like no one got their hands dirty. (Terkel, quoted in Smith, 1991)

Said Abe Peck, a professor at Northwestern University and author of the book *Uncovering the '60s*: "Keep in mind, we're talking about a very emotional nine years versus a very clean-cut 40 days" (Peck, quoted in Smith, 1991).

### "CAUSE ROCK"

If the generation of the late 1960s and early 1970s seemed determined to tear society apart, from the early 1970s to the present rock music has been used to build things up, or at least to relieve some of the misery in the world. We've already discussed the use of music to support the Gulf War (and the apparent lack of any music opposed to the war). But another attempt by musical artists to change the world has led to something known as "cause rock," the efforts by numerous artists to support innumerable social causes.

Music in support of social causes has been around for years. In the 1940s Woody Guthrie and Pete Seeger were writing songs for migrant farm workers and for unions. Even while "Eve of Destruction" was reverberating around the world, George Harrison launched one of the first cause rock concerts with the 1971 "Concert for Bangladesh." Such concerts are intended not only to raise money but to provide national or international publicity for the causes themselves.

A simple electronic database search reveals a number of concerts and albums connected with cause rock, illustrating the wide variety of issues and artists involved in these humanitarian benefit concert efforts. Some of the concerts, in fact, are now annual events.

1971—Concert for Bangladesh
    George Harrison
    Ravi Shankar

1979—No Nukes
    MUSE—Musicians United for Safe Energy
    Bruce Springsteen
    Bonnie Raitt
    Jackson Browne

1984—"Do They Know It's Christmas" (Ethiopian relief)
    Bob Geldof and Band Aid

U2
Sting
Duran Duran
Boomtown Rats
Midge Ure

1985—USA for Africa ("We Are the World")
Michael Jackson
Bob Dylan
Huey Lewis
Kim Carnes
Bette Midler
Cyndi Lauper
Dan Akroyd
Kenny Rogers
Bruce Springsteen
Ray Charles
Diana Ross
Stevie Wonder
Paul Simon
Willie Nelson
Tina Turner
Billy Joel

1985—Live Aid (African relief)
Simon Le Bon (of Duran Duran)
Tina Turner
Mick Jagger
Led Zeppelin
Phil Collins

1985—"That's What Friends Are For" (AIDS awareness)
Dionne Warwick
Elton John
Stevie Wonder
Gladys Knight

1985—Farm Aid
Willie Nelson
John Cougar Mellencamp

1986—Conspiracy of Hope (for Amnesty International)
Peter Gabriel
Brian Adams
Lou Reed
Joan Baez
Police
Jackson Browne

1987—Faith No More ("We Care a Lot," a parody of all the "Aid" efforts)

1988—Human Rights Now! (Amnesty International)
  Bruce Springsteen
  Peter Gabriel
  Sting
  Tracy Chapman
  Youssou N'Dour

1993—Concert for rape victims in Bosnia-Herzegovina
  Nirvana
  L7
  Breeders
  Disposable Heros of Hiphoprisy

1996—Tibetan Freedom Concert
  Beastie Boys

1999—"No Boundaries" benefit album for Kosovar refugees
  Pearl Jam
  Alanis Morissette
  Rage Against the Machine

1999—Net Aid (anti-poverty)
  Sheryl Crow
  Jewel
  Puff Daddy
  Sting

Perhaps the most notable effort was "We Are the World," written for USA (United Support of Artists) for Africa. The song was written by Michael Jackson and Lionel Richie, produced by Quincy Jones, with organizational efforts led by manager Ken Kragen. At an all-night recording session following the annual American Music Awards, more than forty-five people performed the song, which went on to sell more than 4 million copies. It reached Number 1 on the *Billboard* charts; but what makes its debut unusual was that when it was released in February 1985, more than 8,000 radio stations played it at the same time. Then, on April 5, 1985, the Friday before Easter, more than 5,000 radio stations around the world played the song simultaneously (numerous radio and television stations throughout the United States reprised the simulcast at noon Eastern Standard Time, Monday, January 30, 1995).

The impact of "We Are the World" was tremendous. According to Ken Kragen, one of the organizers for the effort, "We raised $61.8 million and we distributed $61.8 million—that in itself is an amazing feat, that 100 percent of the money raised was distributed" (quoted in "A 'World' without End," 1995). Said Peter Gabriel, in words that could have been taken from social activists writing songs in the 1930s and 1940s: "You can shape and mold and direct [young people's] intentions positively with music. Music itself doesn't change the world, people change the world, but music can be a powerful instrument of information" (Gabriel, quoted in Hilburn, 1988).

Although efforts to support causes attracted a great deal of attention, there is always a question of just how much good a concert can really do. One cynical assessment has put it this way: "In retrospect, maybe it was naive to think that a Led Zeppelin pseudo-reunion, sets by Phil Collins on two continents and a duet between Mick Jagger and Tina Turner would end the plight of starving Africans. Back then, though, anything seemed possible. . . . And if they can't save the planet, at least some have found a way to save their careers" (Soeder, 1999). An even more cynical opinion questions the sincerity of artists who find causes to which they can attach their name and performances. In fact, these efforts may have run out of steam, as more and more artists produce albums rather than give concerts, "which raise money and awareness without subjecting fans to political sermons or grief-stricken pleas for cash" (Christensen, 1997). And though the concerts and records may have led to short-term relief (some concerts raised hundreds of millions of dollars), long-term solutions to poverty, hunger, and disease seem more difficult to achieve. There is also concern that the public, and the artists themselves, are tired of trying to change society: In October 1999 Willie Nelson called off his annual "Farm Aid" show in Dallas after only 8,000 people bought tickets for the 50,0000-seat venue. Problems, such as liability insurance for such large events, can gradually destroy an artist's enthusiasm for a particular cause.

## CONCLUSION

As we have seen, not all music is created strictly for its aesthetic or entertainment value. Quite often the music has a message, political viewpoint, or cause in which the songwriter or artist believes. The question remains, however, Should music performers use their celebrity status to garner publicity for their personal viewpoints? Artists are blessed, undoubtedly, with a bully pulpit to which few other people have access.

During times of war, particularly Vietnam and Desert Storm, music was often used to define opposing sides: antiwar sentiment versus patriotism. Yet, some listeners and performers preferred music that entertained rather than lectured. Some critics have even made jibes about performers who, they feel, used social causes more than served them.

Perhaps it is not possible to detach music from social causes. One might see an inseparable relationship between music and the human behavior it describes. Such relationships had been foreseen by the "father

Willie Nelson has taken an active role in creating Farm Aid, a music festival to support independent farmers who suffer economic hardship. This is just one example of how artists support causes in which they believe. (Photofest)

of sociology," Emile Durkheim, who noted that ideas and society are related; that the society one lives or works in will determine what ideas one has. Thus, the work of a singer-songwriter is directly related to the kind of society in which that person lives.

## TOPICS FOR DISCUSSION

1. How does protest music, which usually speaks against the dominant culture, become commercially successful?
2. How do you think societal differences in the 1960s and 1990s made a difference in songs dealing with the Vietnam War and the Gulf War?
3. Do you think cause rock is losing its popularity? Are there some social causes in the twenty-first century that might be attractive to those promoting benefit concerts? Why?
4. Should songwriters be less concerned with social issues in order to spend more attention on basic human emotions, or should social issues be a primary focus of song lyrics?

## REFERENCES

### Books

Denisoff, R. S. (1972). *Sing a Song of Social Significance*. Bowling Green, OH: Bowling Green University Popular Press.

Kingsbury, P. (1995). *The Grand Ole Opry History of Country Music*. New York: Random House.

Orman, J. (1984). *The Politics of Rock Music*. Chicago: Nelson-Hall.

Plato. *The Republic*, trans. Francis MacDonald Cornford (1945). New York: Oxford University Press. Book IV, p. 424.

### Magazines, Journals, and Newspapers

Anderson, R. H. (1989, June 4). Ayatollah Ruhollah Khomeini, 89, the Unwavering Iranian Spiritual Leader. *New York Times*, p. 39.

Anderson, T. H. (1986). American Popular Music and the War in Vietnam. *Peace and Change* 11:52.

Berlau, J. (1996, August 19). The Battle over "Okie from Muskogee." *Weekly Standard*, p. 43.

Boehm, M. (1989, September 16). Airplane, Haggard to Retrace '60s Battle Lines in O.C. *Los Angeles Times*, Calendar, p. 1.

Boehm, M. (1993, July 22). Material Matter: Merle Haggard Thinks of Himself as the Competition, Not Newer Country Stars. *Los Angeles Times*, OC Live, p. 4.

Carey, J. (1969, May). Changing Courtship Patterns in Popular Songs. *American Journal of Sociology*, p. 730.

Catlin, R. (1995, March 13). Pete Seeger and the Wisdom of Songwriting. *Hartford (Connecticut) Courant*, p. E1.

Christensen, T. (1997, September 22). Musicians Are Questioning Whether Charity Shows Can Help Save the World. *Dallas Morning News*, Entertainment News.

Clark, J. (1995, November 18). Would Our Lives Be Different If They'd Never Got Together? *(London) Daily Mail*.

Denisoff, R. S. and M. H. Levine (1971). The Popular Protest Song: The Case of "Eve of Destruction." *Public Opinion Quarterly* 35:117.

Dimmock, T. H. (1998, June 25). Philosophers Are Right That Classical Music Ennobles Our Children. *Baltimore Sun*, p. A22.

Dominic, S., and M. V. Moorhead (1999, October 28). Recordings. *Phoenix New Times*.

Finn, T. (1999, May 15). Wicked Words: Uproar over Modern Lyrics Fails to Recognize Tradition of Mayhem. *Kansas City Star*, p. E1.

Goldstein, R. (1973, June). My Country Music Problem—and Yours. *Mademoiselle*, p. 114.

Harrington, R. (1985, September 15). Rock with a Capital R and a PG-13: The Debate over Steamy Lyrics Goes a Long Way Back. *Washington Post*, p. H1.

Harrington, R. (1991, January 30). Country Music Goes to War. *Washington Post*, p. B7.

Hilburn, R. (1988, December 18). Rock 'n' Responsibility: More Than Ever, Rock's Creative Pulse Centers on Conscience and Heart. *Los Angeles Times*, Calendar, p. 80.

Hirsch, P. (1971, January). Sociological Approaches to Pop Music. *American Behavioral Scientist*, p. 374.

Horton, T. (1969, May). The Dialogue of Courtship in Popular Songs. *American Journal of Sociology*, pp. 569–578.

Ivins, M. (1992, June 29). Ruby, Don't Take This Job and Hold It against Me. *Seattle Times*, p. A9.

King, F. (1974, July). Red Necks, White Socks, and Blue Ribbon Fear: The Nashville Sound of Discontent. *Harpers*, pp. 30–31.

Mayhew, D. (1994, July 3). Rock's Roots in American Rebelliousness. *Fresno Bee*, p. F11.

Menconi, D. (1999, April 11). Fight Songs. *(Raleigh, N.C.) News and Observer*, p. G1.

Morse, S. (1999, April 16). Merle Haggard Still Calls the Tune: Returning to the Region, the Country Legend Pulls No Punches on Drug Laws, Nashville, and Life on the Road. *Boston Globe*, p. C5.

Morthland, J. (1991). Liner notes for "AM Gold: 1962." Warner Special Projects.

Morthland, J. (1992). Liner notes for "AM Gold: Late 60s Classics." Warner Special Projects.

Morthland, J. (1993). Liner notes for "The Time-Life History of Rock 'n' Roll: Folk Rock 1964–1967." Warner Special Projects.

Nominees for Country Music Hall of Fame Announced (1993, July 1). *Business Wire*.

Pate, J. (1992, September). Barry Sadler's Last Project. *Soldier of Fortune*.

Peter Seeger: A Link in the Chain Celebrates His Decade on Columbia, 1961–1971 (1996, September 3). *PR Newswire*.

Peyton, A. T. (1999, March 8). "I See by Your Outfit": Exposed Navels and Other Reasons for the Decline of Country Music." *Weekly Standard*, p. 36.

Pisik, B., and J. A. Hewitt. (1991, February 4). "I'll Be a Cranky Old Yank in My Clanky Old Tank on the Streets of Yokohama with My Honolulu Mama Doing the Beat-O, Beat-O, Flat on My Seat-O Blues" and Other Songs of War. *Washington Times*, p. E1.

Rockwell, J. (1990, January 21). Pop View: Why Rock Remains the Enemy. *New York Times*, sec. 2, p. 24.

Rodda, R. (1999, September 30). In Control: The Hag Reprises More Than 40 Songs. *Buffalo News*, p. G30.

Simon, S. (1998, June 20). *National Public Radio Weekend Edition*.

Soeder, J. (1999, October 10). Cause-rockers Back, Beating Their Drums. *(Cleveland) Plain Dealer*, p. I2.

Smith, P. (1991, March 10). Gulf War: Quick Blitz Nixes Hits. *Boston Globe*, p. B1.

van Vleck, P. (1999, October 15). Haggard's New Double CD Packs a Solid Punch. *(Durham, N.C.) Herald-Sun*, p. D2.

Vranish, J. (1995, November 19). All in the Family: Pete Seeger and Granddaughter Give the PBT a Sense of Family Values. *Pittsburgh Post-Gazette*, p. G1.

A "World" Without End: Ten Years Later, Music Industry Still Feeling Effects of Song (1995, February 1). *Washington Post*, p. D7.

# 4

# Parody and Sampling: Borrowing or Stealing Copyright?

*Note: The reader is cautioned that copyright is a vast and complex legal area. Anyone with a particular, or detailed, copyright issue is urged to seek the advice of an attorney.*

It's been said that imitation is the sincerest form of flattery. If someone is copying your song or melody, however, you may be losing a great deal of money. How? Because as the songwriter, you have a right to be paid every time your music is played on the radio, included on a CD or tape, or downloaded from the Internet. Every time someone makes an unauthorized copy of a CD or illegally downloads a song off the Internet, the songwriter, along with the publisher, producer and record label, loses money. Many people feel justified copying music because they believe they are hurting only "big record companies" or "millionaire recording artists." Unfortunately, many "little people" work for the large record labels, and songwriters are usually the ones who suffer most from this type of loss of income. Songwriters should receive payment when others use their artistic creations. Unfortunately, that is not always the case.

Napster, the Internet system that allows individuals to trade recordings over the Internet, has made many music consumers aware of copyright laws. As discussed in chapter 1, Napster initially angered major labels and precipitated several lawsuits regarding copyright infringement. Ironically, after resolving all lawsuits, Napster entered into a strategic partnership with BMG, one of the major label groups that had filed a lawsuit against Napster. Perhaps BMG adopted the strategy of "if you can't beat 'em, join 'em."

What if someone writes a song that "sort of" sounds like yours? Or what if someone makes a version that spoofs your song? It's a different song, but it "sort of" sounds like yours. Here lies the heart of issues dealing with copyright protection, sampling, and parody, the three major concepts discussed in this chapter. The first, copyright, deals with what rights songwriters, publishers, producers, labels, and singers have regarding the music they create and market. The last two, sampling and parody, deal with what recording artists other than the originator are actually doing with a given set of musical notes, sounds, or words that have already been created by someone else (the copyright holder). Because copyright is the overarching concept affecting both sampling and parody, we will start our discussion with a general look at copyright law.

## COPYRIGHT

Arguments regarding the need for stronger or weaker copyright laws tend to be generated by two groups. One group, users of existing copyrighted material, characteristically argue for greater ease of access to creative works. Therefore, they would like to see less-restrictive copyright laws. The other group, those who control copyright protected works, almost always fight to get more powerful copyright laws enacted.

Federal laws that provide our copyright protection are rooted in English law. The term "copyright" was originally used to describe the right to copy a book. After movable type was invented, reproducing books and sheet music in large quantities became much easier than copying by hand. Therefore, the earliest copyright laws were designed to help the creator of a song or composition collect payments from anyone wishing to duplicate the work. As uniquely American arts and entertainment creations increased, our federal government recognized a need to protect intellectual property of an artistic nature. Hence, the concept of copyright protection was gradually extended to other artistic creations in addition to literary works. American copyright laws were intended to encourage people to create works of art by providing them the right to own and profit from their works.

The first book published in the United States was the *Bay Psalm Book*, a collection of liturgical texts set to music. As technology evolved, the concept of reproducing music changed drastically. One piece of new technology was the player piano, a piano played automatically by rolls of paper containing punched holes that pneumatically triggered piano keys to play contemporary songs. Because no existing statutes protected this type of reproduction of music—piano rolls—new copyright laws needed to be enacted. Permission to make a mechanical piano roll, like sheet music, was controlled by the publisher. The permission to make mechanical devices to recreate music became known as a mechanical license. The basic concept of a mechanical license is still used today, except the mechanical device licensed is typically a CD or tape.

The most comprehensive copyright laws in this country were enacted in 1976 after many years of vigorous lobbying from persons who used copyright-protected music (television, radio, and restaurant interests) and persons who controlled copyrighted music (songwriters and publishers). Although the new copyright act addressed changes in commerce and technology, it left questions to be answered in the courts.

The Copyright Act of 1976 governs the use of all artistic and literary creations, including music, lyrics, and visual arts. The body of copyright law enacted in 1976 was so comprehensive that Congress gave the public two years to adjust to the changes. The 1976 Copyright Act thus actually took effect on January 1, 1978. The act requires persons who use copyrighted music to obtain permission from the person or company in control of the copyright before using a musical composition or song to create a new derivative work. For example, a film is a work derived from many existing copyrighted works—from a musical score, individual songs, a script, and others. If the film uses several different songs, the film's producer must obtain permission from each copyright holder before using the songs in the film. A song is considered intellectual property and is, therefore, protected by federal copyright. Unlike tangible property, such as a car or house, intellectual property can take many forms. For example, a song—basically a melody with lyrics—can be contained on a recording, notated in sheet music, or arranged and used in a television commercial.

Although a songwriter might have a wonderful song in his or her head, the song is not protected by copyright laws until it is fixed in tangible form. To put a song into a fixed form, the creator usually creates a recording of the song or writes the melody and lyrics using traditional music notation. To establish a date of ownership, professional songwriters register their songs with the Office of Copyright in the Library of Congress using a form PA (http://lcweb.loc.gov/copyright). A songwriter puts the letter *c* inside a circle, along with the songwriter's name and the year of creation, on all copies of the song to indicate the song is protected by copyright.

After fixing the song in tangible form, songwriters typically want to earn income from their creation. To do this, they must have help from other industry professionals. The first step is usually to secure a publishing contract. A publishing deal is conceptually quite simple: In exchange for a percentage of the income derived from the song (usually 50 percent), a publisher will gain control of the copyright. In turn, the publisher will exploit the song in the marketplace and then share the income with the songwriter. The publisher first makes a demonstration recording (song demo) of the song using professional singers and instrumentalists in a recording studio. The publisher then tries to entice producers and artists to listen to the song demo and ultimately use the song on their recording. If the song is used on a recording, the record label must obtain permission from the publisher in the form of a mechanical license, which defines how much money—usually a few cents per unit manufactured—the publisher and songwriter receive. Payments are based on the number of units sold and are called mechanical royalties. Most publishers use the services of the Harry Fox Agency in New York to administer their mechanical licenses.

A performance, another use of a song, is also protected by copyright law. In a legal sense, a performance can take the form of a live performance, a radio broadcast, or television broadcast containing the song. The newest type of performance is a digital transmission across the Internet. Because it would be impossible for a publisher, even a very large one, to monitor the performances of thousands of radio stations, television stations, cable operators, concerts, and clubs, most publishers and songwriters affiliate with a performance rights licensing organization, such as the American Society of Composers, Authors and Publishers (ASCAP), Broadcast Music Incorporated (BMI) or SESAC (formerly the Society of European Stage Authors and Composers, but now only known by the acronym), to collect performance rights royalties.

Mechanical rights royalties and performance rights royalties typically represent the bulk of income songwriters and publishers earn from a song. However, generous amounts of money can also be earned from derivative uses of the song. If a song is used in synchronization with a film or television production, an additional license is required. In concept, one needs a synchronization license to create a film that includes the song and a performance license each time the film is shown. In practice, however, a film producer can obtain a combination synchronization and performance license to use a song in their film.

Keep in mind, the foregoing procedure covers only the song, not the recording of the song. Once a song is recorded, another copyright protects the recorded musical performance. Sound recording copyright includes everything beyond the melody and lyrics. Rights to the sound recording are typically owned by the record label. This copyright, like the song itself, should be registered with the Office of Copyright. The sound recording copyright is registered using form SR, and a letter $p$ inside a circle denotes sound recording copyright (http://lcweb.loc.gov/copyright).

The copyright laws in the United States grant exclusive rights to owners of copyright. Exclusive rights protect the following activities:

1. making physical copies of the work, for example, sheet music and recordings;

2. distributing copies, commonly recordings, for sale, rental, or lease;

3. performing the work in public;

4. making derivative works; and

5. transmitting the work in digital form.

In addition, copyright protection includes visual arts, such as artwork that might appear on the CD insert.

There are two important caveats to consider, however. First, the copyright act does not allow protection for ideas themselves (you cannot, for example, copyright the *idea* of rap or rock or country music). Second, the act makes exceptions to copyright protection for uses it terms "fair use" (sec. 107), and it is this concept that causes the most trouble in the music industry.

Fair use, according to our copyright laws, makes exceptions to the exclusive rights of the copyright owner. The fair use concept means the exclusive rights of the copyright owner apply to all uses of the song, *except* under certain circumstances. The act attempts to list fair use exemptions, but qualifies the list with the phrase "such as." Examples of fair use include limited reproduction of a work for face-to-face teaching in a classroom, use of excerpts for literary criticism and reviews, and parodies. The act also says the courts, in determining copyright violation, are allowed to use subjective standards such as how much economic damage was done to the original copyright holder and how much of the original work was copied. The only thing agreed on by the industry in 1978 was that the new laws did not define the concept of fair use very well.

## COPYRIGHT INFRINGEMENT

Several factors come into play when trying to ascertain whether or not a sample or a parody has infringed on the copyright of another work. These factors include (1) how much of the original work was used; (2) how much damage to the commercial viability of the original work has been caused by the new work; and (3) the purpose of the new work. Anyone who uses music without the permission of the copyright owner "infringes" on the owner's rights. Remember, copyright laws are federal laws. Therefore, copyright infringement is a federal matter.

One of the best-known examples of musical "borrowing"—or copyright infringement, depending on whom you ask—involved former Beatle George Harrison. A musical group called the Chiffons claimed Harrison's song "My Sweet Lord" was too much like their song "He's So Fine," written by Ronald Mack and recorded by the Chiffons for Bright Tunes Music in 1962. The catchy tune contained repetitions of two basic phrases as shown in Figure 4.1 and Figure 4.2. Phrase A

Figure 4.1. Phrase A.

Figure 4.2. Phrase B.

(Fig. 4.1) was played four times, followed by four repetitions of Phrase B (four groups of the notes shown in Figure 4.2). Experts said the two sets of notes were not by themselves unique; however, the "four-and-four" pattern, they said, was "very unique" (*Bright Tunes*, 1976). In addition, as shown in Figure 4.3 (Phrase C), there are several instances of a grace note—a very short note—added to the notes in Phrase B. "My Sweet Lord," recorded in 1970 by George Harrison, used four repetitions of the same Phrase A followed by three repetitions of the same Phrase B. In place of the fourth repetition of Phrase B, Harrison used a different pattern, but he kept the grace note of the Chiffons' Phrase C in the same position.

The harmonies in both songs, experts said, are identical. It should be noted, however, that this is not unusual: Chord progressions that create harmonies for popular music tend to be very similar or even identical. The melody and lyrics are, therefore, the prototypical basis of infringement suits. Although there is some confusion as to how the song actually came to be written, it is generally conceded that Harrison and R&B gospel singer Billy Preston collaborated in producing the song for Harrisongs Music, Ltd. (*Bright Tunes*, 1976). In 1971, the owners of the copyright for "He's So Fine," Bright Tunes Music Corporation, sued for copyright infringement. When the case was finally settled, twenty years later, in 1991, Harrison was required to pay $587,000 in damages for his "unknowing" use of the melody (*Bright Tunes*, 1976; *ABKCO Music*, 1981; *ABKCO Music*, 1983; *ABKCO Music*, 1988; *ABKCO Music*, 1991).

Although the copyright infringement issues surrounding "He's So Fine" and "My Sweet Lord" are significant, they did nothing to define precisely what someone can actually "borrow" from someone else's work. In addition, the judgment addressed only the use of the underlying composition, or song rights. It did not provide a legal precedent for "borrowing" a portion of sound recording rights. Questions that

Figure 4.3

would result from evolving genres, such as rap, that depend on digital technologies and sampling were not answered.

Courts have been forced to look at infringement claims case by case. There is a common misconception that one can use a few bars of a song without infringing on copyright. However, this concept is without legal merit. As explained by copyright expert Brett I. Kaplicer, "Whether it is one note, two notes, or even three, the trier of fact in each case should ultimately determine whether the defendant has appropriated, either qualitatively or quantitatively, enough of the plaintiff's original expression to rise to the level of substantial similarity" (Kaplicer, 2000). Therefore, sampling any recognizable portion of the song or sound recording without permission could constitute infringement.

## SAMPLING

As one can see, using someone else's music treads on several forms of protection. A common, and sometimes controversial, way of using parts of someone else's song and sound recording is called sampling. Rap artists often take small segments of several different recordings and incorporate them into a new work that involves using the sound recording as well as the underlying song (melody and lyrics) incorporated into the recording. Therefore, the person who samples a small segment of a recording must obtain permission from the record label (for the sound recording) and publisher (for the melody and lyrics).

The earliest form of sampling was called "Musique Concrete." It was developed by a French radio broadcaster name Pierre Schaeffer in 1948 (www.musespace.com). The French term "Musique Concrete" refers to the use of "found" sounds that exist in nature. The first composers to experiment with this technique used analog tape recorders to record naturally occurring and acoustically generated sounds. Then, they edited pieces of different sounds together to create long sound collages. In order to create a five-minute composition, many hours of cut-and-paste editing were needed.

In addition to early attempts to sample existing sounds, Musique Concrete composers developed a technique for repeating recorded sounds of short duration to make a repetitive, and often rhythmic, piece of music. This technique was called "looping," from the practice of splicing a length of analog tape into a circle. The circle, or loop, of tape would travel over the tape head repeating the sounds for as long as the composer wanted.

Conceptually, creators of dance music and rap songs do the same thing as Musique Concrete composers: sample existing music, then edit and loop it. However, the development of digital recording has made the process much easier. The digital recording process, as opposed to analog recording, converts sounds into digital information in the same way that a word processor converts typed letters to digital codes and back again. This digital information can be modified, edited, and played back with amazing speed and accuracy. Small digital samplers are readily available and fairly inexpensive.

The merger of digital recording, computer storage systems, and music-specific software has lead to a new system of creating music called musical instrument digital interface (MIDI). As MIDI equipment became more sophisticated and less expensive over the past twenty years, it has transformed the way recordings are made. MIDI technology has also created new controversies regarding music copyrights that were not addressed in the copyright act.

Songwriters, composers, and producers no longer have to rely on traditional recording sessions to create their music. For example, a producer might imagine a wonderful orchestral string section in the background of the song they are producing. Because of MIDI technology, the producer has several options. He or she might choose the traditional way: hire several violinists, violists, and cellists to record in a studio. Or the producer can use synthesized sounds of violins, violas, and cellos using a synthesizer keyboard and MIDI equipment and software. The last option, and the most controversial, is to sample an actual orchestral section of another recording and edit it, using MIDI techniques, for the new recording.

The question we must ask ourselves is, have any of the options presented above infringed on the sound recording rights of the original recording? If a producer has used a portion of the vocalist singing the lyrics and the melody, has that producer infringed upon the song rights as well? One artist, Leo Nocentelli, of the New Orleans funk band the Meters, recalls his introduction to sampling: "I was on a session and the guy pressed one note on the keyboard and it made 'Whooaahh! Good God!' like James Brown. It blew me away. It was James Brown's voice by the press of a finger and I saw the trouble in that" (Snowden, 1989, p. 61). James Brown himself, quoted in an article by Randy S. Kravis, was even more emphatic: "Anything they take off my record is mine. Is it all right if I take some paint off your house and put it on mine? Can I take a button off your shirt and put it on mine? Can I take a toenail off your foot—is that all right with you?" (Kravis, 1993).

In addition to the confusion regarding legal interpretations of the copyright law, interpretations of what sampling means, from a utilitarian standpoint, vary. For example:

"Sampling" means very different things to different people. To a synthesizer manufacturer, a sample is the discrete sound of a piano or drum recorded on a chip. To a composer [or producer], it's riff played by an ace guitarist—or a symphony orchestra, for that matter—on a sample CD. To a rapper like Puffy Combs, it's the Police's "Every Breath You Take," which Combs reincarnated in his Grammy-winning hit, "I'm Missing You." And to a musicologist, sampling is an entirely new method of composing, in which sounds, not notes, are the vocabulary of choice, and virtually any sound can belong to anyone. (Lyon, 1998)

Whereas fine art electronic music applications of analog sampling have been around since 1948, commercial entertainment applications of digital sampling are a fairly recent phenomenon. In the 1960s disc jockeys began to mix different sounds together into a single work called a "dub." A soft rock example is found in two recordings of the same song, "You Don't Bring Me Flowers," recorded by Neil Diamond and by Barbra Streisand at about the same time in the late 1970s. Realizing that the songs were in the same musical key, DJs began to play both at the same time, thus "mixing" them (other versions of the story say DJs took audiotapes of the two songs and spliced them together). The response from listeners was apparently so enthusiastic, Diamond and Streisand later recorded the song as a duet.

While radio DJs were mixing their own song collages for broadcast, a new artform, called rap, began in 1974 (see Chapter 8 for a more in-depth discussion of the evolution of rap). Rap producers typically began the recording process by creating an instrumental bed over which the MC (as in master of ceremonies) would rap. By using synthesizers, digital samplers, and MIDI technology, rap producers sampled and mixed existing sounds (Kravis, 1993). Thus it can be seen that sampling is not simply copying another artist's work. Sampling can, of course, involve direct copying, unchanged by digital manipulation. How much has been copied is certainly a relevant question here. Some examples of early recordings that used this kind of sampling are Run DMC's "Walk This Way," which uses portions of Aerosmith's recording of the same song, and "U Can't Touch This," by MC Hammer, which uses a distinctive riff from "Super Freak" by Rick James.

Another use of sampling is taking the original sound and manipulating it to make another sound. In some cases, the original sound is completely lost in the process. Still another use is to take an existing natural sound (i.e., a jackhammer, an airplane, or the crack of a bat hitting a ball) and digitize it and use it in a song. Artists such as Nine Inch Nails and Moby use such sound effects as overlays to lyrics and traditional musical instruments. Of course, natural sounds do not have copyright protection like music does.

Regardless of how the music is sampled, the use to which it is put, or how much is used, the question still arises: Is sampling stealing and thus prohibited by existing copyright laws, or is sampling one more artistic technique that is, in fact, protected by U.S. copyright laws? One way to avoid sampling problems is to ask permission or, in terms of industry practice, obtain a "license" to use the original work, or portions thereof, for specified purposes. In order to use a part of the melody and lyrics, the producer or record label of the new work needs permission for two things. First, permission is needed to create a derivative work that contains the song. Second, permission is needed to distribute the new work for sale, rental or lease. Those permissions are typically obtained through the publisher of the song in question and are a license, which will often be based on a "per unit" cost. For example, the publisher might give a license that costs the producer or label a few cents for each unit—CD or tape—sold. Thus, in order to use a portion of the sound recording, the producer or record label for the new work must obtain a license from the label of the recording to be sampled, with said license based on the number of units sold.

Although it seems intuitively logical to obtain the necessary licenses for songs and recordings sampled, some artists, producers, and labels fail to do so. One problem involves time and the difficulty of identifying who controls the copyrights. Another problem concerns the number of samples that must be licensed on an album. A producer who wants to include an average of four samples per song on an album of ten songs, for example, will have to negotiate eighty licenses: forty song permissions and forty sound recording permissions. It should be noted that the publisher typically controls the copyright and does not "sell" a song outright. Rather, the owner will "license" a song; that is, for a fee, the owner will allow someone to use the song for very specific purposes. In the music industry, obtaining licenses for all sampled music is referred to as "clearing" the samples.

As rap, as well as rap-influenced music, has come to command a large proportion of recordings sold in this country, publishers and labels have become increasingly concerned about sampling. For example, rap and R&B accounted for a robust 42.2 percent of all records sold in the United States in 1998, according to SoundScan, a company that monitors record sales. In addition, some alternative rock acts have also followed the lead of rap producers and have incorporated sampling into their recordings. There is a growing concern among publishers that all samples be properly licensed.

Few court cases have involved infringement as a result of sampling. The reason is not that instances of infringement haven't occurred; it is that most have been settled out of court. The first significant case that involved sampling involved rapper Biz Markie. In his production "I Need a Haircut," Markie used three words and a portion of music from the Gilbert O'Sullivan song "Alone Again." The court ruled in favor of the publisher, Grand Upright Music Ltd and found Warner Brothers Records guilty of infringing on the song (Grand Upright Music Ltd, 1991). In order to emphasize the court's attitude about sampling, the court began its decision with the biblical phrase, "Thou shalt not steal."

Because the amount of music sampled by Markie was substantial and obvious, the case did not clearly define the amount of music that must be sampled in order for the sampling to be considered infringement. Therefore, another case involving sampling worked its way through the judicial system. The case involved songwriter and artist Boyd Jarvis, who sued A&M Records for using portions of his song "The Music's Got Me" on a recording called "Get Dumb." The court agreed with Jarvis that his song copyrights had been infringed. More importantly, the court explained that a sample should be judged by how qualitatively, as well as quantitatively, it reflects the original work. In other words, even if a small quantity of melody and lyrics is appropriated, the quality and recognizability must also be considered.

The problem with these court cases is they do not provide clear explanations for sampling sound recordings, only for sampling melody and lyrics or songs. Litigation involving the use of melodies from another song usually require note-by-note comparisons of the melodies to determine if they are substantially similar. Lyrics, like melodies, are easily compared to determine infringement. However, proving that a portion of a new recording is a sample of an existing work is much more difficult because the combination of music elements—melody, texture, tempo, rhythm, harmonic progression, dynamics—are so complex. In addition, digitally altering one or more elements, such as dynamics and tempo, might make detection of the other sampled elements difficult.

In all likelihood, litigation regarding digital sampling of sound recordings will increase in the future. The lack of case histories to define legal parameters of sampling only adds to the probability that cases decided in the lower courts will be appealed to higher courts. As digital technology continues to improve and prices for sampling equipment and software decrease, more self-produced artists will venture into sampling, looping, and MIDI techniques. Many young musicians and producers have come to believe music available on the Internet and through other digitally recorded formats is free for the taking. A new generation of music producers and performers might soon take their position of greater access to the courts. Perhaps then the courts will decide exactly how much of a sound recording can be sampled before it is considered infringement.

## PARODY

Parody is a literary device that is not a copy of another work but, rather, an imitation designed to make fun of the original work. Thus the parodist might make fun of a play by Shakespeare by writing a play that uses the same kind of language and literary techniques, but is a totally separate work. The writer, of course, expects the reader to recognize the original work and the fact that what is now being read is a parody. Likewise, a songwriter may write a song that is a parody of someone else's song. The question that arises, of course, is, "Is the parody an original work of art, or is it a derivative work that belongs to the owner of the parodied song?"

Whereas sampling is a direct copying of another work, parody is a different work based on an original. We also need to distinguish between parody and satire: Whereas a parody is a new work based on, and designed to poke fun at, the original work, a satire is a new work based on an original, copyrighted work, but designed to poke fun at something else.

The major debates dealing with musical parody involved the 1964 country rock classic by Roy Orbison and William Dees, "Oh, Pretty Woman," and a parody created in 1989 by Luther Campbell and 2-Live-Crew, "Pretty Woman." The original song, "Oh, Pretty Woman," was written by Roy Orbison and William Dees in 1964. As is the common practice in the recording industry, Orbison and Dees assigned the publishing rights for the song to a publisher, in this case Acuff-Rose Music. Thus Acuff-Rose would administer the licenses for any users who wished to use the song. Orbison then recorded the song with the Candymen, and it was distributed by Monument Records. Orbison's record entered *Billboard*'s Top 40 chart on September 5, 1964, where it remained for fourteen weeks. The song eventually reached the Number 1 position and remained there for three weeks (Whitburn, 1985, p. 235).

In 1989 Luther Campbell of the group 2-Live-Crew wrote "Pretty Woman," which he said was intended, "through comical lyrics, to satirize the original work" (*Campbell v. Acuff-Rose Music*, 1994). In July 1989, 2-Live-Crew wrote to Acuff-Rose Music and said they were willing to pay a license fee for their use of the song and would credit Acuff-Rose Music, Orbison, and Dees as publisher and authors (songwriters) of the original song. The group also included a copy of the lyrics and a recording of the parody. As might be expected, Acuff-Rose refused permission. Nevertheless, in summer 1989 2-Live-Crew released the song on their album (records, CDs, and tapes) *As Clean as They Want to Be*. The albums credited Acuff-Rose, Orbison, and Dees.

Over the next year the song sold nearly 250,000 copies, and Acuff-Rose filed a copyright infringement suit in Nashville. The federal district court ruled in favor of 2-Live-Crew, noting that even though the group had made commercial use of the original song, that use still falls under "fair use," and that it was "extremely unlikely that 2-Live-Crew's song could adversely affect the market for the original" (*Acuff-Rose Music v. Luther R. Campbell*, 1991, 1157–58). In reaching this conclusion, the court said the song was obviously a parody and that the rap group had used only a minimal amount of the original to establish it in the minds of the listeners. Acuff-Rose appealed the decision to the 6th Circuit Court of Appeals in Cincinnati, which reversed the U.S. District Court ruling and ruled in favor of the publisher. The appellate court, relying on the U.S. Supreme Court's decision in *Sony Corp. of America v. Universal City Studios*, said the "blatantly commercial purpose . . . prevents this parody from being a fair use" (*Campbell v. Acuff-Rose*, 1992, 1439).

As could be expected, 2-Live-Crew then appealed this decision to the U.S. Supreme Court, where Justice David Souter wrote what is essentially a primer on the issue of parody and fair use. Souter said a parodist is entitled to make "fair use" of the original work, which is generally considered only enough to establish the nature of the original. What the 2-Live-Crew decision did not address was parody as it relates to using a portion of a sound recording. Therefore, a producer in the future might assume that sampling existing songs, then looping and editing them to form a collage, might be considered a parody. If that line of logic is used, another lengthy set of trials might develop to decide the issue.

## CONCLUSION

Most law-abiding citizens would never think of taking a piece of lawn furniture from a neighbor's yard without permission. But many performers and producers don't view intellectual property such as songs and recordings the same way: They freely take portions of songs or sound recordings for their own use. Most persons who sample a recording or create a parody of a song believe they are not stealing. They rationalize "I only used a small portion of your work to create my new and different work." Just as they did when phonograph records were first invented, the judicial and legislative branches of the federal government continually work to create guidelines that define what is permissible use of songs and recordings for derivative works.

As technology improves, society as a whole will be forced to ask some tough questions: If someone samples your music, how much is "too

Songwriters such as Roy Orbison have found their work "borrowed" by other artists and discovered that not all copying is illegal. (Photofest)

much"? And, if someone makes a parody of your song and earns a large amount of money from it, should he share some of his income with you? These are serious questions that have taken up a great deal of time in our legal system. With the creation of any new technology comes social and economic change, and laws and regulations have a difficult, if not impossible, task of catching up with the social and economic consequences of the new technology. Computers and the associated music technology they provide have opened up a whole new area of debate about the ethical and legal aspects of the industry. Providing a balance between access to new works and protection of those works will not be easy in the future. The debates have begun, and there are no signs they will end any time soon.

## TOPICS FOR DISCUSSION

1. Could a law be written that would allow artists to sample another artist's work, yet at the same time protect the interests of the original copyright holder?

2. Is all music simply a variation on a limited number of themes and therefore should limited sampling be tolerated?

3. Is there a difference between sampling the melody line and sampling the lyrics? Should there be different rules for sampling the melody or the lyrics?

4. Suppose Congress amends the Copyright Act to allow unlimited sampling so long as proper credit is given and monetary compensation is provided. After this law passes, Harley Schmedlap and the Frog Stompers samples a song owned by Out of Tune Records. Out of Tune sues. Argue the case for Harley. Argue the case for Out of Tune.

## REFERENCES

### Books

Overbeck, W. (2000). *Major Principles of Media Law*. New York: Harcourt College Publishers.

Perkins, W. E., ed. (1996). *Droppin' Science: Critical Essays on Rap Music and Hip Hop Culture*. Philadelphia: Temple University Press.

Whitburn, J. (1985). *The Billboard Book of Top 40 Hits*. New York: Billboard Publications.

### Legislative and Judicial Proceedings

*ABKCO Music v. Harrisongs*, 508 F.Supp. 798 (S.D.N.Y. 1981).

*ABKCO Music v. Harrisongs*, 722 F.2d 988 (2d Cir. 1983).

*ABKCO Music v. Harrisongs*, 841 F.2d 494 (2d Cir. 1988).
*ABKCO Music v. Harrisongs*, 944 F.2d 971 (2d Cir. 1991).
*Acuff-Rose Music v. Luther R. Campbell AKA Luke Skywalker*, 754 F.Supp. 1150 (MD Tenn. 1991).
*BMI v. Claire's Boutiques*, 949 F.2d 1482 (7th Cir. 1991).
*Bright Tunes Music Corp. v. Harrisongs Music Ltd*, 420 F.Supp. 177 (S.D.N.Y. 1976).
*Campbell v. Acuff-Rose*, 972 F.2d 1429 (6th Cir. 1992).
*Campbell v. Acuff-Rose Music*, 510 U.S. 569 (1994).
*Copyrights*, 17 USC 102 (1999).
*Copyrights*, 17 USC 107 (1999).
*Edison Brothers Stores v. BMI*, 954 F.2d 1419 (8th Cir. 1991).
*Fairness in Music Licensing Act of 1998*, 105 P.L. 298; 112 Stat. 2827.
*Grand Upright Music Ltd v. Warner Brothers Records*, 780 F.Supp. 182 (S.D.N.Y. 1991).

## Magazines, Journals, and Newspapers

*Cardozo Arts and Entertainment Law Journal* (2000). *Cardozo Arts & Ent LJ* 18:227.
Chuck D. (2000, May 31). Napster: Sharing or Stealing? *CNN Burden of Proof.*
Durst, F. (2000, May 31). Napster: Sharing or Stealing? *CNN Burden of Proof.*
Kaplicer, B. I. (2000). Rap Music and De Minimus Copying: Applying the Ringgold and Sandoval Approach to Digital Samples.
Kravis, R. S. (1993). Does a Song by Any Other Name Still Sound as Sweet?: Digital Sampling and Its Copyright Implications. *American University Law Review* 43:231.
Levy, S. (2000, June 5). The Noisy War over Napster. *Newsweek*, p. 47.
Lyon, R. (1998, May 1). Viewpoint: Ample Samples. *Creativity*, p. 7.
Snowden, D. (1989, August 6). Sampling: A Creative Tool or License to Steal? *Los Angeles Times*, Calendar, p. 61.
Watson, Margaret E. (1999). Unauthorized Digital Sampling in Musical Parody: A Haven in the Fair Use Doctrine? *Western New England Law Review* 21: 469.

## Web Sites

http://fairuse.stanford.edu/
This website provides a wealth of information about copyright and fair use. It also provides access to other websites related to copyright legislation and case law.

http://lcweb.loc.gov//copyright
An extensive official site for information about copyright. This site offers instructions on how to register songs and recordings with the Office of Copyright, Library of Congress. It also has downloadable forms.

# 5

# Messages of Death: Satanic Messages, the Promotion of Evil, and Rock Music

It's hard to know for sure when critics first made the supposed connection between rock 'n' roll and evil. Some people, equating sex with evil, trace the term "rock 'n' roll" back to a blues term alluding to sex. Apparently, the assumption was that Satan influenced behavior of sinners who listened to the primal drums of rock music. Another accusation made of rock music has been its ability to induce a primal trance-like state in listeners and dancers. A few critics even believe evil forces enter one's body during those rock-induced trances. This is understandable because one can visit almost any dance club and notice persons who appear to be totally lost in the music. But are they in a trance, or are they merely concentrating on their dance moves? If entranced, would they necessarily be that way because of some evil power? And would they be more susceptible to control by Satan while in their hypnotic state?

Some critics believe rock music was fairly benign until the time of the Beatles and their alleged backward masking (reversed speech) and hidden lyrics. Still others see heavy metal performers such as Alice Cooper, with his sinister makeup, and Ozzy Osbourne, who allegedly bit the head off a live bat, as true links to satanism. Do artists who don frightening makeup and costumes really worship Satan, or are they merely using theatrical techniques to sell more concert tickets and recordings?

No one knows for sure if any artists have ever been influenced by "dark forces," but the fear has been revitalized in recent times. The tremendous popularity of some sinister-appearing bands, such as Nine Inch Nails, the admittedly satanic White Zombie, and, of course, the singer many people see as evil incarnate, Marilyn Manson, have ignited the flames of fear for many parents. Are these and other artists who have come under attack because of what they may, or may not, be doing to the hearts and souls of supposedly impressionable teenagers really dedicated to "converting" listeners to some new belief?

While the accusations fly and apocryphal stories and urban myths abound, some people believe certain combinations of music and lyrics ensnare unsuspecting listeners into satanism and then influence them to do evil. Others contend the loud sounds and depressing lyrics are simply organized noise that has no real power. Not all who loathe occult subgenres of music such as death metal, black metal, and dark metal are members of conservative groups. Music critic Rick De Yampert said of the genre, "Its ear-splitting guitars sound (and feel) like a jet engine is sucking out your brains. The genre's guttural vocals sound like a guy who's screaming and devouring a live Chihuahua at the same time. The genre's lyrics often extol The Guy With Horns and Tail Who Lives in the Hot Place" (De Yampert, 1999).

Some members of the media, including critic Michael Deeds, are neither impressed nor intimidated by this genre of music. Said Deeds about death metal band Eyehategod, "These creatures attack almost mechanically with a feedback-laced, sloth-paced, pain-faced journey into the murky depths of the very swamps from which they emerged" (Deeds, 1993). Of the group Tomb of the Mutilated, he said, "This is without a doubt the most repulsive album cover to emerge from the grave in 1992, complemented by some of the most standard death metal to get flushed down the toilet" (Deeds, 1992). Whereas Deeds and some other music critics dismiss death metal as the musical equivalent of a mosquito, others—parents, clergy, and government officials—fear it is a threat to society. As teenagers adopt the stereotypical deathlike makeup, black clothing, and Gothic accessories, parents wonder if the transformation will go beyond appearance. Each time a fan of death metal commits an antisocial or illegal act, music is the suspected cause.

## EVOLUTION OF THE OCCULT IN MUSIC

Although there is a great deal of disagreement regarding the way music affects one's behavior, there is also absolutely no doubt that some rock music past and present contains references to Satan and the occult. Many of these references are obvious in band names, album titles, lyrics, and CD artwork. Some titles with satanic references are the following:

- "The Conjuring" by Megadeth
- "Highway to Hell" by AC/DC
- "Anti-Christ Superstar" by Marilyn Manson

- "Bark at the Moon" by Ozzy Osbourne
- "Sabbath, Bloody Sabbath" by Black Sabbath
- *Their Satanic Majesties Request* by the Rolling Stones
- "In League with Satan" by Venom

The first rock album to flirt blatantly with occult references was *Their Satanic Majesties Request* by the Rolling Stones in 1967. The album cover featured Mick Jagger dressed in a sorcerer's costume. The cover also contained a plastic square that contained a dual-image illustration. Looking at the cover art from different angles made the images of the musicians appear to move. The album that contained these and numerous other unorthodox images was the first of many Rolling Stones albums alluding to the occult over the next thirty years. Other albums whose covers contained mystical symbolism and titles included *Beggar's Banquet* (an album that included the song "Sympathy for the Devil"), 1968; *Goat's Head Soup*, 1973; and *Voodoo Lounge*, 1994.

Shortly after the Rolling Stones released *Their Satanic Majesties Request*, a new artist, Alice Cooper, whose real name is Vincent Damian Furnier, released an album called *Pretties for You* in 1969. It was not so much the music as it was his over-the-top theatrical stage show that made him instantly infamous. Thus, Alice Cooper started what many pop music historians believe was the first true prototype for heavy metal.

Because hard-driving, loud rock bands have never garnered significant amounts of radio airplay in this country, most of the emerging hard rock and heavy metal bands have depended on concert touring to promote their recordings. As Alice Cooper's stage shows gained him increasing publicity—he was considered extremely bizarre at the time—his stage shows and albums capitalized on his Halloween image. Also, his lyrics began to be more aggressive: A later album contained a song titled "Lay Down and Die, Goodbye." His previous efforts were considered strange by most adults, but it was his third album, *Welcome to My Nightmare*, that began to worry some parents. Songs from the album included "Devil's Food," "Black Widow," and "Only Women Bleed." His concerts included a feigned self-decapitation, a mutilated female mannequin, huge live snakes, and giant spider props.

Around the same time Alice Cooper was touring to support his first album, a British band called Earth changed their name to Black Sabbath. In 1970, Black Sabbath released their debut album *Black Sabbath*. While Black Sabbath began to perfect instrumental and vocal sounds that helped define the genre of music now called heavy metal, it was their lead singer, Ozzy Osbourne, who emerged as the most infamous performer of heavy metal. In 1978 Black Sabbath fired Ozzy Osbourne from the band. Two years later, in 1980, Ozzy released his first solo album with new back-up musicians. The album, *Blizzard of Ozz*, soon went gold and was later certified platinum. It would eventually sell 4 million units. After his name became synonymous with the bizarre occult style of heavy metal, he formed "OzzFest" in 1996 to package the top metal bands for touring.

Another band instrumental in defining the heavy metal genre was Led Zeppelin. Led Zeppelin's maiden album release on Atlantic Records in 1969, modestly titled *Led Zeppelin*, was the first of many successful releases. Like most metal bands, Led Zeppelin received very little airplay. Although four Led Zeppelin albums are on the list of the top one hundred best-selling albums (www.RIAA.com), the highest any single made it on *Billboard* was Number 4.

Led Zeppelin's album covers added to the groups alleged satanic mystique. Their album artwork contained mystical symbols rumored to have hidden meanings. Their fourth album, *Led Zeppelin IV*, lacked a printed title on the album cover, and the only identifying names on the album were mysterious symbols printed on the inner record sleeve.

Without a doubt, Led Zeppelin was the band that brought the genre to the attention of industry executives. Just four of their albums—*Led Zeppelin II, Led Zeppelin IV, Physical Graffiti*, and *Houses of the Holy*—sold more than 60 million units. *Led Zeppelin IV* sold 22 million alone and is the fourth highest-selling album ever (www.RIAA.com).

Heavy metal seemed to have cycles of popularity. During one of its down cycles in the 1970s, a new subgenre developed. The new stylized metal bands were influenced by the punk scene as well as metal. Many of the true punk bands of the period sang (or shouted) angry lyrics over minimalistic instrumental backgrounds. The guitar sounds were often extremely fast and loud.

The union of punk and metal gave birth to thrash metal and speed metal. Bands such as Motorhead, Ace of Spades, and Overkill were able to attract both "punks" and "metal heads" (www.hardradio.com). One characteristic of punk audiences was an affinity for freeform dancing and bumping into others on the dance floor. This style of dancing, called "slam dancing," was reincarnated in the form of moshing during the early 1990s.

As many of the established heavy metal bands began to rise in popularity once again in the 1980s, mainstream heavy metal began to sound more lyrical and pop. At the same time, speed metal bands like Metallica, Megadeth, Anthrax, and Slayer slowly built a fan base for speed metal. After Metallica's *Master of Puppets* album was certified gold by RIAA in 1986, speed metal was recognized by major labels.

In a reaction to what some musicians felt was the commercialization of metal, an undercurrent of angry post-punk bands took some of the psyche from thrash metal and developed death metal. Death metal is as challenging to listen to as it is to perform: Tempos change from extremely fast to funeral march slow; full guitar power chords are amplified and distorted to extremes; vocal styles include screaming and growling that make understanding lyrics impossible.

Offshoots of death metal include black metal. Black denotes a definite association with satanism, or Satan worship—no longer mere theatrical trappings or symbolism. A slower, but equally satanic, sibling to black metal is doom metal, or simply doom. Doom returned to some of the classic Black Sabbath sound, but it added elements not seen or heard in metal. Doom began to incorporate orchestral movements and operatic vocals, reminiscent of Wagner operas. The most innovative variance doom adopted was inclusion of female singers.

Although black metal can be found in the United States and most European countries, it is most active in Norway. What troubles many people who have been following the development of black metal is its serious, rather than theatrical, approach to the occult. In 1982 the British band Venom released "Black Metal," a song that gave name to this subgenre of music. A subculture to accompany this angst laden music has also evolved.

In their in-depth investigation of black metal and the musicians who create it, *Lords of Chaos: The Bloody Rise of the Satanic Metal Underground*, authors Michael Moynihan and Didrik Soderlind reveal the seriousness of this cult-based music (Moynihan and Soderlind, 1996). They found black metal musicians who advocate church burnings, murder, and suicide. Indeed, if anyone doubts how dangerous the black metal musicians and fans can be, they should consider the actions of Varg Vikernes (The Count), a leader in the movement. Vikernes was responsible for burning more then ten churches and is serving a twenty-one-year prison sentence for killing a fellow Norwegian black metal musician Oystein Asseth in 1993 (Introvigne, 1997).

The black metal subculture is definitely not smoke and mirror theatrics. It is a social movement that, some fear, too closely resembles neo-Nazism's hatred of organized religions, especially Judaism and Christianity. Varg Vikernes published what he calls his *Sacred Text* and has championed Vidkun Quisling (1887–1945), a Nazi collaborator and alleged racialist (Introvigne, 1997). Varg Vikernes continues to write music and magazine articles from his prison cell.

## SATANIC MUSIC AND HUMAN BEHAVIOR

Whenever fans of satanic or occult music do something to harm themselves or someone else, the inevitable question arises, "Did the music make the listener do it?" As we discussed in Chapter 2 about drugs and music, there are many theories about whether music causes behavioral changes in listeners. Those same unanswered questions surround the debate about music associated with the occult and satanism.

The notion that some kinds of music contain satanic messages that cause listeners to act in certain ways is predicated upon one of two ideas. The first is that the brain can be influenced subliminally by garbled words whose "true" meaning is somehow directly grasped by the subconscious mind. The second is that the mind translates reversed speech (backward masking) into clear speech where the true meaning is understood by the subconscious mind. In either case, the subconscious mind allegedly then directs the conscious mind to believe bad things or do bad deeds. There is, however, no reputable evidence such mental processes exist.

The belief in the existence and efficacy of backward satanic messages probably derives from the ancient practice of mocking Christianity by saying prayers backwards at the witch's Sabbath. One such example is the Beatles' allegedly putting backward or subliminal messages in their recordings. They supposedly announced that Paul McCartney was dead, but of course he was very much alive and well. Another example is Jimmy Page's allegedly inserting the backward message "my sweet Satan" in Led Zeppelin's song "Stairway to Heaven."

Obviously, then, the subject of demonic influence in music is not as simple as it first sounds. Although the questions, "Is there demonic content in secular music?" "Is 'Christian Rock' really Christian?" and "Can rock music have a subconscious influence?" may seem separate and distinct, they are, in fact, interrelated.

## CRITICISM FROM CHRISTIAN GROUPS

Whereas organizations such as the Fundamental Evangelistic Association may be concerned about rock lyrics in general, the Christian Family Network (CFN) has taken on Marilyn Manson—whose name is really Brian Warner—himself. Interestingly, in what almost looks like a paean to the rocker (the CFN website includes photographs, news stories, quotes, audio clips, and concert reviews of Marilyn Manson), the CFN home page proclaims, "This site is committed to providing the truth about Marilyn Manson from a Christian perspective. We believe that Mr. Manson will be thrilled by any discord this causes, but God has placed us in this arena to battle the wickedness that Marilyn and his band symbolize" ("The Truth about Marilyn Manson," 1999).

Although many conservative Christian groups seem content merely to distribute information, the American Family Association takes a more proactive stand by distributing suggestions for combating what the groups sees as Manson's satanic influences, including working with police and other officials to set up "citizen's oversight committees," and it

Lead singer of the shock rock band Marilyn Manson performs at "OzzFest '97" at Giants Stadium on Sunday, June 15, 1997, in East Rutherford, New Jersey. (AP/Wide World Photos)

appeals to city officials to strictly enforce laws regarding drug and alcohol use at concerts ("What to Do When Marilyn Manson Comes to Town," 1999). First Amendment advocates insist that parents, not government, should regulate what young consumers listen to. It appears, then, that the American Family Association is alerting parents to do just that.

Even established church leaders such as the late John Cardinal O'Connor have entered the fray. In a 1990 sermon at St. Patrick's Cathedral in New York City, the cardinal denounced the demonic influences of some rock music, calling the music "pornography in sound" and asserting, "Some music is a help to the devil" ("Cardinal: Two Devil Exorcisms Recently," 1990).

Not all critics of occult music have used acceptable methods, such as protest rallies or speeches, to voice their dissent. On March 1, 1995, a fan was arrested backstage at a Robert Plant and Jimmy Page concert in Detroit. The assailant, armed with a pocket knife, allegedly wanted to stab guitarist Page. The former fan of Led Zeppelin believed Plant and Page were performing satanic music (*Entertainment News Wire*, 2000).

## CHRISTIAN ROCK: AN OXYMORON?

One would expect some secular groups that include occult-looking costumes and scenery in their performances to come under fire from conservative religious groups. But what about Christian groups? Well, they too have come under criticism for supposedly promoting satanism. How, you might ask, can that be? Many fundamentalist religious groups and denominations decry rock music in general. To many of these groups, even worse is so-called Christian rock. Some fundamentalist religious groups consider established contemporary Christian acts such as Amy Grant, Petra, Steve Greene, and Twila Paris to be as reprehensible as secular bands like White Zombie and Marilyn Manson ("What about Soft-Rock Music," 1999).

Why? Simply because such Christian acts do not meet the Fundamental Evangelistic Association's (FEA) criteria for a truly "Christian" song: The song must be doctrinally correct (according to the FEA's interpretation of the Bible); it should not contain syncopation ("Does it stir the flesh to 'boogie,' or the spirit to praise the Lord?"); and it must be politically correct ("The character of much of what is called "Christian" music may best be characterized as charismatic . . . universalist, socialist . . . utopian . . . idealistic"). In short, rock music in general, and Christian rock in particular, is suspect: *"How can rock music, with its origins in demonic activities, and with its proven adverse medical and 'emotional' effects, apply to the Gospel of the Lord Jesus Christ?"* (" 'Christian' Rock Music," 1999, emphasis in original).

Other organizations such as Dial-the-Truth Ministries chastise Christian rock groups for failing to adhere to the prohibitions of II Corinthians 6:14f (i.e., uniting the righteous with the unrighteous): "Be ye not unequally yoked together with unbelievers: for what fellowship hath righteousness with unrighteousness? And what communion hath light with darkness?" (Noebel, 1999).

Christian rock groups faulted by Dial-the-Truth include the following:

- Stryper: Faulted for an upside-down crescent moon "which to occultists is the sign of the witchcraft goddess, Diana. You'll also discover the tiny splotch of black blood" (Dial-the-Truth Ministries, 1999). Dial-the-Truth also notes that the group's producer, Enigma Music, has connections with secular satanic music.

- Frontline: Two aqua-colored triangles, "the color of the Age of Aquarius" (Marrs, 1999).

- Amy Grant: Dressed in a red robe in her video "That's What Love Is For," and on the palms of her hands is a six-pointed star—A HEXAGRAM! Sean Sellars, a former satanist on death row for sacrificing three people to Satan, says in his book *Web of Darkness* (p. 51), the hexagram "is said by some to be *the most powerful and evil sign in satanism and of all the occult world.* The hexagram is used mainly in witchcraft to summon demons from the underworld. The word hex, which means to place a curse on someone, originated from this sign." And the primary point of contact in the transmission of spirits is the hand (Watkins, 1999, emphasis in original).

  It should be noted that both *Webster's New World Dictionary* and *The American Heritage Dictionary* say the word *hexagram* is derived from the Greek word *hexa* meaning "six." The word *hex*, as in "curse," is derived from a German word, *hexe*, meaning "witch." Thus the word *hexagram* has no linguistic connection with witches or the occult. The six-pointed star is also known as the "Star of David," and sometimes as "Solomon's Seal," and it is also a symbol of the State of Israel.

- Michael W. Smith: Smith's name is written backwards and the *M* and *T* are "part of the runic alphabet. Runes are the oldest form of occult knowledge and magic . . . their use sets a person against God" ("Is This Christian," 1999a).

- Carman: According to Terry Watkins, head of Dial-the-Truth Ministries, Carman's videos contain blasphemous images as well as occult symbols such as satanic tarot cards, pentagrams, and "the satanic salute (index and pinky finger displayed)" (Watkins, 1999). Although Watkins equates the "index and pinky finger" gesture with satanism, the hand motion is also used by fans of the University of Texas Longhorns as a "hook 'em horns" salute.

- Point of Grace: Criticized for using zodiac signs, Egyptian signs, pyramids, and hexagrams (Watkins, 1999).

For some devout Christians, however, contemporary Christian and Gospel music is merely another tool to "win souls for Christ." Even the venerable Christian evangelist Billy Graham uses Christian rock and rap groups such as Jars of Clay and dc Talk in his crusades.

Perhaps the most paradoxical form of music to emerge in recent history is called "Christian metal" music. Like its secular analog, Christian metal has subgenres: hard rock/melodic metal; heavy metal/classic metal; speed metal/thrash metal; death metal; doom metal; and black metal. A well-organized website, Metal for Jesus, offers the following explanation: "Christian Metal is just as brutal and heavy as the Secular [sic] when it comes to the music. What differs is the lyrics" (Metal for Jesus, 2000). In addition, the Metal for Jesus site presents a comparison chart to help persons switch from secular metal to Christian metal. For example, those who like Marilyn Manson should listen to Rackets and Drapes. Fans of Nine Inch Nails are instructed to listen to the band Detritus.

It should be noted that Christian rock also has millions of supporters, even among the ministry. Said Frank Breeden, president of the Gospel Music Association, the organization that sponsors the Dove Awards, the Christian music equivalent of the Grammies, "There really is no such thing as a Christian B-flat. Music in itself is an amoral vehicle" (Sclater, 1998).

## POLITICS AND SATAN'S MUSIC

Not only have various religious and civic groups gotten involved in satanic and occult music, but Rep. Robert K. Dornan of California once proposed a bill in Congress that would require record companies to put labels on records, similar to cigarette warning labels, to warn against backward masking (Grove, 1985). The measure, which would be nearly impossible to police, was defeated (Harrington, 1982). That such a law was even considered shows the concern some citizens have regarding satanic and occult music. (See more on record labeling in Chapter 10.)

At hearings on the measure, Led Zeppelin's "Stairway to Heaven" was played and its alleged "backward masked" lyrics exposed. Although offered a chance to reply, Mark Weinberg of Swan Song Records merely said, "Our turntables only rotate in one direction" (Brenner, 1982a; Ferguson, 1982; Brenner, 1982b). The *Washington Post*, on what was apparently a slow editorial day, took the congressman to task in a somewhat tongue-in-cheek editorial:

> Those of you who may not be in the habit of halting your turntable's forward motion and forcing the stylus backward through the record's grooves may be wondering what this is all about. Mr. Dornan was inspired by a similar bill introduced in the California legislature by Republican assemblyman Phil Wyman. Both Mr. Wyman and Mr. Dornan are concerned about subliminal messages extolling the worship of Satan that are audible when records are played backward. Mr. Dornan and Mr. Wyman assure us that they do not dislike rock music (Mr. Wyman says that "Stairway to Heaven" is one of his favorite records); but they are afraid that subliminal messages may affect unknowing consumers. They have not, however, given us any inkling of how the human brain goes about sorting out from the multitude of sounds perceptible on a rock record being played forward a message that is both inaudible and backward. ("I Love Satan?" 1982)

## IS SATANIC MUSIC TO BLAME?

In addition to the considerable controversy about the alleged occult nature of rock music, both secular and Christian, are also questions about what kind of influence music, particularly heavy metal, death metal, or black metal, has on young listeners. Here, as with drug-related lyrics, the evidence is far from conclusive. Interestingly, none of the events cited above deal with the alleged satanic influence of rock music. Indeed, satanists themselves would apparently decry the violence in both society and in the media: "Satanism isn't about taking drugs, and it isn't about harming animals or children. . . . Satanism respects and exalts life. Children and animals are the purest expressions of that life force, and as such are held sacred and precious in the eyes of the Satanist" (Church of Satan Youth Communique, 1999). Nevertheless, for the alleged connection between music and violence, one can turn to three enduring suicide stories that are often cited as evidence of the evil effects of rock music.

- On October 26, 1984, John McCollum, a nineteen-year-old, killed himself while listening to Ozzy Osbourne's music.
- On December 23, 1985, Raymond Belknap and his friend, James Vance, shot themselves in a suicide pact. Belknap died immediately from the gunshot wounds, but his friend survived. Vance was left horribly disfigured and died three years later from his

injuries. Both had been listening to the Judas Priest album *Stained Class* before the incident.

- On May 3, 1986, Michael Jeffery Waller committed suicide. In this case it was alleged Waller killed himself after repeatedly listening to an Ozzy Osbourne tape.

Although these three events were certainly tragic, they brought into sharp focus the ongoing debate about the effects of rock music and the paucity of evidence supporting the idea that rock music can make someone do something.

On October 26, 1984, nineteen-year-old John Daniel McCollum shot himself in his right temple with a .22 caliber handgun while lying on his bed listening to the final side of a two-record Ozzy Osbourne album, *Speak of the Devil* (*McCollum et al. v. CBS, Inc., and John "Ozzy" Osbourne, 1988*). McCollum had a problem with alcohol abuse as well as serious emotional problems. During the time before his death he had listened to side one of an Osbourne album, *Blizzard of Ozz*, and side two of another Osbourne album, *Diary of a Madman*. These albums were found on a stereo in the family's living room. However, he had gone into his bedroom and was apparently listening to *Speak of the Devil* at the time of his death. He was found the next morning (October 27, 1984), wearing a headset. The stereo was still running, with the needle in the center of the still-turning record.

A year later, on October 25, 1985, McCollum's parents sued both CBS Records and Osbourne, claiming the music caused the youth's suicide. They later amended their suit, claiming negligence, product liability, and intentional misconduct. On December 19, 1986, Judge John L. Cole of the Los Angeles County Superior Court dismissed the complaint. The McCollums appealed, and in July 1988 a California court of appeals affirmed the dismissal. The court of appeals agreed that "the message he [Osbourne] has often conveyed is that life is filled with nothing but despair and hopelessness and suicide is not only acceptable, but desirable." The court also noted, however, that suicide is a common theme throughout literature:

- Hamlet's "to be or not to be" soliloquy is about suicide.
- There are sixteen suicides in Shakespeare's plays.
- Tolstoy's Anna Karenina dies by throwing herself under a train.
- Willie Loman in *Death of a Salesman* plans to commit suicide.
- The operas of Puccini, Menotti, and Verdi all contain suicides.

- The theme song from the movie and television program *M\*A\*S\*H* is titled "Suicide Is Painless." (*McCollum et al. v. CBS, Inc., and John "Ozzy" Osbourne*, 1988, p. 995).

In affirming the lower court's dismissal of the action, the court of appeals made several assertions: The First Amendment bars the plaintiff's action, and the plaintiffs did not show any basis for recovery. That is, they did not present any evidence to support their charges.

In regards to the First Amendment, the court said, "Entertainment, as well as political and ideological speech, is protected; motion pictures, programs broadcast by radio and television, and live entertainment, such as musical and dramatic works, fall within the First Amendment guarantee" (*McCollum et al. v. CBS, Inc., and John "Ozzy" Osbourne*, 1988, p. 999). The court did note that First Amendment protections are not absolute, but only in cases where direct, immediate harm has been shown to be caused by the communication would sanctions be considered. It is this standard of "direct, immediate harm" that is difficult to overcome.

In terms of the actual impact of the music, the court noted that McCollum's parents had not presented any evidence to show such an effect: "It can not be said that there was a close connection between John's death and defendants' composition, performance, production and distribution years earlier of recorded artistic musical expressions. Likewise, no moral blame for that tragedy may be laid at defendants' door." (*McCollum et al. v. CBS, Inc., and John "Ozzy" Osbourne*, 1988, pp. 1005–6).

The court also made it clear that artists should not be expected to consider the impact their music might have on the most susceptible members of society: "It is simply not acceptable to a free and democratic society to limit and restrict their creativity in order to avoid the dissemination of ideas in artistic speech which may adversely affect emotionally troubled children" (*McCollum et al. v. CBS, Inc., and John "Ozzy" Osbourne*, 1988, p. 1005).

The second incident, that of December 23, 1985, involved two attempted suicides, one of which was successful. In this case there surfaced the issue of scientific evidence for mind control by music. According to the Washoe County District Court, both James Vance and Raymond Belknap had serious emotional and social problems, and although the parents tried to link the shooting to the Judas Priest album, there was evidence that James, at least, was contemplating suicide even before the boys began listening: "Later in the afternoon Vance and Belknap had a discussion with Rita, Raymond's sister. During that discussion James asked Rita whether she was willing to name the child with which she was pregnant after Raymond if anything were to happen to him. She said that she would. After having said this, Raymond gave her a hug and kiss and told her he loved her" (*Vance v. Judas Priest*, 1990, pp. 14–16). The court then went on to describe the rest of the afternoon and noted that although the boys had been chanting something that sounded like "Just do it, just do it," these lyrics do not appear in the album in question.

Of more significance was the testimony of the plaintiffs' and defendants' witnesses as to the effect of record lyrics on the mind. Unfortunately for those looking for a cause-and-effect relationship between Judas Priest and the suicide, even the plaintiff's chief witness, Dr. Howard Shevrin, said that the connection was not certain and that someone "must be predisposed to do a particular act before a subliminal message will have an effect on behavior" (*Vance v. Judas Priest*, 1990, p. 11). The defendants' witness, of course, was even more emphatic: Dr. Anthony Pratkanis and the defendants' other witnesses testified that a subliminal message can have no impact on behavior. Rather, the "deceaseds' actions were caused by depression resulting from a combination of alcohol, marijuana, personality disorders, and employment and family problems" (*Vance v. Judas Priest*, 1990, p. 13). Thus the court issued two "Findings of Fact": First, "The scientific research presented does not establish that subliminal stimuli, even if perceived, may precipitate conduct of this magnitude." Second, "There exist other factors which explain the conduct of the deceased independent of the subliminal stimuli" (*Vance v. Judas Priest*, 1990, p. 14).

The third incident often cited by those who think "the music made me do it" involved the supposed connection between the suicide of Michael Jeffery Waller and, once again, Ozzy Osbourne. In this case most of the court record deals with alleged subliminal messages in the song "Suicide Solution" on the album *Blizzard of Ozz*. Few details of the life of Waller are available, except to say he was a "troubled adolescent" (*Waller v. Osbourne*, 1991).

As in the previous cases, the plaintiffs were given every opportunity to prove their contention that the music somehow led directly to violent, suicidal actions. They were allowed to rely on psychologists and sound engineers to prove their contention. And as in the previous two cases, they were unable to do so. Said the court: "Viewing the facts in a light most favorable to the plaintiffs, the song 'Suicide Solution' can be perceived as asserting in a philosophical sense that suicide may be a viable option one should consider in certain circumstances. . . . Nevertheless, an abstract discussion of the moral propriety or even moral necessity for a resort to suicide, is not the same as indicating to someone that he should commit suicide" (*Waller v. Osbourne*, 1991, p. 1151).

## CONCLUSION

As we noted above, for over thirty years there have been references to Satan and the occult in band names, album titles, and song lyrics. In addition, some very popular artists use demonic-looking clothes, makeup, and staging to present an eerie image to the public. Therefore, as one might expect, parents, church leaders, and lawmakers have often criticized heavy metal and its derivative subgenres.

Whether or not we agree with those who criticize such music, we probably understand why parents may be concerned that their children not only listen to the music but also adopt the lifestyle and image of the artists who play the music. Marilyn Manson has mocked Christian hymns in his concerts and declared, "I am the god of (expletive)" (De Yampert, 1999). He and others have used broken glass and other sharp objects to perform acts of self-mutilation on stage. Many parents don't understand the purpose of such performances by Manson and by other artists, such as Alice Cooper and G. G. Allin. They wonder how the music and the milieu it creates might affect their children. Statements such as "If you're a strong person, you're not going to convert to satanism," offered by Manson concert attendee Terri Vasquez, twenty, cause one to wonder if the not-so-strong are being converted (MacCormack, 1999). So, as with other species, parents try to protect their offspring from potential harm. Yet according to Stuart Fishoff, professor of media psychology at California State University, Los Angeles, "The research shows, unequivocally, people who are predisposed to violence are attracted to violent media," and not the other way around (Thomas, 1999).

Many musicians whose music is associated with the occult admit they don't take satanism seriously. Alice Cooper compares his act to a circus sideshow and denies any deep, let alone mysterious, meaning to his music (Beckerman, 1999). Ian Scott, guitarist with Anthrax, observed, "Every name on the bill [Clash of the Titans Heavy Metal tour] has to do with killing, but it's just imagery" (Gunderson, 1991).

Dave Sirulnick, head of the news department at MTV, believes most teenagers seek a group of peers with whom that can associate. Furthermore, he thinks following a subculture based on a particular artist or style of music provides that needed peer group. "They're into something; it's the kids who withdraw that you have to worry about," said Sirulnick (Thomas, 1999). This need for peer group identity is evident in Gothic, or Goth, fans, who wear dark clothing that makes them look like extras for a Dracula film and thus gives them membership in an identifiable group. Troy Hunt, an organizer of a national Goth convention, described a sense of "us" that the event provided. "You could bump into people in the hallways of the hotel and just strike up a conversation with no introduction whatsoever," said Hunt (Chen, 1999).

Unfortunately, too many adults today vividly recollect an organized movement of young people wearing the same-colored outfits: the brown uniforms of the Nazi Jugen Bund. Perhaps the uniform look of teenage aficionados of the many subgenres of music with occult trappings dredges up those memories many parents and grandparents have tried to forget. Whether or not musicians really worship Satan or merely use occult references for effect, their music and behavior will continue to upset a percentage of the population. As Brian Warner said of his alter ego, "What good would Marilyn Manson be if no one hated Marilyn?" (quoted from a 1994 interview in MacCormack, 1999).

## TOPICS FOR DISCUSSION

1. Is the concern with satanic and occult music with the way the song is presented or with the message itself? Or is it with both?

2. Some people contend that recording artists who perform satanic and occult music are only putting on a performance; that they are, in fact, ordinary people who don't believe a thing about what they are singing. Do you think this is true? Can you sing about one lifestyle yet live another?

3. Part of the concern about occult music is that it promotes evil. Suppose a group called The Square Triangle records a song promoting "good" magic. How do you think parent and religious groups would respond? Would it make a difference if the song had a hard driving beat or if it were "light and sunny"?

4. Respond to the accusation that songs that promote environmentalism and world unity are satanic.

5. The Goth movement has spawned some forms of music that use pagan symbolism and rituals. Is this type of music satanic or merely theatrical?

6. Is it possible for fans of death metal or black metal to remain devout Christians or Jews?

## REFERENCES

### Books

Campbell, R. (1998) *Media and Culture*. New York: St. Martin's Press.
Introvigne, M. (1997). *The Gothic Milieu: Black Metal, Satanism, and Vampires*. Torino, Italy: Center for Studies on New Religions (www.cesnur.org).

Moynihan, M. and D. Soderlind (1998). *Lords of Chaos: The Bloody Rise of the Satanic Metal Underground*. Los Angeles: Feral House.


## Legislative and Judicial Proceedings

*McCollum et al. v. CBS, Inc., and John "Ozzy" Osbourne*, 202 Cal.App.3d 989, 249 Cal.Rptr. 187 (1988).
*Vance v. Judas Priest*, 1990 WL 130920 (Nev.Dist.Ct.), 1990.
*Waller v. Osbourne*, 763 F.Supp. 1144 (1991).


## Magazines, Journals, and Newspapers

Beckerman, J. (1999, October 22). Shock-Rocker Gets the Chills, Alice Cooper Does Halloween. *Bergen (N.J.) Record*, Your Time, p. Y2.
Brenner, E. (1982a, July 6). Congressman Warns of Satanic Messages on Rock Records. *United Press International*.
Brenner, E. (1982b, July 5). Satan Is Everywhere—Especially on Rock Records. *United Press International*.
Cardinal: Two Devil Exorcisms Recently—Blames Heavy Metal. (1990, March 5). *United Press International*.
Chen, S. (1999, October 28). Gothic Houston: Nationwide Goth Music Conference Inspired by Houstonian. *Houston Press*.
De Yampert, R. (1999, June 17). Famous Devilish Rockers Really on the Fringe of Fright. *Tennessean*, p. 4F.
Deeds, M. (1992, October 16). Alternative Reviews. *Idaho Statesman*.
Deeds, M. (1993, February 19). Alternative Reviews. *Idaho Statesman*.
*Entertainment News Wire* (2000, March 20). Led Zeppelin Fan Arrested.
Ferguson, E. (1982, July 6). Style: Personalities. *Washington Post*, p. B3.
Grove, L. (1985, April 4). Bob Dornan, Combat Ready: The Controversial California Congressman Shooting from the Lip and Aiming for "Wimps." *Washington Post*, p. C1.
Gundersen, E. (1991, May 23). A Holiday for Headbanging Rockers. *USA Today*.
Harrington, R. (1982, December 26). Baby, What'd He Say? *Washington Post*, G9.
I Love Satan? (1982, July 10). *Washington Post*, p. A22.
MacCormack, Z. (1999, March 27). Christians Try to Win Hearts of Manson Fans. *Washington Times*, p. A12.
Moore, T. E. (1996, November 21). Scientific Consensus and Expert Testimony: Lessons from the Judas Priest Trial. *Skeptical Inquirer*.
Sclater, A. (1998, June 6). Christian Rock "Satanic," Minister Says. *Montgomery Advertiser*, p. 1C.
Siskind, L. J. (1993, November 29). The Folly and Futility of Censoring Violence. *Connecticut Law Tribune*, p. 21.
Stark, S. (1995, June 11). Politicians Criticize Rock-n-Roll, as Usual. National Public Radio.
Thomas, K. (1999, April 22). Surrounded by Sound and Fury, Whirlwind of Violence, Hate Sweeps Kids, On Line and Off. *USA Today*, p. 1D.

Wickham, S. K. (1996, December 1). Raunch 'n' Roll: Lyrics Offend Many. Explicit Nature of Modern Songs Offends Many. *Union Leader*, p. A1.

## Web Sites

"Christian" Rock Music: Christian or Satanic? (1999, February 23). Dial-the-Truth Ministries. *http://www.av1611.org/crock/crock1.html*.

"Christian" Rock Music: Christian or Satanic? (1999, February 20). Fundamental Evangelistic Association. *http://www2.dynamite.com.au/wayne/crock1.htm*.

Church of Satan Youth Communique, Church of Satan. *http://www.coscentral.net/cos/home.html*, March 18, 1999.

www.hardradio.com/history. This website provides a very thorough history of heavy metal and its derivative subgenres of music.

Is This Christian? (1999a, February 26). Dial-the-Truth Ministries. *http://www.av1611.org/msmith1.html*.

Is This Christian? (1999b, February 26). Dial-the-Truth Ministries. *http://www.av1611.org/stryper4.html*.

Marrs, T. (1999, February 23). The Dragon's Hot Breath Unmasking the Awful Truth about "Christian" Rock Music. Dial-the-Truth Ministries. *http://www.av1611.org/crock/crocmars.html*.

Noebel, D. A. (1999, February 23). Christian Rock: Paganism in the Church. Dial-the-Truth Ministries. *http://www.av1611.org/crock/crocknob.html*.

www.riaa.com. This site allows a researcher to search by band or artist name and learn the sales level of all albums released.

The Truth about Marilyn Manson. (1999, February 20). Christian Family Network. *http://www.cfnweb.com/manson*.

Watkins, T. (1999, February 26). Christian Rock: Blessing or Blasphemy? Dial-the-Truth Ministries. *http://av1611.org/crock.html*.

What about Soft-Rock Music Like Steve Greene and Twila Paris? (1999, February 24). Dial-the-Truth Ministries. *http://www.av1611.org/question/cqok.html*.

What to Do When Marilyn Manson Comes to Town . . . or Your Child's Bedroom. American Family Association. (1999, February 20). *http://www.afa.net/alert/marilyn_manson_report.htm#Part 3*.

# 6

# The Glass Ceiling: Women in the Music Industry

Imagine an energetic young woman, fresh out of college, arriving for her job interview at a record label that has some of the most popular artists on its roster. As she enters the office of a senior vice president, she can hardly contain her excitement. She learned of a job opening through a college friend, a young man recently hired in an executive position at the label. The first question she hears is, "How fast can you type?" Although she is surprised at the question—she thought that she was interviewing for an executive position like her male counterpart—she answers cordially, "My last typing score was sixty-three words-per-minute with two mistakes." "That's a little slow, most of the girls around here type at least seventy-five, but you'll be on the switchboard most of the time."

Five minutes into the interview, she realized the job of "executive assistant" for which she was interviewing was actually much different than the job her college friend got. Ironically, his position has the exact same job title! This well-educated young industry hopeful knew she had two choices: take the secretarial job, smile, and try to move up in the company and recording industry; or ask why female "executives" are expected to start as receptionists whereas males aren't. Obviously, if she chose the latter course of action, she would probably not be offered the job and would have an arduous task if she chose to file a gender discrimination claim.

Some women in the music industry have pointed out that whereas other industries have moved beyond the "good ol' boys" system of hiring, the music industry often acts as if it is above the law. The obvious gender bias described in the previous hypothetical situation happens at record labels, music publishing companies, and other music firms. According to reports from women, this happens because the industry continues to rely on gender stereotypes that have been around for years.

## ARE WOMEN UNDERREPRESENTED IN THE MUSIC INDUSTRY?

A population estimate released by the U.S. Census Bureau on June 1, 1999, indicated that there are 133,230,000 males and 139,406,000 females in our country (www.census.gov). Women can, therefore, be considered the majority (51 percent) gender in the United States. That proportion is also true of undergraduate college enrollments. In addition, the average age for females in this country is almost thirty-eight, whereas for men it is thirty-five. It is intuitively logical, then, to expect females to be well represented in managerial positions in the business world.

The proportion of females in the workforce has increased dramatically since 1940. Women represented one quarter of the workforce in 1940. By 1997 women represented half of all persons employed in the United States (Smith and Bachu, 1997). The motivation behind the Family Medical Leave Act was to help companies retain more female employees after childbirth. Clearly, females are well represented in the population of employees! If half the population of college-educated job seekers is female, half the workforce is made up of women, and they tend to have longer professional lives than males, should we not expect parity in mid- and upper-level management?

In order to determine if females are well represented in music industry occupations, one must look at different types of businesses such as record labels, publishing companies, artist management firms, and booking agencies. These types of companies tend to be clusters of "small businesses," or divisions, often loosely aligned under a larger corporate umbrella. Because of the numerous autonomous divisions, these types of companies often do not have centralized human resources departments, or summary data, for all employees. Typically, they do not have the readily available data about the proportion of females in different levels of management such as a company like IBM, Ford Motor Company, or Prudential Insurance. Therefore, it is difficult to accurately define the number of females vis-à-vis males employed by record companies, publishers, or other music business firms. Audio engineers and record producers, in contrast, tend to be freelance occupations that are even more difficult to analyze from a gender distribution standpoint.

A glance through the employee roster of a record label usually reveals quite a few female employees. As one moves up the corporate ladder toward upper management, however, the gender pattern becomes decidedly male. The 1999 *Recording Industry Sourcebook*, a directory of music industry personnel, lists seventy-two senior-level executives at major labels in the United States. A senior-level executive, in terms of this research, was someone at a record company who was listed as holding the title of chairperson, CEO, or president. In total, there were nine chairpersons, twenty-one CEOs, and forty-two presidents. Of those seventy-two senior-level label executives, there were three females: one chairperson and two presidents. In other words, this analysis revealed that 4 percent of the senior-level executives at major labels were women.

The *Los Angeles Times* list of pop music's "Top 40 people who will shape the industry in the 90s and beyond" (The Top 40, 1996) included only one female. She was not one of the few female CEOs in the industry. She was Madonna! Her industry "clout," according to the publishers, emanated from her ability to sell 500,000 copies of her book, *Sex*, in one week.

The executive boardroom isn't the only place where women struggle for recognition in the recording industry. The likelihood of a female being hired as the audio engineer ("first engineer" or "mix engineer") for a major label recording is probably the same as being struck by lightning. The absence of females in engineering roles in the music industry is not, however, much different from the absence of females from engineering in general. Women account for only 8.5 percent of engineers in the United States! Yet, with the large number of females involved with music technology—as performers who use synthesizers, amplifiers, and other electronic gear—one would expect to see more women entering the field of audio engineering.

One frequently cited reason why females are not promoted to upper-management positions is their lack of experience. As the theory goes, females tend to have less work experience than their male counterparts because of child-rearing duties. For example, a woman with two children might have stopped working for a few years in order to be with her children during their preschool years. After her last child started first grade, she reentered the workforce. The males, against whom she must now compete for promotions, have more on-the-job experience than she does.

Research conducted by the Population Division of the Census Bureau tends to refute the theory that childbearing causes differential experience in women. About 60 percent of all women who discontinue work for maternity reasons return to work within six months of giving birth to their child. Amazingly, 60 percent also continue to work while pregnant. The Family Medical Leave Act has given added incentive for females to "freeze" their job while on maternity leave (Smith and Bachu, 1999). It is unlikely that the percentage of females who work throughout their pregnancy and then return to their careers will decrease in the foreseeable future.

## WHAT PROBLEMS DO WOMEN FACE IN THE MUSIC INDUSTRY?

Potential problems a woman faces in the music business begin with finding the job she really wants. This, the first big hurdle, requires that she resist any pressure to accept an "alternative" job instead of the one she is truly seeking. If she is one of the fortunate few who isn't steered away from the job she really wants and into a more "feminine" job, she might be hired. Next, she might encounter her second obstacle: an environment that neither supports nor appreciates female employees. She may encounter an environment that is unpleasant for all "non-male" employees or for her in particular. She could even get the message, "You've come a long way baby . . . now make us some coffee!"

At the end of a productive day on the job, she might grab some samples of upcoming album releases and take them home to play while she relaxes. If she's lucky, the albums won't include songs with titles like "Smack My Bitch Up," a song from British rock band Prodigy's album released by Maverick Records, Madonna's label, and distributed by Warner Brothers. Unfortunately, it is likely that Madonna's label might make huge profits off that very type of music—music that creates a distinct feeling that women are, first and foremost, sexual objects.

Recording industry firms are susceptible to sexist work environments that evolve as a result of the lyrical content of the music they sell. It is, obviously, difficult for many males to spend a lot of time working on recordings and videos that reduce the female image to a sexual object and not let that attitude carry over into their interpersonal relationships in the office. But the judicial system has made it clear that the responsibility for preventing what is termed a "hostile environment" for women in the workplace rests on the shoulders of the company as well as on those of the harassing individual. If a record company creates an atmosphere in which sexually explicit artwork is present, lyrics that denigrate women are played in work areas, and jokes of a sexual nature are common, one might describe it as a "hostile environment" for women. Such an environment has been the basis for claims of sexual harassment in recent years in many different industries, including the music industry.

Although the music industry has always offered a platform for social reform, it does not follow its own example. It seems sadly ironic that a large number of recording artists eagerly support social causes, such as shelters for battered women, yet work for record companies that are blatantly sexist in promoting music that refers to women as "bitches" and "whores." In her scathing indictment of the industry, Annie Fort (1992) asked, "Will all the artists performing at Farm Aid this year care as much about the secretaries who work at their labels as they do about farmers they have never met?"

Her point is well taken. Do artists such as Jewel, Shawn Colvin, and Alanis Morissette sing with passion about problems women face while their record labels promote violence against women? Or are they even aware of the environment that female executives, producers, and engineers endure to make and sell their respective gold records?

## GENDER STEREOTYPING

Females are, without a doubt, major consumers of music. The percentage of recordings purchased by women has increased such that they buy slightly more records (51.3 percent) than males (www.RIAA.com). In addition, female consumers buy a large percentage of albums created by female artists. For example, performers such as Jewel, Sarah McLachlan, Sheryl Crow, Whitney Houston, Brandy, and Mariah Carey perform on many of the recordings bought by women (Sudo, 1990). If women are active in the creation and consumption of recorded music, then one might assume that females would be equally well represented in boardrooms of record labels. That assumption is, however, quite far from the truth.

An explanation of why there are fewer females in leadership positions in the industry might lie in gender stereotyping. Perhaps women are funneled into the types of jobs that seldom lead to upper-level management promotions. Dyana Williams, president of the International Association of African-American Musicians (IAAAM), stated that women are "locked out of some jobs" in the music industry. According to Williams, "There are females in publicity and there are a lot of female singers, but there are few sales executives, audio engineers and producers." She gave an example of a female friend who was pursuing a job in the sales division of a record label. "My friend was steered away from sales because it is considered a job for males—not females" (Williams, 1999).

Why would females not be welcome in some departments? Dyana Williams feels that sometimes male record label employees do things they don't want women to know about. At very least, some think that their male clients would feel uncomfortable having women around at certain times. It has been rumored, for example, that record promotion executives provide perks for radio program directors in order to get radio airplay for the label's records. Several current and former promotion executives, who spoke on the condition of anonymity, admitted to providing "adult entertainment" to radio executives on occasion. When pressed about these activities, Williams (1999) stated, "The practice of promotion staff providing prostitutes and strippers for radio executives at conventions is not uncommon. This type of behavior happens all the time!"

A woman interviewed for a *Los Angeles Times* exposé (Becklund and

Philips, 1991) told the journalists that she left her job in a promotion department because "she could not comfortably take men to strip joints!" A male promotion executive who has worked for major and independent record labels spoke candidly about the "sex for airplay" rumors. He asked to remain anonymous, but confirmed that promotion staff members often have an official hotel suite at conventions plus an unadvertised and confidential suite for special guests. The two types of special guests are men from radio stations and strippers or prostitutes hired by the label. "A stag party atmosphere, complete with booze and women, is offered to important radio contacts," he said. He also noted that though there is no overt agreement that the radio executives will play the label's records, the inference is there. The goal is to establish a "good buddy" relationship with key radio personnel. The presence of female promotion executives would, obviously, put a damper on the party.

## SEX DISCRIMINATION AND THE LAW

Media coverage of sexual harassment in the music industry became so frequent in the 1990s that some people began to think it was a regular part of this quirky business. Some veteran executives—both males and females—go so far as to criticize females who file charges alleging sexual harassment or hiring discrimination. They defend unorthodox behavior by stating, "If you can't handle the environment of the music industry, then go work somewhere else."

"It's no worse in the music industry than in other fields" is a common response to allegations of sexual harassment and employment discrimination in the music industry. That line of defense attempts to explain gender bias as "human nature." Accusations of sexual harassment leveled at persons in high-profile positions such as senator, Supreme Court justice, and president have not resulted in substantial sanctions against harassers. The sexist behavior of powerful government figures sends a subtle message to other males: "Boys will be boys." Is such behavior simply a result of gender differences? Even if it is, sexual harassment is now considered totally inappropriate in the workplace, and laws have evolved to support that philosophy.

The federal government has enacted laws that address the various types of discrimination that might confront women in any workplace. Sex discrimination is protected by Title VII of the Civil Rights Act of 1964. Specifically, Section 703(a) of Title VII explains: "It shall be an unlawful employment practice for an employer . . . to fail or refuse to hire or to discharge any individual, or otherwise to discriminate against any individual with respect to his compensation, terms, conditions, or privileges of employment, because of such individual's race, color, religion, *sex*, or national origin" (emphasis added).

President Lyndon B. Johnson signing the Civil Rights Act of 1964 on July 2, 1964. This legislation gave women and minorities many rights, including legal protection against discrimination in the workplace. It is ironic that no females appear in this photograph of this historic act. (Lyndon Baines Johnson Library, Austin, Texas. Photographer: Cecil Stoughton)

The number of legal actions dealing with discriminatory hiring practices evolved quickly after passage of the Civil Rights Act of 1964. Although most litigation tended to deal with racial discrimination, it established firm footing for gender-based lawsuits that followed. The area of discrimination unique to treatment of females centered around the new concept of harassment in the working environment. To most high school–aged women, sexual harassment is an expression they understand. To their grandmothers, however, it is a recent phenomenon.

In order to further clarify its position on sexual harassment and to declare it a form of gender-based discrimination, the Equal Employment Opportunity Commission (EEOC) issued guidelines in 1980. In declaring sexual harassment to be a violation of the Civil Rights Act, the EEOC defined the circumstances under which an employer might be held liable for sexual harassment, what constitutes harassing behavior in the workplace, and steps an employer should take in order to prevent sexual harassment.

In general terms, sexual harassment is unwanted or unwelcome conduct of a sexual nature. An employee who willingly has an affair with a supervisor would have difficulty defending a claim of sexual harassment at a later date. If the sexual advances made by a supervisor were unwelcome, however, the employee might be able to establish a harassment claim. It should be noted that it is not uncommon for an employee, usually a female, to be coerced into having sex with a supervisor. The supervisory person has the power, but not the legal right, to fire or to retaliate in some other way against the harassed employee if she refuses to provide the sexual favors requested. Such sexual conduct obviously remains unwelcome and unwanted.

The EEOC's guidelines were subsequently reviewed and affirmed by a 1986 Supreme Court decision in *Meritor Savings Bank v. Vinson* (106 S. Ct. 2399, 40 EPD paragraph 36,159). An additional, and extremely important, outcome of the case was recognition of two types of sexual harassment by the judicial system. The most obvious form of harassment is referred to as "quid pro quo." This Latin expression basically means "something in exchange for something else." If an employer asks for, or merely infers, that sexual favors will result in some benefit or detriment to an employee's job status, then quid pro quo harassment has occurred. The second, and less obvious, form of harassment is called "hostile environment" sexual harassment. If a woman is subjected to crude jokes, pornography being viewed in her presence, or sexually explicit music being played in the work area, then she may very well have grounds for a hostile environment harassment claim. The expression "hostile environment" infers an atmosphere of ongoing sexually oriented activities in one's place of work.

A lawsuit filed against Price Waterhouse by Ann Hopkins, an accountant, established a firm legal precedent because it was appealed to and decided by the U.S. Supreme Court. The act of gender stereotyping by an employer was the legal issue decided in this case. Specifically, the Supreme Court decision declared gender stereotyping by an employer to be grounds for sex discrimination claims. The case of *Hopkins v. Price Waterhouse* (and later, *Price Waterhouse v. Hopkins* in appellate courts) also had a significant impact on subsequent legislation dealing with civil rights. It may also provide the legal precedent for female employees in the music industry who experience gender stereotyping.

Hopkins joined the accounting firm of Price Waterhouse in 1978 and worked in their Office of Government Services for five years. It was common practice for accountants at the firm to apply for partner status after several years of successful employment. In 1982 Ann Hopkins applied for partnership. At that time there were 662 partners, 7 of whom—1 percent—were females. Of the 88 persons seeking partner status that year, Hopkins was the only female. Twenty-one candidates were rejected, 47 were accepted and 20, including Hopkins, were held for consideration the following year. After learning that it was unlikely she would win partner status the next year, she filed a lawsuit against Price Waterhouse.

When Hopkins' employment records were examined during her U.S. District Court trial, it was apparent that she accomplished many things one would expect from partners. Records revealed that she "played a key role in Price Waterhouse's successful effort to win a multi-million dollar contract with the Department of State" (*Hopkins v. Price Waterhouse*, 287 U.S. App. D.C. 173; 920 F. 2d 967, 1990 U.S. App.). The trial court proceedings indicated that her clients were pleased with her work and that none of the partners had been as successful in the year preceding her application for partnership.

The firm justified not awarding Hopkins partner status by pointing to negative comments made by partners. The negative comments referred to her problems with interpersonal skills. During her trial Judge Gesell concluded that "both supporters and opponents to her candidacy indicated that she was sometimes overly aggressive, unduly harsh, difficult to work with and impatient with staff" (*Price Waterhouse v. Hopkins*).

Both written and spoken comments made by partners showed a definite pattern: The partners' major concern was that Hopkins' behavior was not "ladylike." Comments from partners about Hopkins' less-than-feminine demeanor included a reference that she was "macho"; another speculated that she "overcompensated for being a woman"; one suggested that she take a "course at charm school"; and several felt that she should not use foul language because it was inappropriate for a woman (*Price Waterhouse v. Hopkins*).

At the trial Dr. Susan Fiske, a social psychologist, testified that the partner selection committee appeared to be influenced by gender stereotyping. The Supreme Court agreed with Dr. Fiske. In the course of reviewing the reasons for denial of her partnership application, Supreme Court Justice O'Connor concluded that Price Waterhouse "permitted stereotypical attitudes toward women to play a significant, though unquantifiable, role in its decision not to invite her to become a partner" (Rothstein and Liebman, 1994). The lower-court trial judge noted that female candidates for partnership were viewed more favorably if they were perceived to be more feminine. He also noted that one partner said he would not support any women for partnership because "women were not even capable of functioning as senior managers (a level below partners)" (*Price Waterhouse v. Hopkins*, 1990).

Ann Hopkins was ultimately awarded back pay of $371,175 and admitted to partnership at Price Waterhouse. The most significant historical outcome of this case was the influence it had on the subsequent revisions of the Civil Rights Act. Debate over passage of the 1991 civil rights legislation made reference to legal issues presented in *Price Waterhouse v. Hopkins*.

On November 21, 1991, President George Bush signed into law the 1991 Civil Rights Act. The intent of the law was to update the existing Civil Rights Act. In doing so, Congress agreed to provide victims of civil rights violations the right to recover monetary damages. Specifically, a plaintiff could be awarded an amount of money that would compensate them for what was lost as a result of the discriminatory act. This award, called "compensatory damages," might include foregone salary or wages. In addition, for cases in which the actions of the employer were committed with "malice or with reckless indifference," the plaintiff can be awarded punitive damages. Punitive damages are intended to discourage the offending party from doing such a thing again (Civil Rights Act of 1991).

## HARASSMENT IN THE MUSIC WORKPLACE

The last decade of the millennium might receive the dubious honor of being dubbed the "Decade of Sexual Harassment Claims." According to the American Management Association, "Between 1990 and 1996, the number of sexual harassment cases filed with federal and local agencies skyrocketed 150 percent, jumping from 6,127 to 15,342" (Reynolds, 1997). Although the exact number of claims filed by employees working in the music industry is not known, media coverage of such harassment cases exploded in the 1990s.

In 1991 the *Los Angeles Times* published an in-depth story about complaints of sexual harassment in the music industry. The two investigative reporters who wrote the article, Laurie Becklund and Chuck Philips, revealed that during the previous eighteen months, female employees at three different record labels had filed harassment charges against powerful male executives at each respective company. The supervisors named in the three separate claims were all well known and powerful industry executives: Marko Babineau, former general manager of Geffen subsidiary DGC Records; Mike Bone, former co-president of Mercury Records; and, Jeff Aldrich, former senior vice president of A&R at RCA Records. At about the same time, Abe Somer, former head of the Music Department at Mitchell, Silberberg & Knupp, a powerful entertainment law firm in Los Angeles, also was the target of sexual harassment charges by a former law clerk.

Some of the women interviewed for the story described corporate environments in which sexual harassment was blatantly ignored and even joked about. The reporters learned of informal networks created by women in the music business to warn one another about sexist males to watch out for. They called those males "bimbo hounds."

Chuck Philips, the male reporter of the investigative duo, continued to investigate and report on sexual harassment in the music industry over the next three and one-half years. Philips seemed to have uncovered a dirty little secret of the music industry: Frequent incidents of sexual harassment perpetrated by specific executives are typically well known throughout a company long before any formal complaints are filed. A few of the executives found to have committed sexual harassment were not even fired. In fact, the females who lodged complaints were sometimes transferred to another area of the corporation while the male offender remained in his job. Apparently, the record labels thought that moving harassed women to a different area was the appropriate way to deal with the problem.

As a result of Philips' relentless efforts to determine how prevalent sexual harassment was in the music industry, other media pursued the topic. *Billboard* magazine published an article that conducted interviews of selected female and male executives. ABC-TV's *Prime Time Live* produced an investigative report that aired on national television. One could say that Chuck Philips was responsible for bringing sexual harassment in the music industry to a national forum.

Finding information about past incidents of sexual harassment in the music industry is quite difficult. When faced with lawsuits that appear to have a good chance of winning in court, music industry firms typically settle out of court. But in order to receive the cash settlement, female plaintiffs must agree not to discuss the case or the settlement with anyone. In rare instances, though, the plaintiff and her legal counsel decline settlement offers and proceed to a civil trial.

Penny Muck, who has been referred to as the "Anita Hill of the Music Industry" (Philips, 1992), filed a multi-million-dollar lawsuit against Geffen Records and its parent company, MCA, over allegations of sexual harassment by her former boss, Marko Babineau, former general manager of Geffen Records' DGC label. Although Muck initially refused to talk to the press about her charges, she eventually agreed to an extended interview with the *Los Angeles Times*. Her graphic description of Babineau's outrageously disgusting behavior prompted numerous other women to give anonymous reports of sexual harassment to the media.

Muck had worked in the music business for eight years, the last two as secretary to Babineau. In her lawsuit Muck alleged that Babineau had fondled her breasts and buttocks. As his behavior grew progressively more repulsive, he began occasionally to masturbate in front of her and two other female employees over a two-month period. His behavior was so bizarre that she feared no one would believe her if she reported it. "After he ejaculated, it was so weird. Like something out of Dr. Jekyll and Mr. Hyde. He just walks back into his office and it's like business as usual" (Philips, 1992, p. 1).

Geffen Records' response to Babineau's behavior was, amazingly enough, just as bizarre. Sources at Geffen told reporters that Babineau had sexually harassed other female employees as far back as 1984, when he became head of promotion at Geffen. Prior to Muck's complaint, two other women had been transferred to other departments when they complained about him. Babineau's punishment at the time? He was promoted to general manager of Geffen's newly formed DGC label when Geffen Records was sold to MCA in 1990!

Penny Muck settled her lawsuit for assault, battery, and sexual harassment against Geffen Records for over $500,000 according to anonymous sources interviewed by the *Los Angeles Times* in 1995 (Philips, 1995). A second sexual harassment case against Babineau, filed a year after Muck's, was settled for $100,000. Although Muck was prepared to be ostracized from the music industry, she found an excellent job as the West Coast representative for an artist management firm.

Not all print media saw the Peggy Muck incident as a symptom of a greater problem worth pursuing aggressively. An article by Chris Morris and Phyllis Stark (1991) in *Billboard* seemed to sugar-coat the issue of sexual harassment in typical showbiz style. Although the article cited quotations from female victims that read like indictments of the music industry in general, the journalists apparently felt a need to cushion those revelations with their version of "boys will be boys." Morris and Stark generalized, "Many observers believe that, while sexual harassment does take place within the music industry, it is no more prevalent there than in any other sector of American business." They seemed to echo Irving Azoff, president of Giant Records, who responded to the *Los Angeles Times* article by saying, "I'm astounded that they chose to limit the story to the record business. As usual, the record business is low man on the totem pole, and we get hit first." But the ultimate head-in-the-sand award goes to Sammy Hagar, of the group Van Halen, who gave his true feelings about sexual harassment in the music business during a backstage interview. Hagar told a reporter, "Can you blame 'em? They hire fine secretaries, then harass 'em. It's a man's nature, I'm sorry" (Willman, 1992).

Perhaps the saddest epilogue to the 1991 *Los Angeles Times* article would be a status report on the three record label executives whose harassing actions were the focus of the article. After leaving Geffen Records in the shadow of sexual harassment charges, Babineau opened an independent record promotion company, MJB & Associates. His first projects as an independent promoter were allegedly records released by Geffen Records and Radio Active Records, two labels distributed by MCA. After leaving RCA with a presumably lucrative cash settlement, Jeff Aldrich began to freelance as an A&R talent scout. RCA hired him several weeks later to work for them as a consultant. After leaving Island Records, Mike Bone was hired by Def American Records, a Time Warner subsidiary. Bone was hired in spite of protests from several of Def American's twelve female employees.

## EQUAL PAY

Even though many women are able to find the job they want in the industry and endure nonsupportive work environments, they are often faced with discrimination in the form of the pay they receive. There is general suspicion among women that men earn more money for doing essentially the same work as their female counterparts in the music industry. It is difficult to conduct salary equity studies in the music industry because most firms are tight-lipped about any personnel information. Therefore, reviewing national data for all types of employment is currently our only alternative.

Because it is a less obvious, but a nonetheless painful, problem for women in the workplace, salary disparity is often overlooked. When music industry companies are asked about gender issues, they typically point to the number of females in their "workforce" and present deceptively impressive statistics for percentages of females hired in recent years. Unfortunately, the number or percentage of female employees does not answer the important question, Are women paid fair and equivalent salaries? If women are locked-out of upper-level positions in the music industry, one would expect average pay for males to exceed that of females. If women are pigeon-holed into vocational specialties that are low paying, it is likely that average earnings for women executives in the music industry are even lower than those of females in other industries.

One would expect that after almost twenty-five years of living under the Civil Rights Act, American women would enjoy salary equity. Unfortunately, the disparity in pay between men and women is quite pronounced. In 1998 the median weekly earnings of females working full time were $456, whereas their male counterparts earned $598 (*Monthly Labor Review*, 1999). Those data translate to women earning 76 percent of what males do.

When the variable "ethnicity" is entered into the equation, the comparison is even less equitable. African American males earned $468 per week; black females earned $400. Clearly, females, and especially African-American females, are still fighting for pay equity in the workplace. This unfortunate phenomenon might be explained by the low percentage of African American females in senior-level positions. The combination of historical discrimination against African Americans plus gender discrimination puts female minorities in the "most underrepresented" category of the national workforce.

Dyana Williams, president of IAAAM, points to the need for a study of African American women in the music industry. "How many African American females head a record label? How many engineers or producers are African American females?" asks Williams. Dyana often speaks to young African American women who aspire to leadership roles in the music industry. She emphasizes the importance of being prepared through education and networking. She asks, "Is it a coincidence that Sylvia Rhone, who is African American, studied business at the Wharton School of Business and later became the only female to assume the role of label chairperson?" She concludes, "Be informed; knowledge is power" (Williams, 1999).

There is a glimmer of hope for the younger generations of females entering the workforce. Women's average earnings, as a ratio of males' earnings, appear to be changing for the better with each emerging generation. When the population of working women was divided into three age groups (25–34, 35–44 and 45–64), the youngest group faired much better than the other two. The youngest group of females with bachelor's degrees in accounting earned 91 percent of what comparable males earned; the older groups earned 80 percent and 64 percent respectively. The youngest group with bachelor's degrees in business earned 86 percent of what their male counterparts earned. The other groups earned 77 percent and 66 percent. One might conclude that the struggle for salary equity is making incremental gains with each successive generation of educated females.

## A SUCCESS STORY

In spite of the numerous obstacles that face women who struggle for recognition in the music industry, some women have won the battle for success. Because it is difficult, and not common, for a female to ascend to the head of a music industry organization, successful women executives shine like beacons of hope for others on their way to the top. One female, Frances Preston, patiently rose from secretary-receptionist to one of the most powerful and influential executives in the industry. Another female executive, Sylvia Rhone, not only ascended to the head of a major record label but also promoted other women to leadership positions in her organization. Their success stories should serve as motivation for other women climbing corporate ladders in the music industry. One must ask, "Why have these women succeeded whereas many others haven't?"

One of the brightest beacons in the music industry is Frances Williams Preston, president and CEO of Broadcast Music Incorporated (BMI). The organization that Preston runs is a performance rights organization. It represents thousands of songwriters and publishers and collects royalties from TV, radio, and live music performances that use music created by BMI songwriters. Because the slightest adverse change in copyright laws could have devastating effects on songwriters and publishers, Preston maintains a close liaison with representatives of the House and Senate to keep track of legislative action. In the course of a day, she might meet with a famous rock songwriter in the morning and a group of senators in the afternoon. She might consider running for a national political office, as many people have predicted, if she weren't having so much fun at her current job!

Unlike many of her male counterparts, Frances Preston started at the bottom of the corporate food chain. She started as a receptionist and worked her way up to a secretarial position. She jokes about her lack of typing skills when she joined BMI, but her communication skills were her obvious asset. Her Ghandi-like persistence to enter the male-dominated ivory tower of music industry leadership was her second greatest asset. In 1986 she was promoted to the top management position at BMI, a role that requires her to maintain dual residences, with a home in New York and another in Nashville.

During her thirty-year rise from receptionist to one of the most powerful people in the music industry, Preston has had her share of problems with the male power structure. "In the old days, guys would even schedule meetings at clubs that didn't allow women," she recalls (Philips, 1993). Once again her persistence and patience paid off. She was the first female admitted to the Friars Club in New York. Another male-dominated organization she joined was the Country Music Association (CMA), headquartered in Nashville. She is now one of only four people who have been awarded the honor of being "Lifetime Directors" of the CMA.

Although Preston is best known for her executive skills, her most lasting legacy will likely be a result of her philanthropic work. The Frances

Frances Williams Preston, President and CEO of BMI, receives the MIDEM 1999 "Person of the Year" Award in Cannes, France, January 24, 1999. She is the first female to be honored with this award, and only six other persons have received it. (BMI Archives Photo Collection. Photographer: Yves Coatsaliou)

Williams Preston Laboratory, a cancer research center, and the T. J. Martell Foundation are ongoing fund-raising activities that she pursues with the same vigor as her full-time job. Her charitable contributions have not gone unnoticed. She was selected "Person of the Year" at the 1999 Cannes MIDEM, an international music industry event. As with many other awards she has received, Frances Preston was the first female to receive this award.

## TOPICS FOR DISCUSSION

1. Females are typically underrepresented in record label divisions such as sales, promotion, and A&R. Do you think this occurs because the jobs in these areas don't appeal to women? Or is gender discrimination preventing them from getting entry-level jobs in these types of positions?

2. Females tend to score higher than their male counterparts on the verbal sections of college entrance exams. There is a larger proportion of females in publicity jobs at record companies; however, publicity jobs are usually lower-paying positions than other divisions at record labels. Do you think women are encouraged to apply for publicity jobs and discouraged from others? Or do you think females are attracted to publicity because of the writing skills required? Are salaries low because women accept lower salaries?

3. It is likely that many women experience sexual harassment in the workplace but do not report it. Should women be encouraged to report sexual harassment in the workplace, even if doing so means sacrificing a good job? Do you think that senior-level executives have a tendency to ignore sexual harassment complaints? Do you think sexual harassment is more prevalent in the music industry than in other industries such as banking or insurance?

4. The common remark made to women who report sexual harassment is, "This is the way the music industry is. If you can't take the environment, then get out of this business." Do you think there is validity to that argument? What, if anything, might be done to change tolerance of sexual harassment in the music industry?

5. Frances Preston has been described as the "most successful woman in the music industry." How did her career path differ from that of her male counterparts? What things did she do to succeed? Why have other women failed while she succeeded?

## REFERENCES AND RESOURCES

### Interviews

Butler, Twiss. Reference Department, National Organization for Women (NOW). E-mail correspondence, August 27, 1999.

Williams, Dyana. President, International Association of African-American Musicians (IAAAM). Personal interview, August 4, 1999.

### Books

*Annual Demographic Survey, 1999*. Washington, DC: Recording Industry Association of America. (This report is a summary of data gathered from 3,051 music purchasers in the United States. It presents trends in the styles of music purchased and other demographic data such as age and gender of record buyers.)

*Recording Industry Sourcebook*, 10th ed. (1999). Emeryville, CA: Cardinal Business Media. (This is one of the most comprehensive directories of persons and organizations in the music industry.)

Rothstein, Sidney D., and Roy Liebman (1994). *Employment Law: Cases and Materials*, 3rd ed. Westbury, NY: Foundation Press. (This book provides a thorough legislative history of the Civil Rights Act. It also provides a very good overview of legal issues surrounding employment and hiring.)

*Sex Discrimination Issues* (1998). Washington, DC: U.S. Equal Employment Opportunity Commission. (This is an extensive explanation of the rights and responsibilities under federal EEOC laws and guidelines. It is written by extremely knowledgable staff and legal counsel of the agency that oversees compliance for employment discrimination in this country.)

Smith, Kristin E., and Amara Bachu (1999). *Womens' Labor Force Attachment Patterns and Maternity Leave: A Review of the Literature*, Population Division Working Paper No. 32. Washington, DC: U.S. Bureau of Census.

Stan, Adele M. (1995). *Debating Sexual Correctness: Pornography, Sexual Harassment, Date Rape, and the Politics of Sexual Equality*. New York: Delta Books/Dell Publishing. (A series of essays by many different experts in the field of women's studies. Most essays deal with contemporary feminist issues that continue to be controversial.)

Wagner, Ellen J. (1992). *Sexual Harassment in the Workplace: How to Prevent, Investigate and Resolve Problems in Your Organization*. New York: American Management Association. (This book was written for management executives, but it is so well written that it is an excellent introduction to the topic.)

*Women's Earnings 76 Percent of Median for Men in 1998*. Washington, DC: U.S. Department of Labor, Bureau of Labor Statistics. (A brief statistical comparison of median weekly earnings of women working full time during 1998. Researchers present comparisons of males, females and ethnic groups.)

## Magazines, Journals, and Newspapers

Baye, Betty Winston (1999, July 25). Leaving the Sisters Behind. *The Tennessean*, p. 4D. (This column by Winston discusses the plight of African American women who struggle against racial discrimination as well as gender bias in the workplace.)

Becklund, Laurie, and Chuck Philips (1991, November 3). Sexual Harassment Claims Confront the Music Industry. *Los Angeles Times*, p. A1, col. 5. (This is the investigative report that revealed three record labels and a prominent entertainment law firm were under investigation for sexual harassment. The article generated heated debate in the music industry and motivated several record companies to review their policies regarding sex bias and harassment.)

*Civil Rights Act of 1964*, Public Law No. 88–352 Sec. 703, 38 Stat. 241, 255 (1964), 42 U.S.C. Sec. 20003–2(a) (1982).

*Civil Rights Act of 1991*, Public Law No. 102–166 (1991).

Collins, Glenn (1988, November 9). At 84, a Spry Friars Club Accepts Women in Its Cast. *New York Times*, p. C19, col. 4. (After eighty-four years of excluding females from its membership, the entertainment industry club agreed to admit women. However, it was only after a sex discrimination complaint was filed against the 1,350-member club.)

Cusolito, Karen (1992, February 13). Hollywood Warned about Sex Suits. *Hollywood Reporter*. (Discusses a seminar about sexual harassment presented to entertainment industry employers and employees in Los Angeles.)

Duggan, Dennis (1993, July 8). Bad Rap for Women. *Newsday*, New York Diary, p. 26. (Covers a press conference by the Coalition of 100 Black Women asking rappers to stop attacking black women in their lyrics.)

Ellis, Bill (1996, November 5). How to Succeed by Trying. *The Commercial Appeal*, p. 1C. (Ellis describes the struggle several females had in Memphis and Nashville music scenes.)

Fort, Annie (1992, March 21). Artists, Wake Up! *Billboard*, Letters to the Editor, p. 14. (An insightful letter that asks why female artists stay on a label that promotes sexist music.)

Hansen, Mark (May 1991). Study Shows Job Bias Changing. *American Bar Association Journal*, p. 34. (An interesting study by the American Bar Association. It revealed that over a twenty-year period lawsuits alleging discrimination changed from predominantly hiring complaints to on-the-job sexual harassment complaints.)

Holland, Bill (1994, February 19). House Panel to Examine Rap. *Billboard*, sec. 1.

Hudson, David (1996). Like It or Not, Gangsta Rap Endures in the Free Marketplace of Ideas. *First Amendment News*, Commentary, October 1996.

*Meritor Savings Bank v. Vinson*, 106 S. Ct. 2399, 40 EPD paragraph 36,159. (U.S. Supreme Court 1986).

*Monthly Labor Review* (1999, January 27). Women's Earnings 76 Percent of Median for Men in 1998. U.S. Dept of Labor Web site, http://www.bls.gov/opub/ted/1999/Jan/wk4/art03.htm.

Morris, Chris, and Phyllis Stark (1991, November 16). Biz Faces Sexual Harassment Onus; L.A. Times Inquiry Turns Up Charges. *Billboard*, p. 6. (Presents differing opinions from female executives regarding how prevalent sexual harassment is in the industry.)

Mulligan, Thomas S. (1997, December 19). Women's Rights Activists Go A-Protesting. *Los Angeles Times*, Business, p. D4. (Describes the confrontation between women's rights activists and Time Warner, Inc. Females objected to Warner's role in marketing music that encourages domestic violence.)

Philips, Chuck (1992, March 5). "Anita Hill of the Music Industry" Talks. *Los Angeles Times*, Calendar, p. F1. (An interview with Penny Muck, the woman whose lawsuit against Geffen Records triggered an industrywide debate over sexual harassment in the industry. She describes shocking—and disgusting—behavior as she discusses her former employer.)

Philips, Chuck (1992, July 21). Controversial Record Exec Hired by Def. *Los Angeles Times*, Calendar, p. F1, col. 5. (An article about Mike Bone, an industry executive who was sued for sexual harassment and was subsequently hired by Def American Records, a Time Warner–affiliated label.)

Philips, Chuck (1993, April 18). She Advanced the Old-Fashioned Way—She Earned the Promotion. *Los Angeles Times*, Business Calendar, p. 10. (An article about Sylvia Rhone, president of Electra Records. Rhone is an African American woman who is one of the most successful executives in the music industry.)

Philips, Chuck (1993, April 18). You've Still Got a Long Way to Go, Baby. *Los Angeles Times*, Business Calendar, p. 9. (An excellent article about female executives who have become successful in the entertainment industry in spite of male chauvinism.)

Philips, Chuck (1995, March 17). Company Town: Hollywood Records Executive Fired Amid Harassment Complaints. *Los Angeles Times*, Business, p. D1. (Coverage of an executive who was fired for sexual harassment at Walt Disney Company's Hollywood Records. The *Los Angeles Times* points to its in-depth investigation several years prior to this firing as the impetus for several companies, including Disney, implementing strict policies against sexual harassment.)

PR Newswire (1992, April 27). IRMA Co-Sponsors Workshop on Women, Violence and Rap Music. *PR Newswire*, Entertainment, Television, and Culture section. (A description of a conference cosponsored by the International Rap Music Alliance. The panels discussed the "complicated question of the relationships between women, violence and rap music.")

*Price Waterhouse v. Hopkins*, 490 U.S. 228 (1989). (A court case decided by the U.S. Supreme Court that established the legal precedent for hiring procedures that involve "sex stereotyping.")

Reynolds, Larry (1997, March). Sex Harassment Claims Surge. *Hrfocus*, p. 8. New York: American Management Association. (A very brief article that presents documented evidence that sexual harassment claims soared between 1990 and 1996.)

Sudo, Phil (1990, May 18). Pop Music's New Women's Movement. *Scholastic Update* 122, no. 18, p. 13. (Describes the historically significant appearance of female artists in the top four chart positions of *Billboard*'s weekly charts.)

Stone, Adrianne (1985, January). W.A.S.P., Rock and Roll Outlaws. *Hit Parader*,

p. 56. (An article that describes the violent and sexist concert stunts of this heavy metal band.)

The Top 40 (1996, November 29). *Los Angeles Times*, Calendar, p. 7. (Lists and describes the forty most powerful executives in the music industry at that time.)

Willman, Chris (1992, January 29). Sweatin' It Out. *Los Angeles Times*, Calendar, p. F1. (This brief article about the Grammy Awards includes the infamous "chauvinist pig" quotation by a member of Van Halen.)

## Organizations to Contact

Catalyst
120 Wall Street
New York, NY 10005
Phone: (212) 514–7600
Fax: (212) 514–8470
web: www.catalystwomen.org
Catalyst is a nonprofit research and advisory firm that specializes in women's concerns and needs. It has a dual mission: "to enable professional women to achieve their maximum potential and help employers capitalize on the talents of their female employees."

National Coalition Against Domestic Violence (NCADV)
P.O. Box 18749
Denver, CO 80218
Phone: (303) 839–1852
Fax: (303) 831–9251
web: http://www.ncadv.org
The coalition is dedicated to empowerment of battered women and their children. It is also active in public policy development and advocacy as it relates to violence against women. Song lyrics that glorify domestic violence represent the antithesis of what this organization advocates.

National Organization for Women (NOW)
733 15th Street NW, 2nd floor
Washington, DC 20005
Phone: (202) 628–8669
Fax: (202) 785–8576
e-mail: now@now.org
web: http://now.org
NOW is the most famous women's rights organization in the world. They have thirteen key issues that include violence against women, women-friendly workplaces, and young feminism. They are a major force in legislation involving women's issues.

## Web Sites

www.census.gov
U.S. Census Bureau
This is a wonderful source for current population estimates as well as the
most recent census data. The bureau also generates demographic break-
downs for ethnic groups and other subpopulations.

www.feminist.org/911/harass.html
Sexual Harassment Hotline Resource List
This is an extremely helpful list of numbers to call if one encounters sexual
harassment in the workplace. It also provides helpful information such
as "What to Do If You or Someone You Know Is Sexually Harassed."
The site is produced by the Feminist Majority Foundation.

www.hrplaza.com/fastfacts
HR Plaza Fast Facts
This site gives summaries of human resources research that include
women's issues. The reports are distilled down to basic factoids, charts,
and graphs.

www.RIAA.com
Recording Industry of America
This site has data on recordings purchased by gender.

www.stats.bls.gov
Bureau of Labor Statistics
This is the most comprehensive site available for data about employment,
unemployment, and trends in this country. The most disturbing table
presents median salaries for men and women.

# 7

# Showdown at the Box Office: The Cost of Concert Tickets

When the average price of a ticket to concerts by acts such as the Rolling Stones, Luciano Pavarotti, and Bob Dylan topped $100, some fans began to wonder why concert prices had become so expensive. Even some touring acts became angry with what they perceived as "soaring ticket prices" and pointed the finger of blame at Ticketmaster, the largest ticket distribution company in the world. More recently, members of the media have accused SFX Entertainment, a company that has acquired many of the largest concert promotion companies in the United States, of pushing ticket prices higher as they have become more powerful (Waddell, 1999). One must ask: Are ticket prices really that high? If so, who or what is the cause?

## TICKET PRICES THEN AND NOW

Members of the media have been accusing the live entertainment industry of unfairly increasing ticket prices for years. In 1989 *Los Angeles Times* journalist Thomas K. Arnold observed that the average price for a concert ticket had almost doubled in a ten-year period (Arnold, 1989). His conclusion was based on the average ticket price of $11.50 in 1979 versus a $20.00 average cost in 1989. But when those prices are adjusted for inflation using a standard consumer price index, the difference in price becomes only $0.48 (Inflation Calculator web site). Practically speaking, there was no significant increase in the average ticket price for concerts for that ten-year period beyond the effects of inflation.

Newspaper articles continued to malign the concert industry for what is often called "spiraling ticket prices" from 1989 through 2000. One thing emerges as one reads those articles: Most accounts of overpriced concert tickets focus on the top tier of ticket prices for what are called premium seats. In addition, the data for "average ticket price" are typically not adjusted for inflation. A review of average ticket prices adjusted for inflation from 1979 to 1996 produces an amazing result: During that seventeen-year period, ticket prices increased $0.74 or less than 2 percent beyond the effects of inflation. That compares quite favorably to the adjusted cost of tickets to movie theaters, which increased 37 percent over the same period.

Unfortunately, the stability of adjusted ticket prices for concerts ended around 1996. Using average ticket prices provided by *Pollstar*, a trade publication about live entertainment, it appears that average ticket prices increased from $25.56 in 1996 to $38.56 in 1999. Even after adjusting for inflation, those changes represent an increase of approximately 50 percent in three years! If one uses the $42.21 average ticket price for 1999 cited in *USA Today*, the increase is even higher.

Use of the standard industry figure called "average ticket price" does not accurately reflect the range of ticket prices from artist to artist. For example, some artists work hard to keep the price of their tickets at a reasonable level. Garth Brooks insists that promoters keep the price of tickets at or near $20 so that his fans can afford to attend his shows. He has refused to play some well-known venues in cities like New York because the higher overhead and expensive union wages would drive his ticket prices higher than he could accept. Garth has also lobbied to get anti-scalping laws in states that don't have them in an attempt to keep prices in line.

Heavy metal bands Poison and Ratt have also purposely kept their ticket prices down in order to accommodate their younger audience members. The rock band Offspring has developed one of the most loyal fan bases in part because of their $20 ticket price. Because modern rock and metal bands attract a younger demographic than do pop and country acts, a lower ticket price makes it easier for teenagers to attend a concert. Plus, if the typical concert attender buys $6 worth of highly profitable tour merchandise, it makes good business sense to fill the venue for every concert.

At the other extreme, many artists have chosen to raise ticket prices because fans have shown that they will pay high prices. It appears that some performers have pushed the price of their tour tickets higher in order to see just how much the market will bear. Patrick Pacheco, a journalist for *Newsweek*, blames the Eagles Reunion Tour of 1994 for starting the trend toward excessively high top-end ticket prices. As Pacheco noted, the $100 ticket for the Eagles concerts met with "very little resistance from their fans" (Pacheco, 1999). Many concert promoters noticed how quickly those expensive tickets were sold and, as one might expect, decided to push prices higher for other acts. Ticket brokers and ticket scalpers also took note of the higher ticket prices and pushed ticket prices higher.

Another factor to look at is the range of ticket prices for individual artists. A rock concert in 1980 probably had one ticket price. As outdoor amphitheaters, or sheds as they are called in the industry, became more popular, different price levels evolved to accommodate less expensive lawn seating versus more-expensive covered seating. More recently, promoters have begun to use several different price levels for tickets, mimicking the way symphony orchestra tickets have been scaled for years. This pricing structure, called "scaling seats," has affected the price of good seats at concerts.

If one were to look at the highest ticket price for the most popular acts over the past ten years, a trend toward very expensive premium seat prices would be obvious. Tickets to see Jimmy Buffett, an artist who typically sells out his concerts, have a top-end price of $400. The Rolling Stones finished their "Bridges to Babylon" stadium tour and decided to play arenas before closing the tour. The arena seats topped out at $600 for premium seats. Even opera impresarios are getting into extremely high price scales, with Luciano Pavarotti tickets going for as high as $910. How high might premium seat prices go? They have already reached levels that would never have been predicted ten years ago: The best seats for the Barbra Streisand Millennium Eve concert in Las Vegas were $2,500 each!

## WHAT THINGS ARE AFFECTING TICKET PRICES?

To determine why ticket costs have escalated in recent years and soared for certain artists, it would be a good idea to look at the economics and the players involved in the business of live entertainment in the United States. In other words, one needs to know where all the money from ticket sales flows and who receives a piece of it! There are a lot of players in the concert promotion process, but only a few lucky ones keep significant percentages of the profits.

### The Cast of Characters in a Concert

In general terms, a concert is presented to the public through the efforts of three basic "teams" of professionals. The performers, referred to generically as "act" or "artist," have the largest and most elaborate team of support personnel. An act without a strong reputation might have relatively few people working on their behalf. A superstar band like the Rolling Stones will have over a hundred employees on the payroll, which contributes to higher ticket prices. An entry-level artist will often have a

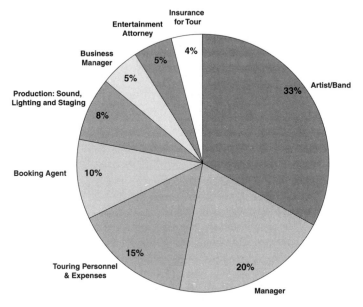

Figure 7.1 Distribution of an artist's or band's income from a concert tour.

minimal team that consists of a personal manager, an entertainment attorney, a booking agent, and a road manager (see Figure 7.1).

The manager may be called an "artist manager," a "personal manager," or simply a "manager." The manager's role is to guide the artist's career in the music industry. Typically, a manager is paid a percentage—called commission—of the artist's total income from music. The commissionable income most often includes record royalties, publishing royalties, merchandising items that include the artist's image, and income from concert tours. Most managers make a commission of 10 percent to 20 percent of artist income. In rare instances, managers can demand and get commissions of 25 percent and higher.

The next person on the artist team is a booking agent. The booking agent's job is to get concert promoters to present the artist in a concert or concerts. Performances that generate income for an artist are sometimes called "bookings" or "gigs." Booking agents are paid commissions only on concerts they obtain for the artist. The booking agent is paid a commission, usually 10 percent of the income an artist makes from the concert.

Income from numerous sources, including publishing royalties, record royalties, and ticket sales, need to be managed. Therefore, income and expenditures are monitored by professionals who specialize in accounting for entertainers. The management of income and expenditures is the job of an industry specialist called a "business manager." A business manager may be paid a number of ways: hourly rates, monthly fees, or a percentage of income. A common commission for a business manager is 5 percent of all music industry–related income.

Another person expecting to take some of the artist's income is an entertainment attorney. Top drawer music industry attorneys ask for a 5 percent commission or an hourly rate of $100–$200. Big-name attorneys can demand $300 or more per hour! If you are keeping track of commissions the artist must pay, we are up to at least 30 percent—probably 40 percent—at this point and we haven't even counted the road musicians and crew members.

A recording artist usually begins to tour to promote a current album release. On tour, the large number of persons who expect to be paid increases dramatically. Because personal managers are the communication point for the record label, publisher, booking agent, and business manager, they cannot go on the road with the artist during a concert tour. The road manager takes over many day-to-day management responsibilities once the artist hits the road. Supervising the road crew, a group of hard-working people called "roadies," is a major responsibility of the road manager. If the tour is somewhat complicated, a tour manager will be hired to arrange the tour, and then the road manager travels with the band to ensure that hotel accommodations, bus or airline travel arrangements, and backstage necessities, for example, are correct.

A tour that involves elaborate set design, sound systems, and lighting will probably also have a production coordinator to oversee all technical personnel—road crew and local crew members—and the equipment necessary to stage the show. Production coordinators are under tremendous stress because the road crew is expected to arrive at the performance venue in the morning and have everything ready to go by the time the audience arrives. Asking the audience to wait an hour or two while the crew finishes setting up sound and lights is simply not an option.

The production coordinator supervises the backstage crews, which are divided into several specialized technical areas such as staging, electric and lighting, props, sound, and rigging. Large international tours like U2, Pink Floyd, and the Rolling Stones often have over fifty crew members on the road with them. Concert tour employees, from tour manager through road crew, are typically paid a weekly salary plus expenses. One of the most well known production coordinators in the world is rumored to earn more than some artists for keeping superstar concert tours running smoothly.

Nonproduction employees on the road might include several truck drivers, tour bus drivers, publicists, the tour accountant, and merchandising managers. Obviously, the larger the tour, the more complicated the tour staff list becomes. The Rolling Stones even had several chefs and bartenders on the road for the "Voodoo Lounge" tour! The bottom line is that they are all paid from income the artist receives from concert ticket sales.

The venue team tends to be less complicated than the artist's team. A venue has relatively few full-time employees, but many part-time employees work the day of the concert. A small venue, such as a 300-seat club, will likely have a skeletal staff. Because clubs are in the business of food and beverage first, music support staff is a low priority. A medium-sized theater might have a technical director in charge of the stage and backstage area, a house manager in charge of the seating and entry areas, and a box office manager in charge of ticket services. Large venues, such as arenas and stadiums, have many employees in the technical, house, and box office areas, but they employ fewer full-time workers than does an artist. Arenas and stadiums that present a lot of concerts might have additional staff members in marketing, security, and in-house booking. To pay for the large facility and its employees, venues are paid substantial amounts of money for rental. A promoter will be charged a flat fee or a percentage of gross ticket sales—8–12 percent—whichever is greater. The venue will also charge for some special services such as modifying the seating arrangement or cleaning the facility after it is used.

The last of the three teams is the promoter's team. Concert promoters have historically been somewhat regional in geographic reach rather than national. Jam Productions established a reputation as a Chicago based promoter; John Scher and Ron Delsener focused on the New York City area for many years; and the concert promotion icon Bill Graham made his reputation in northern California. A recent phenomenon is one company, SFX Entertainment, acquiring regional concert promoters in order to create a powerful international live entertainment corporation. Even though SFX has bought many regional concert promoters, each concert promotion company bought appears to have retained much of its regional flavor and design.

A concert promotion company often begins with one person doing all the necessary things to present concerts. As the number of events the company promotes increases and as the size of venues utilized increase, the solo promoter must hire staff to support the evolving enterprise. Staff members might include a receptionist, a marketing specialist, a sponsorship manager, a production or technical coordinator, and a budgeting and finance executive. The numerous other employees needed to stage a concert are hired on a part-time basis.

As one can quickly see, the artist has the largest number of full-time staff persons on the payroll. The venue, depending on its size, will have the next largest roster of full-time personnel. The concert promoter is, by comparison, least burdened by a large overhead of staff salaries. This is an important factor to remember when we look at the distribution of ticket sales. Artists may receive a large percentage of the box office receipts, but they have a lot of mouths to feed.

### The Storyline of a Concert

Conceptually, promoting a concert is quite simple. First, the concert promoter needs to find an artist willing to perform the show for an agreed-upon amount of money. Next, the promoter needs to rent the venue for a day when the artist is available in the region. Then, all that's left to do is advertise the event, sell tickets, set up and tear down the show, and count the money. However, in practice, each stage of the process has a unique set of challenges. The first stage, finding an artist with strong name recognition, is quite difficult. Most concert promoters read trade publications such as *Pollstar, Amusement Business,* and *Performance* to learn what acts are touring and how successful they have been in other markets. As one might expect, whenever a promoter sees a tour developing for a well-known artist, every competing promoter in the area also learns of it. To make matters worse, some artists, through their booking agents, prefer to work with established promoters rather than with less well known or novice promoters. Acts that agree to perform for a percentage of ticket sales prefer to go with a proven promoter rather than with an unknown commodity. Therefore, a new or emerging concert promoter has a difficult time getting major recording artists to promote.

In the early days of live concerts, artists would ask for a specific amount of money, called a "guarantee," for a concert performance. A guarantee means that the promoter pays the agreed-upon amount irregardless of how many tickets are sold for the concert. As rock stars developed more business savvy, they began to ask for a guarantee against a percentage. Such a fee arrangement means the artist is paid a percentage of ticket sales or a guaranteed amount, whichever is larger. This fee arrangement provides the best of both worlds. If ticket sales don't go well, the artist will still receive the specific guaranteed amount of money and the promoter might lose money on the concert. If, in contrast, the concert is a sellout, the artist receives a major percentage of the box office revenues.

To make the guarantee against percentage deals more equitable, artists often take a percentage of the net, rather than gross, ticket sales. Net sales are defined as gross ticket sales minus certain agreed-upon expenses such as venue rental fees, advertising, and production costs. This type of net deal sounds like a great deal for the promoter, but it is not unusual for a well-known artist to receive 85 percent of the net box office receipts. John Scher, president of Metropolitan Entertainment, a major concert promotion company in New York, said that 15–20 percent of the arena concerts his company promotes do not show a profit (Holden, 1990). The art of negotiating guarantees is, therefore, a major factor in the success or failure of a concert promoter.

The contract between the artist and the promoter is quite complicated because it includes attachments, called "riders," that specify detailed lists of things the artist expects the promoter to provide. The technical rider spells out everything from electrical power needs to how many local stagehands are needed to set up, run, and tear down the show. The hospitality rider includes some real necessities, such as how many meals to cater backstage, but also might include some ridiculous things such as what color limo to provide the artist, what brand and year of champagne to have in the star's dressing room, and what color wallpaper the dressing room can have. The most infamous request was for five pounds of M&Ms with all the green ones removed. The promoter allegedly did not remove the green ones and was sued for breach of contract!

At the same time the artist's contract is being negotiated, the promoter must scramble to obtain a rental agreement for the venue. Because the probability of personal injury to an audience member increases with the size of the crowd, most large venues require the promoter to obtain liability insurance for at least $1 million before signing the rental agreement. The style of music tends to dictate how expensive the insurance will be. Rap groups, for example, or any rock bands that typically have mosh pits, will likely be very expensive to insure. If insurance for a rock concert costs $3 per seat, then that amount will, in all likelihood, be added to the price of the ticket. Venue rental agreements also have lists of services provided, such as custodians, ticket takers, ushers, and security officers, along with their costs. In addition to the costs associated with these services, venues often receive a percentage of ticket sales as a part of the rental fees.

The advertising stage involves media buys for radio and print media. In a competitive market, it is not uncommon for a promoter to budget $4–$6 per seat for advertising. Fortunately, radio stations often agree to become the media sponsor and help publicize and advertise the event in exchange for signage and name recognition. A media sponsor is somewhat like a co-promoter. Radio stations might offer reduced ad rates plus on-air give-aways of shirts, CDS, and tickets to help promote the show. If the advertising campaign has been effective, lots of people will want to buy tickets in advance of the concert. The lure of buying early, rather than at the door, is getting good seats. Unfortunately, the best seats are often not available even to the first person in line to buy tickets. Although the facts behind this phenomenon are difficult to verify, it is likely that prime tickets are set aside for large ticket brokers, record label executives, and friends of the touring artist.

Promoters of events in small venues, such as a bar with a seating capacity of 300, may not bother with selling tickets at numerous locations. In contrast, promoters of shows in large venues must have many locations for ticket sales. The choices are to establish one's own ticket sales locations or to use an established ticket distribution company. Although Ticketmaster is the best-known ticket distributor in the country, many other companies are available to promoters. Most promoters opt to use a professional ticket distribution company because most of the fees are charged to the customers rather than to the promoter. In addition, the option of ordering tickets by telephone and charging the costs to a credit card attracts many buyers. The alternative—driving to a central box office located in the venue—is less attractive to most consumers.

Production costs such as sound, lights, and staging for small venue shows can be a significant part of the total event budget. Artists who don't tour with their own sound and lighting equipment require the promoter to provide the equipment and operators. Artists who perform in large venues such as arenas and stadiums typically carry their own sound, lights, staging equipment and operators rather than depending on local promoters. Obviously, artists who provide their own production equipment will demand larger guarantees that reflect the added cost of production. Either way, production costs cut into the bottom line for the promoter.

The day of the show involves dozens—sometimes hundreds—of hourly wage workers. The first part-time workers to arrive are the stagehands who help the roadies unload the sound system, lighting equipment, and set pieces from the trucks. The stagehands, supervised by the road crew, erect the set, hang lights, and set up sound equipment in the concert venue. Closer to show time, numerous other employees arrive to work as ticket takers, ushers, security, and concessions salespersons, and at other service related jobs. If everything happens according to the plan, the local and road crews have the production equipment erected and fine-tuned by the time the band arrives for sound check. The audience arrives safely and orderly with enough time to buy food, beverages, and tour merchandise before the show begins. Once the performance begins, the promoter can relax a little, but the work is not over yet.

At a certain point in time, usually intermission, a meeting takes place to determine how ticket sales revenues will be distributed. This meeting, called "box office settlement," includes representatives from the venue, the promoter, the touring artist, ticket services, and, unfortunately, the state taxation office if an entertainment tax is levied on ticket sales. Settlement allows each person present to discuss all the expenses the promoter is allowed to deduct before the percentage splits are calculated. The meeting is somewhat like an IRS audit because every expense deducted from ticket revenues must be documented and justified. The typical response from someone observing a box office settlement for the first time is, "I had no idea there were so many expenses to put on a concert!"

Once the expenses are agreed upon, it is merely an arithmetic process to determine the various splits, or shares, of the money. Again, the gross ticket sales minus agreed upon expenses, including any entertainment tax, equals net ticket sales. If the artist has agreed to 85 percent of the net, then that amount is calculated and given to the artist immediately or at a later date. The venue is paid the agreed upon percentage plus the total of services provided.

It is interesting to see how much money the different business entities get from a modest sized concert. Figure 7.2 shows the distribution ticket revenues for a concert.

### The Big Question: Why Does a $21.50 Ticket Cost $30.05?

As early as 1990, consumers began to complain about additional fees added to the price of a concert ticket. Those fees, added by the ticket distribution company, continue to be a source of animosity for many people. Ticketmaster, the largest and best-known computerized ticket distribution company, has weathered lawsuits, artist boycotts, and governmental investigations related to the service fees it adds to tickets. But Ticketmaster wasn't always the biggest kid on the concert ticketing block. In 1968 Ticketron dominated ticket distribution in the United States. Then in 1976 two students at Arizona State University developed innovative computer software that would change the industry. The two young men, computer programmer Peter Gadwa and box office specialist Albert Leffler, started their company by licensing their software and selling hardware for ticketing systems. After their company evolved, the two entrepreneurs sold much of their stock to the Pritzker family of Chicago in 1982. The Pritzker family moved the company, called Ticketmaster, to Chicago and began to compete aggressively with Ticketron.

Fred Rosen, an attorney who had done legal work for Ticketmaster, was appointed CEO of Ticketmaster soon after the Pritzker family became major stockholders. Fred Rosen aggressively pursued exclusive deals with concert and athletic venues. By 1985 Ticketmaster was operating in thirty U.S. cities. The key to Rosen's success was his pursuit of facilities and promoters rather than customers. Ticketmaster charged higher fees than Ticketron and gave some of that money to venues and promoters in exchange for frequent—often exclusive—patronage. Rosen's strategy of giving "preferred customer rebates" to promoters and venues worked and in 1991 Ticketmaster bought Ticketron. Ticketmaster has remained the largest computerized ticket distribution company since its merger with Ticketron.

Along with their success, Ticketmaster also gained the dubious honor

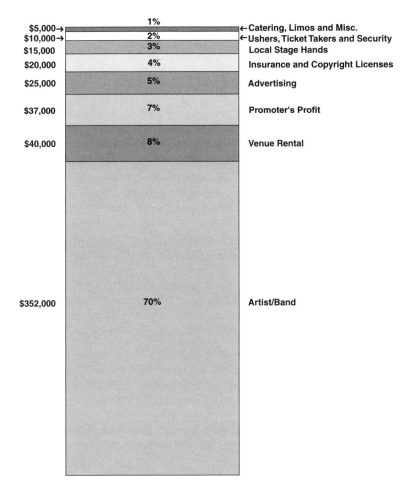

| | | |
|---|---|---|
| $5,000→ | 1% | ←Catering, Limos and Misc. |
| $10,000→ | 2% | ←Ushers, Ticket Takers and Security |
| $15,000 | 3% | Local Stage Hands |
| $20,000 | 4% | Insurance and Copyright Licenses |
| $25,000 | 5% | Advertising |
| $37,000 | 7% | Promoter's Profit |
| $40,000 | 8% | Venue Rental |
| $352,000 | 70% | Artist/Band |

Figure 7.2 How $504,000 of income from ticket sales for a rock concert is distributed. This concert was in an 18,000-seat venue and the average ticket price was $28.

of becoming a lightning rod for criticism directed at ticket prices. Investigative reporter Chuck Philips explained the fees added to a $21.50 concert ticket as follows: $2.00 for a facility fee; $5.00 for a convenience fee when charged by telephone; and $1.55 processing fee charged per order (Philips, 1991). These types of add-on fees, ranging from 22 percent to as high as 44 percent, are what caused a group of consumers to file two $100 million class action lawsuits in 1992. The lawsuits accused Ticketmaster of unfair competition and deceptive advertising (Philips, 1992). The suits were settled with Ticketmaster not acknowledging any wrongdoing, but agreeing to give away $1.5 million worth of tickets to charitable organizations.

At about the same time as the lawsuits were being settled, the rock group Pearl Jam decided to carry the lance against Ticketmaster. In March 1994 Pearl Jam notified promoters that they would perform only at venues that charged no more than $18 per ticket and charged no more than $1.80 for service and handling fees (Philips, 1994). What Pearl Jam apparently did not understand was that Ticketmaster had exclusive agreements with the largest promoters and venues in the United States. Most promoters who were asked to choose between Pearl Jam and Ticketmaster did not have to think about their decision very long: Pearl Jam was forced to cancel their summer tour.

Pearl Jam submitted a complaint to the United States Justice Department on May 6, 1994, accusing Ticketmaster of exerting monopolistic control over ticket prices. In addition, Pearl Jam accused the ticket company of using its power to keep promoters from presenting them on the summer tour. Pearl Jam lost round two of their battle against Ticketmaster when, after a year-long investigation, the Justice Department announced that it was dropping the investigation but would continue to "monitor competitive developments" (Blumenthal, 1995).

Beginning in 1992 Fred Rosen, CEO of Ticketmaster, gave his first of many rebuttals to complaints about service fees added to ticket prices (Rosen, 1992). He pointed out that the largest fee is a "convenience fee" charged only when a customer orders by telephone and charges with a credit card. To accommodate the millions of telephone calls it receives, Ticketmaster must employ many operators who are trained to answer questions and take orders. Rosen noted that five out of six callers do not order tickets, they merely ask questions. Ticketmaster nonetheless pays operators even when they make no sale.

Ticketmaster representatives repeatedly remind critics that ticket buyers have the option of going directly to the venue box office, where they can pay cash and avoid convenience fees. The point is well taken. Although Ticketmaster has been the focus of much criticism regarding ticket prices, no one has refuted one important fact: If you don't want to pay convenience fees for charging by phone, you have the option of traveling to the box office to purchase your tickets.

## TICKET BROKERS AND TICKET SCALPERS

Ticket distribution companies like Ticketmaster enter into a clearly defined business relationship with promoters to sell tickets to concerts. In this symbiotic relationship, the promoter establishes the face value of the tickets after discussing it with the artist's representatives. The sanctioned distributor then sells tickets to the public by taking phone orders and selling at established ticket outlets.

An unauthorized, but legal, alternative distributor of tickets is a ticket broker, who buys tickets at face value and then tries to resell them for a higher price. Most often, a broker will pay people to stand in line to buy tickets. "We've seen busloads of people delivered to specific outlets where an individual gave them money to purchase tickets," said Fred Rosen (Philips, 1990). What infuriates most artists and promoters is the markup of tickets by brokers. It is not unheard of for brokers to charge ten to twenty times the face value of a ticket. Several years ago, for example, a broker sold $30 face value tickets to a Madonna concert for $600. In Superbowl 2000, the lowest priced tickets to the Tennessee Titans versus St. Louis Rams showdown were $325, but the only tickets available to the general public were advertised by brokers for $1,500 to $4,000. Members of the public have made one thing quite clear: They will pay high prices for tickets to events that are high on their priority list.

As reports of brokers selling tickets for much higher than face value surfaced, artists and their managers began to believe that concert tickets were undervalued. As a result, ticket prices for some major artists and premium seats are on the rise. "Why shouldn't artists increase the face value of a ticket if brokers can?" is the operative logic.

Another unauthorized channel for ticket sales is the ticket scalper. The process of ticket scalping is similar to that of ticket brokering, except that tickets are generally sold near the entrance to the concert. Some cities, including New York and Los Angeles, have laws that prohibit ticket scalping. Ironically, those cities permit ticket brokers to operate. Many people in the industry think that the only real difference between a broker and a scalper is their place of business. Yet some cities, such as Nashville, do not have laws against ticket scalping. Garth Brooks, a champion of reasonable ticket prices, lobbied aggressively to get laws making ticket scalping illegal in his home state of Tennessee. Unfortunately, Tennessee politicians decided that if people want to pay excessive amounts of money for tickets from scalpers, it is their right to do so.

Determined to outwit ticket scalpers, Garth Brooks works closely with promoters and Ticketmaster. Even if Garth intends to do several performances in a particular city, he asks promoters to advertise only one show at first. After the show sells out, promoters advertise the "additional" show. That way, scalpers are often stuck holding a lot of tickets as new ones go on sale at face value. If all artists were as vehement as Garth about keeping ticket costs down, brokers and scalpers would probably have a more difficult time reselling tickets. At the very least, they would not be able to demand—and get—extremely high ticket prices for otherwise reasonably priced concerts. Ironically, Garth Brooks might be netting more income on his tours than artists whose tickets are more expensive. By making his concerts accessible to more people, he is able to sell out more shows. Larger audiences result in more merchandise—programs, T-shirts, hats—being sold at his shows. Unlike tickets sales,

A ticket scalper sells tickets in Nashville, where scalping is legal.
Some cities have enacted laws that make ticket scalping illegal.
(Photograph © Jerry R. Atnip)

artists typically have to give the venue only a portion, 10–25 percent, of merchandise income.

Persons who oppose ticket scalpers and advocate anti-scalping laws have a difficult time justifying their position based on ticket price alone because many sell-out events have extremely high ticket prices. If patrons will pay over $900 for an opera ticket, why should a scalper be prohibited from buying $450 tickets to other entertainment events and reselling them for $900? Shouldn't supply and demand determine how high ticket prices rise? Thus advocates for anti-scalping legislation also argue that such laws will help deter the sale of counterfeit tickets. As the quality of computer scanners and color printers improves, making counterfeit tickets becomes easier. Patrons who buy tickets to a concert should, they argue, reasonably expect to get into the event and be allowed to sit in the seats designated on the tickets. If patrons buy from a scalper tickets that turn out to be counterfeit, police cannot investigate as they would with brokers, who do business out of a physical location and are easier to locate if consumers file a complaint. In addition, advocates argue, brokers collect and pay appropriate taxes, whereas scalpers are less likely to do so.

## CONSOLIDATION STRIKES LIVE ENTERTAINMENT

During the last few years of the twentieth century, much media attention focused on the consolidation that occurred among record labels. While a handful of international record companies bought and consolidated many of the most successful independent record labels, one company, SFX Entertainment, quietly began to acquire many of the regional concert promotion companies in the United States. At the same time, New York–based SFX also acquired many concert venues across the country. In just three years SFX spent over $1 billion to acquire eighty-two venues in the top fifty markets in the United States. In addition, SFX consolidation efforts brought three of the top concert promotion companies under its live entertainment enterprise: Delsener/Slater in New York City, Bill Graham Presents in the San Francisco Bay area, and PACE Entertainment's national venue and promotion operations.

SFX is the brainchild of investment and operating executive Robert F. X. Sillerman, whose first venture into media and entertainment was SFX Broadcasting, a company that owned three stations when he took it public in 1993. After quickly acquiring seventy-one radio stations, he just as quickly brokered the sale of the broadcasting entities to Texas-based Capstar Broadcasting Corporation for $1.2 billion. Sillerman, who owned 20 percent of SFX Broadcasting's stock, structured the deal to retain the live entertainment entities through a spinoff to shareholders, thereby creating SFX Entertainment.

Amazing as it sounds, Sillerman holds three high-level and obviously powerful positions: chairman and CEO of the Sillerman Companies; executive chairman of SFX Entertainment, Incorporated; and, chancellor of Southampton College, a campus of Long Island University. If that isn't impressive enough, consider this: In little over two years, Sillerman made SFX Entertainment into the world's largest diversified promoter, producer, and venue operator for live entertainment events. Of course, there is a downside to SFX's speedy rise to the top of the live entertainment food chain. Criticism from media and from competitors materialized as quickly as Sillerman's success. Concert promoter John Scher blamed SFX for paying artists high guarantees in order to beat out competing promoters. "Guarantees are escalating out of control, and ultimately the public is paying for it," said Scher (Waddell, 1999). Other independent promoters around the country also identified SFX as a primary cause of the rise in ticket prices in the late 1990s. Jack Orbin, an independent concert promoter from San Antonio, was even more pointed in his criticism of SFX's consolidation efforts; he said national promoters like SFX "worry about hot dogs, beer, parking and sponsorships, as opposed to airplay, ticket sales, and the music" (Waddell, 1999).

As the debate continues to rage on, one thing remains clear: Ticket prices for superstar tours are not what they used to be. It will be interesting to see if consolidation of the live entertainment industry will have a positive effect on ticket prices. As SFX negotiates with artists to perform in its thirty-one amphitheaters across the country, we might see the company strike some hard bargains with artists eager to perform before shed crowds. That possibility, along with economies of scale in purchasing insurance and securing sponsorship dollars, could provide less-expensive tickets for emerging and mid-level artists. As Robert Sillerman stated emphatically, "We think consolidation will mean more presentations, which means you'll see everybody making more money: artists, managers, agents, buildings and promoters" (Matzer, 1998). Who knows, perhaps SFX will follow the model of mass marketing retailer Walmart, offering lower-priced products and making profits on them through higher volume. Just don't expect to get an $18 ticket to see Barbra Streisand during a flashing blue-light special.

## TOPICS FOR DISCUSSION

1. Considering how money from ticket sales is distributed and how artists distribute their earnings, do you think any specific persons or entities are paid too much money for services they provide the artist? Are any of them paid too little relative to what they do for the artist?

2. There has been much heated debate regarding fees that ticket distribution companies like Ticketmaster add to the face value of a concert ticket. Are these fees excessive? Or are they equitable considering the level of convenience they provide a customer?

3. Do you think concert ticket prices have increased dramatically over the past ten years as alleged by some members of the media? Do you agree with the theory that ticket prices were "undervalued" for many years and have recently risen to logical levels in response to market demand?

4. Should ticket scalping be against the law? If so, should ticket brokers be against the law too? If not, what things can be done to protect consumers from buying counterfeit tickets?

5. The concert promoter takes most of the financial risk in live entertainment because the artist and venue have minimum amounts of money guaranteed no matter how many tickets are sold. Should the venue and artist assume more risk? Is the distribution of income from ticket sales shown in the example in this chapter fair for each person or entity?

## REFERENCES AND RESOURCES

### Correspondence

Finalborgo, Jane. (1999, November). Finalborgo is director of public relations for Southampton College, Long Island University, where Robert F. X. Sillerman is chancellor. She graciously provided biographical information about Robert F. X. Sillerman and SFX Entertainment, Incorporated. E-mail and ground mail correspondence.

### Books

Boswell, William R. (1997). *Life on the Road*, 3rd ed. Needham Heights, MA.: Simon & Schuster Custom Publishing. (A good introductory textbook about stage production techniques for live entertainment.)

Stein, Howard, and Ronald Zalkind (1979). *Promoting Rock Concerts*. New York: Schirmer Books, a division of Macmillan Publishing Company. (Although this book is out of print and somewhat dated, it is still the best introduction to the business of promoting concerts.)

Trubitt, David Rudy, ed. (1993). *Concert Sound: Tours, Techniques and Technology*. Emeryville, CA: MixBooks, a division of Act III Publishing. (This is a collection of hands-on articles about concerts and touring. Although most of the chapters deal with sound technology, there are some good ones about entry-level jobs for persons wanting to be roadies.)

Vasey, John (1993). *Concert Sound and Lighting Systems*, 2nd ed. Newton, MA: Focal Press, an imprint of Butterworth-Heinemann Publishing. (A good primer for anyone interested in sound, lights and staging as it relates to concerts.)

Vasey, John (1998). *Concert Tour Production Management: How to Take Your Show on the Road*. Newton, MA: Focal Press, an imprint of Butterworth-Heinemann Publishing. (This is a good handbook of terminology, forms and procedures necessary to manage a band on tour.)

### Magazines, Journals, and Newspapers

Adelson, Andrea (1988, July 4). Radio Entrepreneur Mixes Fun and Money. *New York Times*, sec. 1, p. 31, col. 1. (A journalist looks at Robert F. X. Sillerman, who sold his broadcast holdings to begin buying venues and concert promotion companies.)

Adelson, Andrea (1997, September 1). Have the Radio Deals Peaked? *New York Times*, p. D6, col. 1. (An analysis of the broadcasting giant, SFX Broadcasting.)

Arnold, Thomas K. (1989, June 28). Ticket Prices for Concerts on an Upward Spiral in San Diego. *Los Angeles Times*, Calendar, part 6, p. 2, col. 1, Entertainment Desk. (An early look at the cost of tickets. It also presents artist guarantee figures that show the beginning of a twenty-year trend.)

Associated Press (1999, July 14). Concert Prices Rock Music Fans' Wallets. *Associated Press Wire Service*, Trends. (An excellent exposé of top end ticket prices charged for superstars.)

Bloomberg News Service (1999, June 24). Money Savvy; Entertainment Prices Outpacing Inflation. *Los Angeles Times*, Business, p. C4. (An investigative report about the rising cost of ticket prices.)

Bloomberg News Service (1999, July 27). Seagrams Plans to Sell Its Concerts Unit. *Los Angeles Times*, Business, p. C9. (The sale of Universal Concerts to House of Blues is described in this brief report.)

Blumenthal, Ralph (1995, August 23). Oddities Continue with Ticketmaster and Pearl Jam. *New York Times*, p. C11. (A summary of the Justice Department investigation.)

Boehm, Mike (1999, September 24). Ogden's Sell-Off Plan Puts Sun in Spotlight. *Los Angeles Times*, Calendar, p. F1. (A staff reporter speculates on the purchase of a food service and facility management company by SFX Entertainment.)

Boucher, Geoff (1999, August 8). Pop Beat; Rock and . . . Whoa! Concert Tickets Soared . . . Public Is Willing to Pay. *Los Angeles Times*, Calendar, p. F1. (A look into the "soaring cost" of ticket prices.)

*Business Wire* (1997, August 25). Hicks, Muse, Tate and Furst and Capstar Broadcasting Corporation to Acquire SFX Broadcasting in Transaction Valued at Approximately $2.1 Billion. (A news release that explains the sale of SFX corporation radio stations. The sale gave Robert F. X. Sillerman the capital to begin acquiring concert promotion companies.)

Citron, Alan, and Michael Cieply (1991, February 26). Ticketmaster to Lick Competition by Buying It. *Los Angeles Times*, Business, p. D2, col. 3, Financial Desk. (A description of Ticketmaster's purchase of Ticketron. This deal made Ticketmaster the largest computerized ticket distributor in the country.)

*Communications Daily* (1997, August 26). Hicks, Muse Announces Even Bigger Media Deal. Warren Publishing. (Details of SFX Entertainment going public after sale of radio stations.)

DeRosa, Robin (1998, August 11). Private Ryan Still Advancing/Pay Up. *USA Today*, Life, p. D1. (This article compares ticket prices in 1988 to those in 1998.)

Hofmeister, Sallie (1997, August 26). Dallas Company to Buy SFX in $2.1 Billion Deal. *Los Angeles Times*, Business, p. D1. (An article that describes the beginning of SFX in live entertainment.)

Holden, Stephen (1990, May 22). Pop Concerts, Once Cheap, Now Rival Broadway in Price. *New York Times*, p. C13, col. 1, Cultural Desk. (An excellent article about the costs of promoting concerts and inflationary factors affecting ticket prices.)

Matzer, Marla (1998, June 18). A Concerted Effort to Do Business Differently. *Los Angeles Times*, Business, p. D1. (An interview with Robert F. X. Sillerman, CEO of SFX Entertainment, Inc.)

Pacheco, Patrick (1999, August 2). The Big Ticket. *Newsday*, p. A13. (A journalist speculates on reasons why ticket prices have risen.)

Philips, Chuck (1990, May 27). Why Does a $30 Ticket Become a $600 Ticket? *Los Angeles Times*, Calendar, p. 8, Calendar Desk. (Journalist Chuck Philips does a great job of investigating ticket scalping and ticket brokering.)

Philips, Chuck (1991, May 10). Ticket Flap. *Los Angeles Times*, Calendar, p. F1, col. 2, Entertainment Desk. (Chuck Philips continues to investigate the fees charged by Ticketmaster.)

Philips, Chuck (1992, June 9). A Tangle Over Tickets. *Los Angeles Times*, p. F1. (A report on two major lawsuits against Ticketmaster.)

Philips, Chuck (1994, May 28). Rock Group Files Complaint over Alleged Tactics of Ticketmaster. *Los Angeles Times*, p. A38, col. 1, Metro Desk. (It seems as though Chuck Philips wrote an article about Ticketmaster each spring. This one deals with the Pearl Jam confrontation with Ticketmaster.)

Ramirez, Anthony (1994, November 6). Ticketmaster's Mr. Tough Guy. *New York Times*, sec. 3, p. 1, col. 2, Financial Desk. (An outstanding and rather lengthy history of Ticketmaster from its roots in Arizona.)

Rosen, Fredric D. (1992, June 22). Counterpunch: Convenience—What Is It Worth? *Los Angeles Times*, Calendar, p. F3, col. 1, Entertainment Desk. (Fred Rosen, CEO of Ticketmaster, provides an excellent rebuttal to criticism of convenience fees.)

Sandomir, Richard (1995, December 21). Sports and Entertainment Group Is Formed by Garden's Ex-Head. *New York Times*, p. D5, col. 3. (A report detailing a new company formed by Robert M. Butkowski, former manager of Madison Square Garden. His company, The Marquee Group, was financed by the owner of SFX.)

Strauss, Neil, and James Sterngold (1998, July 20). The Concert Juggernaut. *New York Times* p. E1, col. 1. (This brief article reveals the companies that SFX Entertainment acquired in less than a year of operations.)

Waddell, Ray (1999, April 17). Touring Season Marked by Vet Acts . . . *Billboard*, Dateline, Nashville. (A discussion of the effects that consolidation in the concert business has had on guarantees paid to artists.)

## Organizations to Contact

Association of Performing Arts Presenters (Arts Presenters)
1112 16th Street NW
Suite 400
Washington, DC 20036
Phone: (202) 833–2787
Fax: (202) 833–1543
e-mail: artspres@artspresenters.org
web: www.artspresenters.org

Members of this organization like to refer to it as Arts Presenters rather than the acronym APAP. It is an organization that represents presenters of cultural arts programming such as chamber music, operas, ballets, and plays. The annual convention of Arts Presenters offers educational workshops, panels, and seminars for cultural arts promoters. It also includes numerous showcases and booking agency booths for people wanting to book cultural artists.

International Ticketing Association (INTIX)
250 West 57th Street, Suite 722
New York, NY 10107
Phone (212) 581–0600
Fax: (212) 581–0885
e-mail: info@intix.org
INTIX, formerly known as Box Office Management International (BOMI), serves as the premier organization for ticketing professionals worldwide. It is a nonprofit organization that provides a clearinghouse for information about ticket services. Its primary focus is the improvement and advancement of ticket management personnel and procedures.

National Association of Campus Activities (NACA)
13 Harbison Way
Columbia, SC 29212–3401
Phone: (803) 732–6222
web: www.naca.org
NACA is a nonprofit organization made up of colleges, universities, booking agents, performers, and campus professionals who present concerts and other programs on campuses. This organization is best known for regional and national showcases at which selected artists perform for student programmers in hopes of receiving bookings. NACA also has a one-week "concert promoter school" during the summer.

North American Concert Promoters Association (NACPA)
Ben Liss, Director
P.O. Box 470463
Brookline, MA 02147–0463
Phone: (617) 739–2121
NACPA is an organization that represents some of the largest concert promoters in the United States and Canada.

## Web Sites

www.billboard.com/charts/boxscore.html
Amusement Business Boxscore
A joint venture site from *Amusement Business*, a trade publication for live entertainment, and *Billboard*. The Boxscore site gives valuable information about concerts performed during the previous week. It provides data for each event, including artists who performed, city where the concert was held, gross ticket sales, ticket prices, attendance, total ca-

pacity, and number of shows. This is invaluable information for regional concert promoters.

www.billboard.com/tourstv/
ToursAndTV Search Site
This site allows you to search for your favorite artists to find out if they are touring or appearing on television. It also offers jump-off buttons to a myriad of *Billboard* magazine's charts and news articles.

http://events.ticketmaster.com/
Ticketmaster Online
This site lets you select any city in the country and find out what shows are available through Ticketmaster. You can buy tickets, as well as tour merchandise, online. Note that this website does not begin with the typical "www" prefix.

www.jsc.nasa.gov/bu2/inflateCPI.html
Inflation Calculator
This site offers a very easy way to adjust the price of things such as tickets from one year to another. It uses the Consumer Price Index as a way of adjusting for inflation.

www.pollstar.com/
Pollstar Concert Hotline Search
Pollstar is one of the trade publications read by virtually every concert promoter. This site offers news about upcoming tours and industry features from the print magazine.

# 8

# Black and White Separation in Music: Marketing or Racism?

Over the years people have had mixed opinions about the nature of our culture. Are we, as a nation, a melting pot in which all our differences are somehow combined into one homogenized culture, or are we more like a salad bowl, each of us maintaining our own distinctiveness, yet still contributing to the whole? On the one hand, we equate separation with segregation; on the other, we celebrate our differences, particularly in the media. When, for example, Kendricks (1998) says, "The African-American experience in film goes beyond the '70s blackploitation era and the more recent wave of gritty, urban dramas spawned by John Singleton's 'Boyz N the Hood.' It stretches back decades before filmmakers such as Spike Lee ('Do the Right Thing'), Charles Burnett ('The Glass Shield') and George Tillman Jr. ('Soul Food') even dared to dream of getting behind a movie camera," he tacitly acknowledges a negative aspect of this separation ("blackploitation"); at the same time, he also affirms that some media products are aimed specifically at black audiences.

Of course, the very nature of "black" films and organizations such as the Black Entertainment Network raises the question, "Are media products produced by or featuring a preponderance of blacks aimed *only* at black audiences, or do they also target white audiences?" This question is even more relevant to the music industry, where "race music," as rhythm and blues was often called, was combined with "white popular," folk, jazz, and country music to form what we now know as rock music.

For most of the youth of America in the 1950s, both black and white, the new rock 'n' roll was simply the music of the new generation. For some adults, however, it was further evidence of the degradation of American society. For some African Americans, the new music was a betrayal of its historic black roots and was being cheapened because white audiences were perceived as unable to truly appreciate the black experience so integral to rhythm and blues. Yet, for record companies, the new music was simply an additional genre that could be sold in order to generate more income.

## THE ROOTS OF SEGREGATED MUSIC

Rock music grew out of a combination of five distinct music genres: rhythm and blues, country and western, white popular, folk, and jazz. The musical genres contributed various elements, as outlined:

- Rhythm and blues: brass instruments, a driving beat, and a frank approach to sex in lyrics.
- Country and western: different guitar styles and earthy topics for lyrics
- White popular: sentimentality (boy meets girl), a history of economic success in the marketplace, and technical expertise in production and engineering studio recordings
- Folk: rebellion against authority and singer-songwriters performing their own works
- Jazz: highly skilled musicians and racial integration

In addition, changes in the licensing structure that determines how songwriters are paid affected the development of rock 'n' roll. Throughout the 1930s and 1940s the major moneymaker for record labels was white popular music, with the music being licensed to radio stations by ASCAP. The economic catalyst for the birth of rock 'n' roll was ASCAP's 1941 doubling of licensing fees it charged radio stations to play music from ASCAP's catalog. In response, many radio stations refused to play songs created by ASCAP songwriters, which in turn left a large "hole" in the broadcast day. To fill the void left by the ASCAP boycott, radio stations began to use artists who recorded songs not licensed by ASCAP, basically songs sung by artists not signed to major labels. Since at that time ASCAP represented predominately mainstream pop songwriters, stations turned to the two music genres outside ASCAP's domain: rhythm and blues, or R&B; and country and western, now known simply as country.

It should be noted that radio was racially segregated until rock 'n' roll became a major economic force: Stations that played R&B were "race music" stations directed toward black audiences; whereas popular stations, like their rural country and western counterparts, were marketed to white audiences. (Note: country and western has become known simply as country.) In the early stages of rock 'n' roll, it was not uncommon for a song to be released to R&B radio stations and later recorded and released to white radio stations by a different band. The second recording, called a "cover" of the original, often sold many more copies than the R&B version. Thus white-oriented stations played "race music" that had been picked up by white artists such as Bill Haley (he covered "Shake, Rattle and Roll," originally by Joe Turner) and the Crew Cuts (they covered "Sha-Boom," originally by the Chords). As pop radio audiences became familiar with "race music" songs covered by white artists, radio stations experimented with playing the original recordings made by black artists. Gradually, white stations began to play the original R&B recordings of songs that appealed to both black and white audiences.

Another phenomenon, called a "crossover hit," emerged as mainstream white radio stations felt more comfortable expanding the mix of music they programmed. A crossover is a song intended for one radio market (e.g., country and western), that is subsequently getting airplay on another station format (e.g., Top 40). At the beginning of the 1950s, several R&B songs "crossed over" into the popular charts: These included "Earth Angel" by the Penguins and "Cryin' in the Chapel" by the Orioles. Thus, in the early 1950s artists began to merge various elements of rhythm and blues, white popular, and country and western, and in 1951 Alan Freed, the Cleveland disc jockey who is credited with coining the term "rock 'n' roll," began to play a mixture of white popular (Frank Sinatra and Al Martino) and rhythm and blues. He also sponsored dances that featured all-black entertainers that attracted large numbers of white teenagers.

Then, in 1954 Bill Haley and the Comets made the final fusion of the three genre with a song that is generally considered the first rock 'n' roll hit, "Rock around the Clock." The song combined country-and-western instrumentation, a hard-driving beat (R&B), and the dance theme so popular in white popular. Even as Haley was hitting the pop charts with his derivative of black music for white audiences, he was also going the other way. In 1955 he released "Dim, Dim the Lights," a pop tune that made it onto the rhythm-and-blues charts, "a particularly unusual phenomenon because 'white' records rarely appeared on the R&B charts" (Stuessy, 1990, p. 34).

Gradually, racial integration of the airwaves became the norm, much to the chagrin of segregationists and adults who objected to the lyrics, beat, or message of the new rock 'n' roll (see Chapters 2, 3, 5, and 10 for examples of reactions to rock music). Through the early years of rock 'n' roll, white artists such as Elvis Presley, Jerry Lee Lewis, the Everly Brothers, and Buddy Holly sang music that had unmistakable rhythm-and-blues roots. In addition, these artists opened the way for acceptance of black artists by white audiences: Little Richard, Larry Price, Fats Domino, and most important, Chuck Berry. Of course, other forms of music were also undergoing transformation as genres were merging and realigning themselves: "Entwined in the music and words of folk-rock are the seg-regated field of race music, white rock and roll, pop music values, and the protest singers and songs generally associated with the student movements of the 1960s" (Dunson, 1966, p. 13).

From this brief history we can see that even from the earliest days of rock music there has been a racial divide between "black" and "white" music and black and white audiences. Even as the racial barriers of radio formats began to fall, however, record companies created their own forms of segregation within their own organizations. Major labels have had many euphemisms for African American music divisions: black, soul, rhythm and blues, and most recently, urban. One must ask, Does such categorization promote racial segregation, or is it a valid form of marketing segmentation necessary to sign artists and sell recordings?

## THE BIRTH OF RAP AND GANGSTA RAP

Depending on whom you ask, rap music began in either the early 1970s or the late 1970s, was itself an outgrowth of urban hip-hop culture, and was seen as a lifestyle as much as a form of music. As with so much popular culture, however, rap did not develop along clearly defined lines in any linear manner. Generally speaking, hip-hop is the overarching umbrella that comprises rap, break dancing, and graffiti. Rap itself has been defined as music with a hard-driving beat, perhaps a reflection of its roots in rhythm and blues, plus spoken or chanted rhyming words instead of sung lyrics (Nazareth, 1999, p. S6). Hip-hop and rap are often used interchangeably; but in the eyes of most musicologists, rap is the musical art form.

Afrika Bambaataa, Grandmaster Flash, and Kool Herc—three inven-tors of what we now call rap—are often referred to as the "old school" or "first wave" of rap. Early rap artist Bambaataa used the term "hip-hop" to refer to his dance gatherings, called jams. "I started naming my jams, 'hip-hop' jams," said Bambaataa (Perkins, 1996). While DJs were mixing and scratching records to create a danceable instrumental back-ground, persons began to step forward to boast about themselves and to talk about the other dancers. Those early front persons became known as MCs and, later, as rappers.

Most sources acknowledge the early contribution of Jamaican music to the development of rap. One early rap artist, Kool Herc (aka Clive Campbell) moved from Kingston, Jamaica, to the Bronx in 1967. He brought with him the tradition of Caribbean ska and reggae beats with the raplike style of Jamaican singers. Some authorities on rap music's origins credit Kool Herc with inventing rap and the hip-hop culture of the Bronx (Perkins, 1996). Then, in 1979, the rap act Sugar Hill Gang released "Rapper's Delight," considered by many to be the first rap single, "a joyous confection of party lyrics and music based on Chic's 'Good Times.' It was good dance music and the accompanying patter over the track (the 'rapping') seemed like an interesting novelty" (Muwakkil, 1998). By the early 1980s hip-hop came into its own with Grandmaster Flash, one of the first technologically savvy rappers. Unlike Herc and Bambaataa, Grandmaster Flash was able to garner financial success for his music. His 1982 single, "The Message," recorded by Grandmaster Flash and the Furious Five (featuring Duke Bootee), was certified gold.

Rap music was not generally embraced by major labels in the 1970s and early 80s, however. After Run-D.M.C. attained commercial success with their debut album *Rock Box*, thanks in part to MTV exposure, labels started to think more seriously about rap as a commercial genre. It was the collaboration of the heavy metal band Aerosmith with Run-D.M.C. that produced the first major hit for a rap album. The instant success of the single "Walk This Way" helped propel the album, *Raising Hell*, to sales of 3 million units.

As major labels began to sign rap acts, rap producers found themselves in an enviable position: There was very little competition from rock producers who weren't familiar with rap. Rap continued to develop its sales base for recordings and concerts throughout the 1990s. Paradoxically, many journalists have criticized the recording industry for transforming rap from a street-based artform to entertainment. While executive editor of Third World Press, Bakari Kitwana criticized commercially successful rap because the artists have "been altered or constructed around being rewarded financially—not for being true to themselves, the artform or rap origins, but to the white corporate elite interest (that which is in the best interest of increasing sales rather than elevating the artform)" (Kitwana, 1994).

Despite any precise definition of rap music, one should not think that rap encompasses just one kind of music. To fans of rap, there are numerous stylistic differences—subgenres—within the rap genre. For example, rappers from the East Coast have tended to use more intricate wordplay, and the words tend to be very fast. Rappers on the West Coast, in contrast, are more likely to use more melodic lyrics. Of course, the same differentiation was once made about jazz: West Coast jazz was seen as "cool," and East Coast jazz was sometimes referred to as "hard bop."

These stylistic differences aside, and even though rap music grew out of African American themes in urban settings, white American youth have adopted rap as their own. Said Bob Santelli, the vice president for education and public programming for the Rock and Roll Hall of Fame and Museum in Cleveland, Ohio: "If you look at American culture today, what is it? It's hip-hop culture. . . . The average kid who buys a hip-hop record is more likely than not to be young, white and suburban. [Hip-hop] is far more than a ghetto phenomenon. . . . This is mainstream American culture" (Santelli, quoted in Nazareth, 1999, p. 56). Noted scholar of rap Nelson George stated his belief that rap was never exclusive to African American audiences: "It is a fallacy that there ever existed a time when hip hop buyers were exclusively black. The first rap hit, 'Rapper's Delight' 1979, was voted single of the year by the National Association of Recording Merchandisers, hardly a collective interested in celebrating singles sold just to black teenagers" (George, 1998, p. 60).

One of the most controversial aspects of rap, the apparent glorification of violence, was launched by the group Ice Cube with their 1989 work *Straight Outta Compton*. The album originated in the wake of the Rodney King riots in Los Angeles, particularly in the Watts and Compton areas. No other aspect of rap music has created more debate than that of gangsta lyrics, particularly anger directed toward authority.

## THE IMPACT OF GANGSTA RAP

The violence in much of rap (particularly gangsta rap, a sub-genre of rap very often containing violent themes also called "hard core rap" or "reality rap") is said to be an outgrowth of two different cultures, again, one on the West Coast and the other on the East Coast. In the east, the birth of gangsta rap was attributed to gang violence between African American, Afro-Caribbean, and Latin gangs in New York. Rather than engage in self-destructive violence, rappers began to "fight" their battles through rap music (Muwakkil, 1998). Still others, such as rapper Kurtis Blow, contend that East Coast rap was mild and that the more violent gangsta rap sprang directly from the urban ghettos of the West Coast:

> Well, at first, rap was fun. It was something that we did as a means of expression in the early days of rap. And then it just progressed.
>
> Each time a rapper would come out, he felt that he would have to outdo the next one. And they started getting harder and harder. The lyrics became more street-oriented. And . . . it was selling. Yes, most definitely. And you know, you had the West Coast come into the picture, and that's when the lyrics really became really hard and a lot of profanity and they were kicking lyrics from the ghetto and from a ghetto mentality, and that's where gangsta rap started. (Blow, 1997)

Whichever coast one believes was the birthplace of gangsta rap, the fact is rap's violent offspring grew out of the urban areas of America's large cities. Because media messages reflect the environment in which they are created, rap's offspring, gangsta rap, reflects dissatisfaction of young

A black BMW, riddled with bullet holes, sits in the police impound lot Sunday, September 8, 1996, in Las Vegas. This scene brings a realistic note to gangsta rap because it is the car in which rapper Tupac Shakur was riding when he was shot and critically wounded the night before. The car was driven by Death Row Records chairman Marion Knight. (AP/Wide World Photos)

adults with the world around them—a world of depressed urban areas. The music thus provides an outlet for the anger of African American youths.

At the same time, rap provides what some critics call a cultural mythology. As stories, through songs, continually reinforce often repeated themes about police brutality, drug use, and gang warfare, they become more believable. In other words, there are those who believe rap lyrics project ideas onto urban youth. Others believe that rap music is the contemporary urban form of journalism: "What we need to realize about gangsta is that while it has been accused of celebrating gang violence, it is also accurate reportage" (Gibb, 2000). Robert "Scoop" Jackson stated in his book *The Last Black Mecca: Hip-Hop* that music does not necessarily change behavior, but it "does 'spark curiosity' and instigate attitudes. The racial attitude in America right now is very tense. Rap music did not cause this, but 'reported' on it" (Jackson, 1994). Both Gibb and Jackson, it seems, believe rap lyrics reflect, rather than create, what is going on in urban settings.

Obviously, the direct impact of gangsta rap is open to debate. In Chapter 2 we discussed the projective-reflective theory of media, which asks, Do the media project a particular point of view on society (and thus lead society in that direction), or do media messages merely reflect what society is already doing? The problem is, violence in predominantly black urban areas was present long before gangsta rap was born. It thus appears that it is the "reflective" part of the theory that is at work.

Nevertheless, there are those who see rap, particularly gangsta rap, as both a symptom and a cause of degradation and violence. Said C. Delores Tucker, chairwoman of the National Political Congress of Black Women, and William J. Bennett, author of *The Book of Virtues* and codirector of Empower America:

> Newspaper editors and television producers veto even the expletive-deleted versions of these lyrics because they are so offensive and obscene. This speaks volumes about just how bad they are.
>
> "Artists" sing about dismemberment and cutting off women's breasts.
>
> This is fair game for an audience of 12-year-olds?
>
> The sponsor behind this kind of music is often Time Warner Inc.
>
> In fact, Time Warner Inc. recently increased its investment in "gangsta rap" and now owns 50 percent of Interscope Records, the record label behind such "artists" as Snoop Doggy Dogg, Dr. Dre, Nine Inch Nails and Tupac Shakur—whose songs of violence are notorious . . .
>
> We are not calling for censorship. We are both virtual absolutists

on the First Amendment. Our appeal is to a sense of corporate responsibility and simple decency. There are things no one should sell.

We met recently with Time Warner executives to outline our concerns. Our recommendation was straightforward: Time Warner should stop its sponsorship and promotion of lyrics that celebrate rape, torture and murder.

Thus far, the appeal has fallen on deaf ears. When we read the lyrics to Time Warner executives and asked if they thought them offensive and ought not to be sold to children, we were told that it was a "complex issue."

It is not a complex issue. There are things on which reasonable people will disagree. But some lyrics of these songs are beyond the pale. (Bennett and Tucker, 1995)

When labels respond to criticism of music lyrics, they typically respond by saying, "It is the *parents of children* who should determine what music their kids listen to, not *record companies*." In reality, parents have a very difficult time policing the music their children listen to. Parents must be alert to radio, cable television music videos, films, and recordings.

On the surface, labels have addressed this issue, but in reality, it is a "bait and switch" situation. Rap singles are often released in two forms. One form, without any profanity, is released to radio as the "clean" version. The other version, complete with profanity, is called the "explicit" version. Therefore, parents might listen to the clean version on the radio and agree to let their child buy the album. Then the child could come home with an explicit version that most parents would have banned from their household had they known more.

Another critic of gangsta rap, Stanley Crouch, has said: "I dislike the side of rap that encourages violence over trivia, theft, drive-by shootings, misogyny, the side of rap that gives young women the impression that in order to rebel, they should become sluts. These things have had a very destructive influence on our society" (Crouch, quoted in Gibb, 2000). Although it is difficult to create the scientifically controlled environment necessary to accurately test the influence of rap lyrics on young listeners, recent abuse of prescription cough syrup may be an example of gangsta rap's perverse effect. After Memphis rap group Three 6 Mafia released its single "Sippin' on Some Syrup," the federal Drug Enforcement Administration (DEA) noticed "soaring sales" of prescription cough syrup. The agency also noted an increase in stolen prescription pads from physicians' offices (Jones, 2000).

Of course, record executives *are* responsive to market forces. A record company is, after all, a business. Labels typically acknowledge that rap

C. Delores Tucker of the National Political Congress of Black Women holds a copy of the cover of Tupac Shakur's album *Makaveli* during a Washington news conference Tuesday, December 10, 1996, to discuss gangsta rap. Tucker, along with former Education Secretary William Bennett, said the album's distributor, MCA/Universal Records, violated a commitment not to distribute profane or violent music. (AP/Wide World Photos)

music contains violence and misogynous messages, but they cannot "censor" an art form that has so many customers. This stance has led to what seems to be a dual standard: Columbia Records refused to distribute the band Slayer's *Reign in Blood* album because of references to the infamous doctor Joseph Mengele, whose Nazi war crimes were still painful memories for many Holocaust survivors in the United States and Europe. One might wonder why Slayer's music was simply "unacceptable for distribution" by Columbia, whereas other albums with lyrics extolling violence against African American women were apparently quite appropriate for distribution. Likewise, Warner Brothers gave mixed messages when the label pulled a Michael Jackson single that was offensive to some members of the Jewish community, yet released "Smack My Bitch Up" by the British group Prodigy in spite of repeated protests from feminist organizations.

Although it may be true that gangsta rap is brutal, supporters contend it is so only because the culture out of which it grew is brutal. However, there is also concern that the lyrics are not merely reflective of a particular society; they are in fact glorifying that society, in which violence plays so large a part:

> The brutality of the music and lyrics undoubtedly reflects the culture from which it comes, which is what makes gangsta rap such a direct and powerful form of communication. Authenticity is all. But when that form of self-expression became big business, the market selected only the most extreme versions. It's a form of cultural cross-breeding that encourages brutality over intelligence, crudity over imagination. . . .
>
> The gangsta identity is deliberately constructed from all the things that scare white America. Yet the unintended result was to provide the perfect soundtrack for white teen rebellion. (Gibb, 2000, p. 5)

One can build a case that some rappers speak from personal experiences with violence and escapist sexual promiscuity in inner-city housing projects. But can one also defend music by white rappers Eminem, Kid Rock, Beasty Boys, and Vanilla Ice as "street journalism" of our day? Perhaps record labels struggle to find any intellectual justification for music that sells many units. And, of course, the ultimate defense of music, no matter how offensive, is the need to protect freedom of expression at any cost.

## THE ECONOMICS OF RAP MUSIC

That a major corporation will give up any profitable music genre unless outside pressures are unbearable is unlikely. Figures show that in

1998, rap outsold country 81 million units to 72 million. Outside pressure would need to be extremely great to cause record labels to restrict their output of rap records, no matter how violent and misogynous they might be.

Perhaps the best (or worst) example of the linkage between white executives and rap music is in the person of Michael Ovitz, one-time president of Disney. After leaving Disney in a deal that included a $90 million golden parachute, Ovitz formed Artist Management Group to manage high-visibility (and high-paying) Hollywood talent. In January 2000, having "seen the future, and the future is hip-hop" (Morris, 2000), Ovitz formed an "urban entertainment division" at AMG, saying, "I want to try to learn this whole urban marketing situation. . . . I see big crossover potential in films, in sports and everything else" (Morris, 2000) "Urban," in case you were wondering, is marketing speak for "African American." To answer the question, "To whom is rap music being aimed?" we must recognize that any major label is going to promote any given act where that act will make the most money. After all, the object of marketing is to generate enough money to show a profit.

Another aspect of the issue is that production and distribution are, in fact, two different areas of the recording industry. This dichotomy can lead to confusion. For example, Death Row Records was a black-owned business, but its music was distributed by Interscope Records, a division of media conglomerate Time Warner, a record distribution entity that employs mostly white executives and handles mostly white artists. Other rap artists affiliated with Interscope include Snoop Doggy Dog, Dr. Dre, and until his murder, Tupac Shakur.

As rock, and its derivative subgenres such as alternative rock, continued to dominate the recording industry, a new form aimed at black audiences was emerging: rap, and its subgenre, gangsta rap. But then something interesting happened: White audiences—predominately teenagers—began to listen to rap music and to take it as their own. As one might imagine, record companies took notice. So, just who was rap supposed to be for: black audiences, white audiences, or both? In today's marketing environment, is any media product, including music, really created for a specific audience, or is it simply one more product to be sold to anyone who will buy it, listen to it, watch it?

Some critics believe that white listeners and performers cannot appreciate the true spirit of rap music. Moreover, they think members of the white majority can never become a part of the hip-hop milieu. Persons taking the opposite viewpoint feel that efforts to exclude whites from rap amount to racism in the guise of Afrocentrism. Their arguments tend to revolve around hypothetical "tables turned" scenarios: If white label heads proclaimed that African Americans would be considered unacceptable artists or audiences for a particular genre of music, would we not cry foul? In other words, reverse discrimination is still discrimination. Such discussions surrounding the alleged separation of "white music" from "black music" characteristically acknowledge historic patterns of racism and their impact on the music industry. One might conclude that the industry was carved into racial divisions by white executives and that things have never changed. However, rap executives should probably not rely on that rationale to justify keeping rap a "blacks only" art form, since that argument is the same as the justification used to maintain segregation in the South, namely, that "it has always been this way."

Another issue that has haunted rap music since its inception is the disparagement of women—misogyny—frequently evident in rap lyrics. Some prominent women's organizations have chastised labels for making money from music that denigrates black women. Misogynous rap lyrics typically take the form of sexual conquest of women, who are often called "Hos"—street vernacular for whores. One might ask, Are labels profiting from rap music at the expense of females?

In addition to misogyny, one can usually notice lyrics that glorify violence in rap music. Male bravado is a popular theme championed in hip-hop culture. It is not uncommon for rap music to sound as if it condones gang warfare, violence directed at police, use of drugs, and treatment of women as objects rather than as human beings. It must be noted, however, that anti-social themes such as anger toward police, use of drugs, and treatment of women as sex objects is not unique to rap music. The rock band Rage Against the Machine and their fans have consistently criticized law enforcement officials. A review of music videos on MTV or VH1—cable channels known for rock and pop rather than rap—frequently portray women as sex objects.

First Amendment rights and the theories discrediting how music affects behavior notwithstanding, one must ask if there are boundaries past which an entire genre of music should not pass. Should we, as a society, cry out against music that is for some people a public form of sexual harassment? Or must society change the conditions described in rap music in hopes that contemporary balladeers—rappers—will change their lyrics accordingly?

Media companies are, of course, concerned with the bottom line and generally less concerned about why white audiences would buy music ostensibly intended for black audiences. Record company executives know a good thing when they see it. And the sale of rap to white audiences is, for the companies involved, a very good thing: It has been estimated that 60 percent of the sales of gangsta rap is to white listeners (Muwakkil, 1998):

> Despite the high profile of black music business executives . . . a shrinking number of multinationals control the business, and their higher echelons remain predominantly white. As is the audience

which buys hardcore rap's tales of bitches, blunts, beatdowns and AK-47s.... Once this credibility is established, then white-owned companies can market young black men and women to the voyeuristic suburban white teens who keep the entertainment industry buoyant. Rappers resent it ... but the dollars keep flowing. (Morris, 2000)

Said Chuck D, founder of Public Enemy, "It's still being controlled by a bunch of white guys in business suits sitting around a conference table. ... When it comes to where the music is going, it's not in the hands of people of color. I feel there has to be a balance" (Chuck D, quoted in Nazareth, 1999).

Lingering racial stereotypes seem slow to die in the music industry, even though it is generally thought of as a liberal industry. Audio engineer Tony Shepperd, who has worked with artists such as Whitney Houston, Al Jarreau, and Madonna, recalls an embarrassing moment during a visit to Nashville. As he bagan to enter the control room, he was told that singers should go through the other door to the studio floor. Of course, the person advising him never imagined an African American gentleman would be an audio engineer (Daley, 1998). Unfortunately, racial stereotypes in the music industry cast African Americans as singers, instrumentalists, songwriters, and producers. Whites are, in contrast, more often seen as engineers, label executives, managers, agents, and entertainment attorneys.

There has also been something of an economic backlash against the violence in rap music revealed in, of all things, country music: Some people who market country music have credited rap with past increases in country music listenership. Jimmy Bowen, former president of Liberty Records and Capital Records Nashville, felt that many young people were turned off by the negativity of rap in the early 1990s and began listening to other genres of music, including country. He believed that country replaced pop and rap music for many youths during the early 1990s, when country artists like Garth Brooks and Reba McIntire soared in popularity. "I hope rap keeps getting stronger and more violent, because it is sending me [country music] customers!" Bowen said in candid sarcasm (Bowen, 1992).

Wayne Halper, general manager for DreamWorks Records, Nashville, had similar feelings, but he emphasized the role of parents in controlling what music their children listen to. The point he makes is that if parents instill a sense of values in their children, they will distinguish between the fantasy of entertainment and reality. Furthermore, he felt that parents should definitely pay attention to what music their children purchase. Said Halper, who noted that his label is predominately country, "The marketplace should be controlled by parents. I don't have a problem with lyric warnings on albums. It could even be a good marketing tool [for country music]" (Halper, 1999).

Further, what makes the distribution of rap music to white audiences even stranger is that the music often deals with places and events middle-class white youth have little or no knowledge of. Gangsta rap tends to focus on fairly specific cities and locations, often referred to as the "hood." Even the rappers themselves acknowledge this somewhat schizophrenic state of affairs. For example, on Mos Def's album *Black on Both Sides* is a cut called "Rock n Roll," which contains the line "Elvis Presley ain't got no soul/Bo Diddley is rock 'n' roll." Interestingly, the album was released by a New York company, Rawkus, which is partially owned by white media mogul Rupert Murdoch, who has even deeper connections to rap. The entrepreneur had a stake in the Warren Beatty movie *Bulworth*, about a fictional character who begins rapping following a breakdown. Here was a rich white man taking on the verbal trappings of the ghetto.

## THE SOCIETAL IMPACT OF RAP

Rap is probably the only genre of music in which the angst of song lyrics is played out off-stage by performers and business executives. There are those who claim the violence in rap music is a deliberate marketing ploy; it not only pits blacks against whites, but also the East Coast against the West Coast, not only in corporate boardrooms but also on the streets:

> You don't have to watch many rap videos on MTV to spot the direct challenge of the "Westside" hand signal—index and third finger crossed over to create a "W"—which shows how the mainstream media has been drawn into this running feud. The coastal conflict has famously spilled over into actual violence; no other musical genre has lost so many of its stars to violence, notably in the murders of big names Biggie Smalls and the late Tupac Shakur. (Gibb, 2000, p. 5)

Others are not so circumspect:

> Many attributed the two murders, which remain unsolved, to an East Coast/West Coast feud, presumably between Wallace and Combs, owner of New York's Bad Boy Records, and Shakur and Marion "Suge" Knight, owner of Los Angeles' Death Row Records. Few deny that considerable hostility existed between the two camps. . . . "I hadn't realized that despite the calm, there were many people still seething about Tupac's death," says Davey D of KMEL-

FM, a popular hip-hop station in Oakland. "Here in the Bay area, kids were actually celebrating Biggie's death." (Muwakkil, 1998, p. 12)

Thus, many people are concerned that white record executives are capitalizing on black rage and thereby trivializing it and profiting from its chaos. Even worse, they are marketing this rage to an audience that has almost no connection to the environment portrayed by the songs and therefore cannot appreciate what the songs are saying. Of course, this situation raises questions about the *purpose* of any given song and whether the listeners' purpose in listening is the same as the artist's purpose in singing or rapping. These questions are not unique to rap music, and in the early days of protest songs there was concern: "Left-wing critics of rock 'n' roll . . . have pointed with horror to teenagers and young adults dancing to civil rights and anti-war songs such as 'Blowin' in the Wind' " (Denisoff, 1972, p. 140).

It must also be noted, though, that rap artists themselves have taken part in what many people consider the American dream of making lots of money. Acts such as Master P, Russell Simmons and Sean "Puff Daddy" Combs are millionaires with their own lines of clothing and restaurants. Roxanne Shante sells soft drinks on television, and Combs has been on the cover of *Fortune*. There is also the indirect financial gain of those involved in subsidiary levels of the industry. Said noted author Nelson George, this money is going directly into black neighborhoods:

Bad Boy (Records) had 20 to 30 [black employees] inside the office in mail rooms, as secretaries and assistants. Street teams plaster the street with fliers and stickers. On the road, stylists, makeup artists and truck drivers. Not all [those jobs] go to black people but a lot of them do. . . .

Master P. employs people. A black woman manages his recording studio. No way that happens if Puffy [Sean Combs, aka Puff Daddy] doesn't exist. He owns a restaurant now—more jobs. Next year a clothing line. Russell Simmons employs people in jobs that wouldn't exist without the music. . . .

There are young black attorneys, black accountants. You notice it more and more. You forget how much money is spilled off by success. (George, quoted by Lewis, 1998, p. E3)

Yet some see gangsta rap as just another form of exploitation of black Americans. Said Stanley Crouch, music critic for the New Republic: "The people who are in it are the same kind of people who were in the slave trade. I mean, if Russell Simmons and those same people had been Africans 300 years ago, they would have been selling slaves. And so what they're doing is they're selling these vile images of black people" (Crouch, 1997).

The equation of black artists, white distributors, and white audiences has become even more confused with what is being called "white rap." Artists like Eminem, Kid Rock, Limp Bizkit, and Korn "have discovered the merits of grafting hip-hop trappings onto rock's power chords" (Dollar, 1999, p. K1). Other white rappers include what is perhaps the original white rap group, Beastie Boys, Everlast (formerly with the Irish American gangsta rap group House of Pain), who do "hip-hop for the coffeehouse crowd" (Dollar, 1999), Eminem (discovered by black rapper Dr. Dre), Warped Tour, and Insane Clown Posse. Said Leslie Farm, program director of WNNX-FM, Atlanta, in an interview with Steve Dollar of the *Atlanta Journal Constitution*: "I haven't seen anything like this since the early grunge days when Nirvana came out of nowhere. . . . It's the biggest phenomenon. Limp Bizkit sold 22,000 records in Atlanta in less than three weeks. Its album (*Significant Other*) debuted at No. 1 and stayed for three weeks against mass appeal acts like Ricky Martin" (Dollar, 1999). In fact, some authorities, such as Jim Kerr of *Radio and Records*, see rock's grafting of rap as a major shift in the music.

> There's nothing artificial about this. Anyone younger than 24 has pretty much lived their entire conscious life with hip-hop. . . . Rock as a genre has transformed itself and embraced a new point of view by including hip-hop elements. Rock has gone through grunge and the corporate rock of the '80s and punk, but it's all various shades of angry vocals over guitar, bass and drums. You haven't seen a whole lot of stylistic change since the Beatles. Nothing in terms of genre-bending has happened to rock like we're seeing now. (J. Kerr, quoted in Dollar, 1999)

As might be expected, however, black rap artists are cool to the ideas that white artists can perform "real" rap. Said Chuck D, with a certain degree of frustration: "I don't know why people keep talking about it. When MTV did 'Yo! MTV Raps' back in the '80s, that right there told us white kids love rap. They didn't put that show on for black kids. So, the white kids tuned in, they've bought into the culture and now people are trying to emulate, do it, incorporate it into their music. What?" (Chuck D, quoted in Dollar, 1999). The questions being raised, however, are far from academic; they affect both the culture and the bottom line. After all, hip-hop and rap ultimately come from an African tradition that white performers cannot possible internalize. So what happens to the cultural identity of rap when it is appropriated by white performers or affected by white audiences? Are these phenomena adding to the culture or taking something away from it?

At another level, one of the foundational premises of rap is that it is "real," in the sense of a reflection (rather than a projection) of life in predominately black inner-city neighborhoods. Yet, perhaps there are also some unintended consequences to the reality of gangsta rap: For white audiences, the only contact they may have with tough urban life is through this music. Further, if this is the only message they are getting, it is also the only view white youth will have. Thus, in this case, in addition to reflecting a particular viewpoint, the producers will also be projecting that view, however stereotypical it might be, onto the white audience. Thus, "the music's blunt lyrics and cinematic qualities offer a vicarious thrill to the millions of whites who buy it" (Muwakkil, 1998).

However, we could ask a similar question of any African American rap artists who make it to the big time: Are they not disavowing the true roots of rap? And is the cross-pollination from one musical genre to another really anything new? Not according to W. T. Lehman, Jr., of Florida State University:

> As soon as whites could observe blacks dancing and singing along the coasts of the new world, they started grabbing those moves, talking and dressing black, and promoting that culture as the ne plus ultra [highest attainable point] of authenticity.... The whole concept of white trash and disdained black forms has been the generative swap meet for Atlantic popular culture since the 1830s— since the onset of the Industrial Revolution. (Lehman, quoted in Dollar, 1999)

## CONCLUSION

The Reverend Jesse Jackson spoke what might be a prophecy in 1989 when he told MTV viewers, "Rap music is here to stay, and to see the youth pick up the bits and pieces of life as it is lived, and transform mess into a message, and be able to uplift people, is a phenomenal art form" (Jackson, 1989). He might not be as supportive of rap in the new millennium, however, if lyrics continue to grow more offensive to the general public.

If rap continues to disparage women, the gender that represents over half the popular and the majority of record buyers, will the industry feel a backlash against labels that distribute it? Even some rap artists and urban label executives think that gangsta rap has gone too far. Joseph "Run" Simmons of Run-D.M.C. said, "When N.W.A. started talking about killing prostitutes on 'One Less Bitch,' it got stupid. It ain't funny no more" (Duggan, 1993).

Perhaps labels have begun to listen to women's groups, concerned parents, and legislators: By the year 2000 most labels had a system of internal censorship in place for rap. In an effort to prevent retailers and radio stations from banning singles or complete albums, labels remix rap recordings to mask certain words or phrases. In order to make Eminem's album *The Marshall Mathers LP* more palatable to the public, his label deleted entire tracks from the album his producer submitted. In addition, the lyrics were "extensively edited—up to 60 times in a single song—to eliminate references to drugs, violence, profanity and hate" (Strauss, 2000). Although most labels have screening committees to recommend changes to rap recordings, few if any executives will admit to self-censoring music.

Will rap continue to grow as a commercially viable genre in the new millennium? If so, debates over whether rap should be an exclusively African American artform will likely continue. If rap continues to dominate album sales, the validity of categories such as "black music" or "urban music" will come under question. If rap becomes the highest-selling genre of music in the United States, and hence the most popular music sold, shouldn't it then be called the new "popular music" or will the industry feel compelled to categorize as "black" any music of predominantly African American origin?

Whatever its category, labels will package, promote, and distribute rap as long as it continues to attract youthful fans. As labels market rap more aggressively, some critics will condemn the industry for profits they will no doubt earn from hip-hop culture. For good or for ill, the thing we know for sure is that rap, and the hip-hop milieu, have made an indelible imprint on American culture.

## TOPICS FOR DISCUSSION

1. What moral and cultural limits have been blurred by rap music? By gangsta rap?
2. Can white audiences really "understand" rap and gangsta rap? Why or why not?
3. Several rap and gangsta rap songs have been criticized for their offensive lyrics, yet the songs themselves contain prosocial messages. Can you justify using "dirty" words to promote worthwhile causes?
4. Women seem to buy rap music in spite of the disparaging terms it often uses to describe females. Why do you think females do not turn away from this genre of music? Do you think rap contributes to degrading stereotypes of women in society?

## REFERENCES

### Books

Denisoff, R. S. (1972). *Sing a Song of Social Significance*. Bowling Green, OH: Bowling Green University Popular Press.

George, Nelson (1998). *Hip Hop America*. New York: Penguin Books.

Jackson, Robert Scoop (1994). *The Last Black Mecca: Hip Hop*. Chicago, IL: Frontline Distribution International, Inc.

Kitwana, Bakari (1994). *The Rap on Gangsta Rap*. Chicago, IL: Third World Press.

Perkins, William Eric, ed. (1996). *Droppin' Science: Critical Essays on Rap Music and Hip Hop Culture*. Philadelphia, PA: Temple University Press. (A collection of eleven works that examine the history of rap and the culture that evolved with this genre of music.)

Stuessy, J. (1990). *Rock & Roll: Its History and Stylistic Development*. New York: Prentice Hall.

## Legislative and Judicial Proceedings

*Plessy v. Ferguson*, 163 U.S. 537 (1896).

*Texas v. Johnson*, 491 U.S. 397 (1989).

*Tucker v. Fischbein*, Civil A. 97–4717, 1999 WL 58585, 1999 U.S. Dist. LEXIS 774 (E.D. Pennsylvania, 1999).

*Ward v. Rock Against Racism*, 491 U.S. 781 (1989).

## Magazines, Journals, and Newspapers

Bennett, W. J., and Tucker, C. D. (1995, June 2). Lyrics from the Gutter. *New York Times*, p. A29.

Blow, K. (1997, March 19). Effect of Gangsta Rap on African-American Culture. *Equal Time*, CNBC.

Crouch, S. (1997, March 19). Effect of Gangsta Rap on African-American Culture. *Equal Time*, CNBC.

Daley, Dan (November, 1998). Black Boxes, White Faces. *Studio Sound*, p. 100.

Dollar, S. (1999, August 1). Hip-hop's Growing Influence: Rock's New Rap; Meet the New Vanguard: Most of Them Are Loud, Some of Them Are Angry, a Few of Them Are Comedians . . . and All of Them Are White. *Atlanta Journal and Constitution*.

Duggan, Dennis (1993, July 8). Bad Rap for Women. *Newsday*, p. 26, City Edition.

Dunson, J. (1966, January 15). Folk Rock: Thunder without Rain. *Sing Out!*

Gibb, E. (2000, January 16). Survival of the Phattest. *Sunday (Scotland) Herald*, p. 5.

Jackson, Jesse (1989, July). Interviewed on MTV.

Jones, Yolanda (2000, July). Sippin' on Some Syrup. *Commercial Appeal (Memphis)*, pg. F1.

Kendricks, N. (1998, February 26). Lost in America; Discovering the Legacy of African-Americans in Motion Pictures. *San Diego Union-Tribune*.

Lewis, G. (1998, December 6). Hip-hop Gives Birth to Its Own Black Economy. *San Diego Union-Tribune*.

Morris, M. (2000, January 26). Black Gold: Fiftysomething White Hollywood Supremo Michael Ovitz Has Announced He's Getting into Hip-hop. It's Not the First Time the Establishment Has Hijacked African-American Culture for Profit. And It Won't Be the Last. The *(London) Guardian*, p. 17.

Muwakkil, S. (1998, March 8). Rap's Dilemma. *In These Times*.

Nazareth, E. (1999, November 14). Rap 'n' Roll History on Its 20th Anniversary, Hip-hop Finally Takes Its Rightful Place in the Rock Museum. *Toronto Sun*, p. S6.
Smiley, T. (1997, March 19). Effect of Gangsta Rap on African-American Culture. *Equal Time*, CNBC.
Strauss, Neil (2000, August 1). Policing Pop . . . Recording Industry's Strictest Censor Is Itself. *New York Times*, p. A1.

## Interviews

Bowen, Jimmy (1992, October). Bowen was president of Capital Records Nashville when he spoke on the campus of Middle Tennessee State University in Murfreesboro, Tennessee.
Halper, Wayne (1999, September 2). Halper is general manager of DreamWorks Records, Nashville.

## Web Sites

http://www.npcbw.org/press/newsobserver.html
National Political Congress of Black Women, Inc.
Dr. C. Delores Tucker has been trying to challenge corporations that produce gangsta rap. She feels that it is exploitation of black youths.

# 9

# "I'll See You in Court": The Strange Relationship between Managers and Artists

The relationship between recording artists and their managers is somewhat like a marriage: Both require an extremely high level of trust, respect, and loyalty. Unfortunately, like the many couples who end their marriages in divorce court, many performers terminate the relationship with their manager through the judicial system. The model of musicians and their business associates settling their disputes in the courts can be traced back to the eighteenth century. As the husband-and-wife team of economists William and Hilda Baumol noted, Prince Karl Lichnowsky filed a lawsuit against Wolfgang Amadeus Mozart in 1791. Prince Lichnowsky was awarded a considerable judgment in what might be considered the first legal showdown between a performing artist and the business person behind his career (Kelleher, 1992).

An artist and manager typically have a contractual agreement, analogous to marriage vows, that tithes a percentage of the artist's income to the manager for long periods of time. Dissolving that agreement, and dividing past, present, and future income, is almost always traumatic. History has shown that managers frequently understand the business environments surrounding the music industry much better than nubian recording artists do. Because of this imbalance of knowledge, managers too often have the ability to take advantage of the artists they work with. Conversely, many managers have helped artists struggle through the start-up phase of their career only to be cast aside in exchange for a more prestigious manager as soon as the artist finds success in the industry.

One thing is certain: Legal battles between artists and managers are not uncommon. Nor are these battles unique to one genre of music. Well-known performing artists who have had legal struggles with their managers include Collective Soul, Billy Joel, Al Kooper, Clint Black, Bruce Springsteen, Jefferson Airplane (aka Jefferson Starship and later simply Starship), Prince (aka The Artist), 'N Sync, the Backstreet Boys, Ozzy Osbourne, Fleetwood Mac, TLC, Mindy McCreedy, Toni Braxton, the Beatles, Jewell, John Fogerty, and Creedence Clearwater Revival.

Contentious litigation between an artist and a manager affects many more people than one might expect. When management commissions come under question, record companies and publishers may not distribute royalties until all lawsuits, countersuits, and appeals have been extinguished. The process could take many years, and royalties could remain in escrow or trust accounts the entire time. Members of Jefferson Airplane were embroiled in numerous lawsuits that lasted over twenty years. During much of that period, RCA/BMG withheld royalties while numerous audits and hearings were conducted.

## THE ROLE OF A MANAGER

In an ideal relationship, a manager directs the career development of a recording artist and oversees many of the artist's business functions. That way, the artist is free to concentrate on creative activities such as writing songs, recording albums, and performing in concert settings. The manager helps procure contracts with record companies, publishers, and booking agencies on behalf of the artist. Because artists need to spend much time away from home, they must trust their manager to sign contractual agreements for them. In order to negotiate and enter into contractual agreements with third parties on behalf of the artist, the manager is usually given limited power of attorney for the artist. That power of attorney is an artist's legal way of saying, "I trust you to handle my money."

Although a manager is crucial to the success or failure of a recording artist, many emerging artists sign management contracts without fully understanding the terms of the agreement. Because experienced managers know the legal and business aspects of the music industry better than the typical band member or singer-songwriter, they have the upper hand during contract negotiations. In addition, most emerging artists have difficulty finding experienced full-time managers. Therefore, when they do find a manager, many artists are eager to sign any contract placed before them for fear of "blowing the deal."

A management contract is conceptually very simple. Unfortunately, in practice it becomes a complicated document written by attorneys to be understood by other attorneys. An agreement between an artist and a manager specifies the following:

1. An explanation of duties the manager will perform;
2. A statement that the manager may represent (manage) other artists;
3. A statement that the manager is the sole personal manager for the artist;
4. A grant of limited power of attorney to the manager in order to sign certain types of contracts for the artist;
5. A detailed section that explains the duration of the management agreement and the terms for renewal of the contract;
6. A description of compensation the manager will receive in the form of commissions, and what types of artist income are subject to a commission;
7. A list of the types of expenses for which the manager will be reimbursed; and
8. An explanation of what happens if the manager or the artist does not live up to promises made in the contract.

Although not specifically discussed in the contract, other things are assumed. It is assumed, for instance, that a manager will make informed decisions that are in the best interest of the artist's career. It is also assumed that the manager will spend the artist's money only on bona fide expenses, not on luxuries to benefit the manager or his friends. It is further assumed that the manager will be honest and not divert money or gifts intended for the artist into the hands of friends, relatives, or himself.

Conversely, the manager assumes that the artist will act in an equally professional manner. The manager should expect the artist to pay the agreed-upon commission for all music related income that is due the manager. The artist should also take the advice of the manager and use it to make logical decisions that are good for their mutual careers. Most of all, the artist should not ignore contractual promises in order to get a new manager before the current contract expires.

It is important to note that a manager often experiences a negative cash flow during the first stage of an artist's career. While artists are in the process of seeking a recording contract, they must spend a great deal of money producing demo recordings and performing showcases. Many emerging acts do not have the funds to invest in these necessary activities; therefore, it is not uncommon for a manager to loan the artist money to get started on the road to success. Even if a manager has negotiated the typical 20 percent commission, an act's commissionable income might be negligible for the first two or three years.

Because managers play a key role in organizing concert tours, their sudden departure as a result of being fired and/or sued usually causes disruptions. For a major artist, touring is a form of promotional support for an album release. Therefore, a canceled tour can also force a label to delay release of the album. As the trickle-down effect manifests itself, income from record royalties, publishing royalties, and concert ticket sales is negatively affected. As one might expect, several corporate entities and their employees are hurt by the diminished flow of money from the artist.

Media, especially trade publications, seem to report artist-manager breakups with the same fervor as artists' divorces. Occasionally, artists and managers feed information to media in an attempt to protect their professional image in the music industry. Not so surprisingly, comments that fly back and forth between artists, managers, publicists, and attorneys grow increasingly more inflammatory as litigation drags on.

After country artist Clint Black terminated his relationship with his manager Bill Ham in 1992, he took advantage of the celebrity status he and his wife, actress Lisa Hartman, held. Black retained his mother-in-law's firm, T. J. Hartman Public Relations, to distribute press releases critical of Ham. As media attention escalated, Ham issued a statement describing his disappointment that Black did not allow their legal issues to "quietly work their way through the court in responsible silence" (Morris, 1992). Ham is not alone in his frustration; most managers prefer to let attorneys argue legal issues in private venues rather than in the media.

## ISSUES THAT LEAD TO ARTIST-MANAGER DISCORD

Artists file lawsuits to change managers much more often than managers sue to drop an artist from their management roster. It is intuitively logical that a manager who is not pleased with an artist will simply stop exerting much effort in the artist's behalf. Therefore, whenever a manager is obviously not interested in continuing the management relationship, an artist is ill-advised to fight the breakup.

Managers occasionally file lawsuits to force artists to pay commissions that have not been forthcoming. With the complex network of revenue streams from which an artist's income—and the manager's commissions—come, determining income that is due the manager is not always easy. In order to recover commissions, a manager might have to conduct accounting audits of the record label and publishing company financial records. Only after an accurate picture of the artist's income is available can the amount due to the manager be determined. Even then, the artist might argue that some of the income is not "commissionable" and therefore not subject to the manager's commission.

If large numbers of artists have sought to dissolve their management contracts in court, one must ask, Why have they become discontented with their managers? Entertainment attorney Jim Zumwalt answers that question with the more rhetorical question, "Why do husbands sue wives and wives sue husbands?" He goes on to explain that "artists generally sue managers for several reasons: To seek relief from the term of the management agreement; for mismanagement; or, for some form of misconduct." Entertainment attorney Douglas C. Anton believes, "Artists sue their managers because they think they are getting ripped-off or the manager is not doing what they should." He adds, "Managers sue because the band has breached the contract or has ceased working with the manager" (Anton, 1999).

"I appreciate all your hard work and financial support while I got my recording career started, but I've found a better manager. You're fired!" Sad as it sounds, those words describe a scenario that happens too often in the music industry. An artist might place confidence in a manager while moving from lounge singer to recording artist, but later the artist comes to believe that the manager is not as knowledgable as other managers in the business. In reality, the manager may be very competent, but other persons—label executives, attorneys, family members—convince the artist that he or she needs a new manager. Of course, sometimes it is sadly apparent that the manager is truly not up to par and is harming the artist's career.

Another reason an artist might seek to drop the manager is simple capitalism. "In business generally, anytime an entity goes from zero or negative earnings to millions of dollars of income, you have the potential for disgruntled participants not getting their fair share or getting cut out of the participation," says Zumwalt. It is not uncommon for artists to resent paying a large portion of their income, in the form of manager commissions, after they have become stars. In such cases, the artists will try to terminate the agreement or have the rate of commission reduced.

Artists who become tremendously successful tend to forget that managers invested much time and money in the early years of their career. A manager who believed in an artist and worked without much compensation during the developmental stage of the artist's career feels quite justified in making millions of dollars after the artist attains superstar status. Artists argue that it is unfair for managers to make more money than the artist simply because of a contract they signed early in their career. It should be noted that in the case of a band, it is not uncommon for the manager to net more money than each individual member of the band. A manager who also retains a percentage of publishing royalties would likely make a great deal more than any one band member.

Artists may also feel as though they have "outgrown" the ability of their manager at some point in their career. In most cases, these artists find someone else—a more experienced manager or a management firm—whom they would rather have represent them. If the new manager is able to negotiate a buyout of the original manager's contract, the transition can be smooth and peaceful. But if the original manager is unwilling to be bought out of the contract, the transition will take a great deal of time and cause a lot of anxiety for all parties involved.

Should the manager not agree to any type of contract settlement, the artist has another option: to make little money so the manager will get little or no commissions. Of course, this tactic is akin to starving oneself in order to kill an intestinal parasite. This strategy might work if the manager finds another artist and decides that fighting the old artist is a waste of time. It is more effective, though, if the time left on the contract is running out in a matter of months rather than years.

## LEGAL RECOURSE FOR MANAGERS AND ARTISTS

Few states have enacted laws to regulate artist managers in this country. Although California and New York have created laws that affect managers, the statutes they enacted are basically intended to help distinguish between booking agents and managers. The main effect the laws have had on managers is to prevent them from procuring employment, such as booking concert performances, for the artists they manage. This impact is minimal because most managers prefer to leave booking to agents so they themselves can concentrate on interfacing with the artist's record label and publisher.

Because artists have little statutory protection to rely on, they most often rely on contract or tort claims when dealing with management contracts (Gilenson, 1990, p. 515). A tort claim is under civil rather than criminal law and revolves around an act that has harmed the artist in some way—usually some form of financial loss to the artist. Contract law, another area of civil law, seeks to enforce and interpret the promises made by all parties who entered into a legal contract. Breach of contract is the legal terminology for not fulfilling one's promises in a legal contract. If an artist signed a legal contractual agreement that promised the manager 25 percent of the artist's gross income in exchange for career advice, then the artist is bound to that promise for the duration of the agreement. Therefore, when a manager alleges that an artist is in breach of contract, the suit is generally a straightforward legal question: Has the artist paid the manager the agreed-upon 25 percent of all income?

An artist claiming that the manager is in breach of contract is in a somewhat more difficult position. If the manager has promised to "advise and counsel in matters related to the artist's career in the music industry," the burden of proof will be on the artist to demonstrate that the manager did not provide adequate advice. Artists have tried, usually unsuccessfully, to demonstrate that the manager's advice caused them to fail in their career. In response, managers can easily point to the high failure rate in the industry and blame a myriad of other factors for the artist's lack of success. If the act has enjoyed some relative success and merely wants to switch to a different manager, the argument for management incompetence becomes even more difficult to argue. Imagine the reaction of a judge when an artist says, "Yes, I earned $20 million over the past three years, but my manager gave me bad career advice." Therefore, one might conclude that "claiming that a personal manager's poor advice and guidance caused the artist's lack of success is not a judicious argument" (Gilenson, 1990, p. 516).

An artist might try to demonstrate in court that the management contract was "unconscionable" when it was created. If the terms of the agreement were unreasonably favorable to one party (manager) over the other (artist), the court system might decide that it was substantively unconscionable and, therefore, should be voided. Artists could also attempt to prove that they were deceived or pressured into signing the contract. If deception or undue pressure can be proven in court, the contract will probably be considered procedurally unconscionable and unenforceable.

In practice, though, managers employ an attorney familiar with the entertainment industry to represent them in contract negotiations. In addition, most managers and their attorneys insist that the artist also have competent legal counsel familiar with industry protocol. The possibility of one attorney pressuring an artist, through the artist's attorney, to sign an "unconscionable contract" is quite unlikely. In addition, the bargaining points of a management contract are fairly consistent throughout the industry. Therefore, an artist attempting to dissolve a management contract based on the argument that it is substantively or procedurally unconscionable will have to assemble very strong evidence.

## MANAGERS AND CONFLICT OF INTEREST

An artist might be more likely to prevail in court, and thus escape a management agreement, through a claim based on tort law rather than contract law. The most common tort claims have revolved around the "fiduciary duties" of a manager. Because a manager handles an artist's money and enters into contracts with third parties on behalf of the artist, the level of trust is assumed to be extremely high. In fact, the term "fiduciary" is derived from the Latin term *fiducia*, or "trust." "A breach of fiduciary duties may arise when a personal manager obtains an interest in a recording or publishing company, thus creating a conflict of interest" (Gilenson, 1990, p. 519).

A conflict of interest occurs, for example, when a manager is motivated to make decisions that are not in the best interest of the artist. The motivation is likely to come from financial or political gain the manager could receive by altering decisions. On July 16, 1991, Peter Mensch, who has managed Def Leppard, Metallica, and Queensryche, told aspiring artist managers at a New Music Seminar panel called "Perfect Managers: Do They Really Exist?" not to be "afraid to make dumb mistakes, [and] don't be afraid to fail." He did, however, stress that managers should fear one thing: conflicts of interest in their relationships with the artists they manage (O'Connor, 1991).

The need to develop strong industry alliances leads some managers into conflicts of interest. A manager's success depends on networking with important decision makers in the industry. The gatekeepers of booking agencies, law firms, music publishing companies, and record labels must be constantly cultivated to ensure their receptivity to a manager's new acts. Ken Kragen, often cited as the most successful manager in history, is so vehement about the importance of networking that he titled a book about his professional success *Life Is a Contact Sport: Ten Great Career Strategies That Work*. Because managers work diligently to develop favorable relationships with industry power brokers, they are susceptible to mixed allegiances. At some point in time, a manager is faced with the unsettling question, "What is more important for my career, becoming a close working friend of this industry heavyweight or getting a slightly better deal for an artist I represent?" The conflict of interest is quite obvious if the manager advises the artist to accept a professional friend's offer even though it is not the best deal available.

Once artists become financially successful, the integrity of their managers is put to a test. Many industry entities—booking agencies, record labels, publishers—try to influence the actions of artists through their managers. Those efforts to influence a manager's decisions are characteristically ethical and legal. Unfortunately, in rare instances those efforts to influence a manager cross the line and are not legal. If a company offers a valuable incentive to the manager in exchange for influencing the artist's decision, for example, that action is considered a bribe or kickback. A bribe is quite obvious: The company pays a manager to advise the artist in a certain way in exchange for something of value, usually money. A kickback is sharing the benefits of a deal with the manager in exchange for the manager advising the artist a specific way. A publisher might, for instance, "kick back" a portion of royalties to the manager for helping sign the artist to the company. In either situation—bribe or kickback—the manager is suddenly faced with a moral dilemma: Should the manager advise the artist to do something that is best for the artist's career or advise the artist to do something that is not necessarily a good career move but is financially profitable for the manager? If an artist proves that the manager benefited financially to the detriment of the artist, the manager will probably face a tort action claiming a violation of "fiduciary responsibility" to the artist.

Another situation that can potentially create a conflict of interest is when the manager assumes more than one role in the artist's career. A manager may, for example, ask for publishing rights to the artist's songs as a part of their deal. Or a manager may own all or part of a record label and ask the artist to sign a recording contract with that particular company. More recently, attorneys have entered the conflict-of-interest arena. Some entertainment attorneys who begin as artists' lawyers later ask for management deals from the same artists. It should be noted that not all instances of a manager's assuming multiple roles create illegal or unethical conflicts of interest.

The problem with a manager owning a publishing company, law firm, or record label is the lack of objectivity in their role as advisor. In an ideal business relationship, the manager is expected to find the *best* recording contract, law firm, and publishing deal for the artist. A manager who owns part or all of a record label may not be aggressive when "shopping" for the best deal. One might consider the occasions when an artist's manager writes a check to the record label on behalf of the artist. "If the manager owns all or part of the label," says Daniel Reynolds, former director of Programs for Leadership Music and former executive with DreamWorks Records, "it is like one hand writing a check and the other hand cashing it."

Entertainment attorney Douglas C. Anton offers the following hypothetical situation to illustrate the ethical dilemma faced by a manager who owns a financial interest in the record label to which the artist is signed:

> The record deal does not contain a "greatest hits" option for Band X. The record company proposes to release a "greatest hits" record for the holiday season. As is customary industry practice, the band won't receive very much money for the use of their previously released songs used on the "greatest hits" album. The members of Band X believe that they, and their music, are already suffering from the over-exposure of their popular hits. Therefore, re-releasing their most popular songs at this time might be overkill. The label will probably make a substantial profit on a holiday release, but the band will not make much money. In fact, the band might be hurt by over-saturating the market with their music. If the manager has a financial interest in the label, a classic conflict-of-interest scenario exists. (Anton, 1999)

Publishing and record companies owned by managers are sometimes referred to as "desk drawer" companies because they are rarely full-service enterprises. Instead, they are sometimes simply a legal means to keep a percentage of royalties earned by an artist in addition to garnering management commissions. In a desk drawer publishing scenario, the manager's publishing company keeps a portion of the publishing rights and brokers a copublishing deal with an actual full-service publishing company. This type of publishing deal is obviously quite good for the manager, but it may not be the best publishing deal for the artist. Perhaps a better publishing company told the manager it wouldn't share publishing royalties. If the manager advised the artist to avoid that publishing company's offer—a better deal for the artist—then a conflict of interest harmed the artist.

Conflict-of-interest debates were extremely heated when MCA Entertainment acquired Front Line Management, an artist management firm, on May 7, 1986. To make matters more controversial, Irving Azoff, then president of MCA Records, owned a majority interest in the management firm. Sidney J. Steinberg, MCA Entertainment's president and CEO at the time, defended the label's ownership of a management firm by stating, "The personal management firm does not negotiate recording deals" (Knoedelseder, 1986). He implied that attorneys, not managers, are responsible for artists' acquiring recording contracts. Steinberg's rationale revolved around an ongoing argument: Do managers "shop" for recording and publishing contracts, or do attorneys actually find them their deals?

David Geffen, a successful artist manager who left management to start his own record label, vehemently disapproved of MCA's ownership of a management firm. Geffen asked, "How can a manager get the best deal he can for his client if the manager also works for the record company? It's very disturbing. If it's legal, it shouldn't be" (Knoedelseder, 1986). He summarized his views on the matter by stating, "You cannot be in the record business and manage artists on your own label—it's a conflict of interest."

## MANAGERS ACCUSED OF STEALING

That managers would steal from the artists they manage is difficult to believe, but allegations of theft are not uncommon in the music industry. One assumes that an artist knows a manager quite well before signing a binding contract. Artists who suspect their manager of taking more than his fair share argue that they didn't really know the manager well enough when they signed a management deal or that the temptation of money gradually corrupted the manager.

Managers are responsible for a tremendous amount of income earned by the artist. The best line of defense an artist can use to keep a manager honest is to employ a business manager. A business manager can be thought of as a hybrid accountant. Often business managers are certified public accountants (CPAs) and undergo annual audits of their financial records. A business manager protects both the artist and the manager by making sure that the manager is paid commissions and reimbursements for expenses and protecting against additional money being diverted by the manager.

Another person who helps keep an eye on the manager's behavior is the artist's entertainment attorney, who must review all contracts before an artist signs them. That way, if a manager attempts to involve the artist in dubious investments, especially those that might benefit the manager, the attorney can alert the artist. The impartial judgment of an attorney and a competent business manager is the best insurance against unethical behavior by a manager. Like good insurance, however, a good business manager and a good attorney cost money.

Even after securing a business manager and an entertainment attorney, some artists suffer financial losses. One of the most contentious and protracted legal battles developed when Billy Joel charged his former manager, Frank Weber, with fraud, breach of fiduciary duty, and federal racketeering statute violations. Joel alleged that Weber double-billed him for music videos and improperly mortgaged Joel's copyrights (Grein, 1989). Frank Weber countered Billy Joel's legal action and alleged that Joel was in breach of contract. Joel was awarded a summary judgment in 1990 and was awarded initial damages of $2 million from Weber. Unfortunately, Frank Weber paid Joel only $250,000 before filing for bankruptcy (Duffy, 1992). Joel continued his relentless pursuit of Weber and was awarded a second summary judgment, this one for $675,670.68, on February 25, 1995.

What made Billy Joel's situation even more upsetting to other artists was his allegation that his former manager worked in consort with the accounting firm Berman, Shaffet and Schain to defraud him of $30 million (MacMinn, 1991). If that weren't enough trauma for one artist, Joel took legal action against Weber's attorney, Frank Conforti, accusing him of having a role in the improper transfer of $1.5 million of Joel's assets. The last thing Joel did in this ongoing battle against his handlers was to sue his former attorney, industry heavyweight Alan Grubman, for fraud and breach of fiduciary duty.

Billy Joel's bizarre story has an equally unusual ending. Sony Music, Joel's label, paid the singer-songwriter $3 million to settle his suit against attorney Grubman. A reporter for the *Wall Street Journal* speculated that Sony "stepped in to end the lawsuit to avoid other recording artists from filing similar suits" (Trachtenberg, 1995). Not so surprisingly, Joel has remained self-managed since his split from Weber.

## ARTISTS ACCUSED OF INFIDELITY

The typical nightmare for a manager is working to make an artist successful, then watching the artist move to another manager after becoming financially successful. Lou "Big Poppa" Pearlman has probably

Billy Joel spent many years in litigation with attorneys, accountants, and his original manager. Joel prevailed after many years of persistence and has remained self-managed ever since. (Maritime Music/Sony Music)

had that very nightmare more than once since creating and managing two superstar acts: the Backstreet Boys and 'N Sync. The Backstreet Boys sold out a fifty-three-show tour in one day and sold 500,000 copies of their CD *Millennium* in the first day of its release. Their mirror image, 'N Sync, sold 7 million copies of their debut album.

If these two groups sound and look similar, it is not by coincidence. Pearlman had a formula for creating his "boy bands." He auditioned dozens of young singers and selected four young men to create his first multiracial vocal group. He then hired voice teachers, choreographers, and producers to cultivate a modern pop sound new to teenagers more familiar with rap music (Moore, 1999). The Backstreet Boys' first record release was not very successful in the United States, so Big Poppa financed a tour of Europe and Asia for the boys. After they established themselves as a successful overseas act, the boys returned to the United States in style. Their concerts sold out and their albums went platinum many times over (Carlson, 1999). Pearlman sensed that other acts would probably emulate the Backstreet Boys' successful style, so he decided to beat any competitors to the marketplace. He followed his boy band formula and created a group he named 'N Sync. Like the Backstreet Boys, 'N Sync quickly became a pop sensation at the box office. But as if in unison, both acts decided to leave Poppa's nest.

In May 1998 the Backstreet Boys filed a lawsuit against Pearlman in an attempt to escape their management contract as well as their recording contract with RCA. In October 1999 the members of 'N Sync decided to leave their label, RCA, and they charged Big Poppa with fraud (Carlson, 1999). Both bands believed that Pearlman had negotiated numerous deals between the bands and the companies in which he held a financial interest. Each band sought to prevent Pearlman from earning as much money from them as he had been. Members of both bands felt that Pearlman was receiving too much income from their efforts. Yet, in the contracts they signed, each had agreed to give Pearlman a hefty percentage of their income from recordings, concert ticket sales, and publishing royalties. The boys were also upset that their manager was getting a large amount of their merchandising sales. They shouldn't have been too surprised, though, because Pearlman had created the band names and had even registered the trademark for the name 'N Sync. Indeed, Big Poppa never attempted to shroud the blessing of wealth he received from his boy bands. As of January 1, 2000, Pearlman had launched eight more bands modeled on the success of the Backstreet Boys and 'N Sync. His ten acts have generated an estimated gross income of about $2 billion. "I have three Rolls-Royces and a limousine. Life is good," according to Pearlman (Carlson, 1999).

Speaking for Pearlman's company, Trans Continental Entertainment, Michael Friedman said, "You can't just skip out on an eight-album deal because someone comes along with another offer" (Pollack, 1999). His point is well taken: Should a group of professional musicians feel justified in ignoring their contractual promises because they resent their manager's tremendous income? Keep in mind that as Big Poppa became extremely wealthy by earning a percentage of each band's income, the band members kept the remaining percentage and also became wealthy. The issue is, of course, "Who should become richer?"

From a manager's perspective, Pearlman literally invented each band and took a great risk each time he contributed all their start-up funds from his own savings. Isn't he entitled to a large portion of the subsequent income as is any other entrepreneur? Band members see it differently. They feel like indentured servants who unwittingly signed contracts that they did not fully understand at a time when they were new to the industry. To them, their manager is not the fatherly figure his nickname implies; he is just another greedy music industry shark who lives the good life at the expense of hardworking performers.

## TOPICS FOR DISCUSSION

1. What are some reasons artists take legal action to dissolve the contract with their manager? Which of these reasons do you think are valid? Which do you think are less than ethical?
2. Do managers have more power in the relationship between them and the artists they manage? Does the level of power seem to shift as an artist becomes more successful?
3. Some very intelligent artists have signed management agreements that they later regretted. Why do you think they accepted contracts that were not in their best interest? What things might an artist do to prevent getting involved with an unethical manager?
4. Do you think it is a conflict of interest for an attorney to manage an artist and also provide legal counsel for that artist? Do you think it is ethical for an attorney to also act as publisher for an artist he or she represents?
5. What things might an artist and manager do to resolve their differences instead of filing lawsuits? What persons might they ask to help resolve their disagreements? Do you think that entertainment attorneys might advise artists to file suit too often? Who benefits most from a lawsuit: artist, manager, or attorneys?

## REFERENCES AND RESOURCES

### Correspondence

Anton, Douglas C. (1999, December 29). Anton is an entertainment attorney who practices on the East Coast. He is a former artist manager.

Zumwalt, Jim (2000, January 4). Zumwalt is senior partner with the entertainment law firm Zumwalt, Almon and Hayes in Nashville. He is also president of Paladin Records.

## Books

Brabec, Jeffery, and Todd Brabec (1994). *Music, Money and Success: The Insider's Guide to the Music Industry*. New York: Macmillan Publishing Company. (The Brabec brothers are twins who have twin careers as entertainment attorneys. They do an excellent job of describing the numerous sources of income an artist can receive. The chapter that describes managers and attorneys is succinct.)

Frascogna, Xavier M., Jr., and H. Lee Hetherington (1997). *This Business of Artist Management*, 3rd ed. New York: Billboard Books, an imprint of Watson-Guptill Publications, a division of BPI Communications, Inc. (This is the only book that deals with artist management in the music industry. The authors are both attorneys, and their advice is based on good legal research as well as many years of experience.)

Kragen, Ken, and Jefferson Graham (1994). *Life Is a Contact Sport: Ten Great Career Strategies That Work*. New York: William Morrow and Company. (In order to illustrate how their ten career strategies work, Kragen and Graham use examples from Kragen's life as manager of Kenny Rogers, Lionel Ritchie, Trisha Yearwood, and Travis Tritt. They also discuss how Kragen produced the fundraising event and album *We Are the World*.)

Passman, Donald S. (1997). *All You Need to Know about the Music Business*. New York: Simon & Schuster. (Donald Passman is one of the top entertainment attorneys in Los Angeles. His book includes practical advice to artists who expect to enter into a contractual agreement with a manager.)

Rogan, Johnny (1988). *Starmakers and Svengalis: The History of British Pop Management*. London: Futura Publications, a division of Macdonald & Company Publishers, Ltd. (Rogan presents a brief description of seventeen different artist managers. He also offers some amusing stereotypes he calls "paradigms of pop management" that include the "Autocratic Manager," the "Concerned Parent," and the "Neutered Lackey.")

## Magazines, Journals, and Newspapers

Aims, Katrine, and Janet Huck (1976, May 10). Hey, Mac! *Newsweek*, The Arts, Music, p. 121. (An explanation of the lawsuit that members of Fleetwood Mac sought to prevent their former manager from using their name for another band.)

*Buchwald v. Katz* (1972, December 19). S. F. No. 22929, Supreme Court of California; 8 Cal 3d 493; 503 P.2d 1376 1972 Cal. Lexis 268; 105 Cal. Rptr. 368. (A test case for the California Artists' Managers Act involving Jefferson Airplane and former manager Matthew Katz.)

Carlson, Peter (1999, November 6). Music Machine: 'Big Poppa' Pearlman Takes Kids and Turns Them into Stars. Then They Sue Him. *Washington Post*,

Style, p. C1. (A lengthy article about the man who found a group of male singers and made them into 'N Sync.)

Citron, Alan, and Robert W. Welkos (1992, November 12). *Los Angeles Times*, Business, p. D1, col. 2, Financial Desk. (An article that explains a very complicated lawsuit involving the law firm representing Prince. Prince's former manager accused the law firm of conflict of interest.)

Davis, Alisha (1999, October 25). Falling 'N to the Sync Hole. *Newsweek*, Arts and Entertainment, Battle of the Bands, p. 82. (A report on the band 'N Sync's decision to tear up their recording contract with Trans Continental Media and BMG Entertainment.)

Duffy, Thom (1992, October 24). Lawyer in Joel Suit Says He's Innocent Man. *Billboard*, Artists and Music, p. 10. (This article explains positions of both Billy Joel and the law firm he sued charging fraud, malpractice, and breach of contract.)

*Entertainment Law Reporter* (1987, July). Jefferson Airplane Obtains Dismissal of Lawsuit by Former Manager. *In the News*, vol. 9, no. 2. (Jefferson Airplane prevailed in the lawsuit by Matthew Katz in which he claimed rights to royalties from the band's first two albums.)

*Entertainment Litigation Reporter* (1990, October 8). California Court Affirms Dismissal of Suit Involving Jefferson Airplane. (A synopsis of the ongoing litigation between Jefferson Airplane and Matthew Katz as of 1990).

Gilenson, Hal I. (1990). Badlands: Artist-Personal Manager Conflicts of Interest in the Music Industry. *Cardozo Arts and Entertainment Law Journal* 9, no. 1. New York: Yeshiva University, Cardozo Law School.

Goldstein, Patrick (1985, July 28). Ry Cooder Takes Blues to the "Crossroads." *Los Angeles Times*, Calendar, p. 65, Calendar Desk. (A brief description of Ozzy Osborne's lawsuit against his father-in-law manager Don Arden.)

Grein, Paul (1989, September 26). Billy Joel Sues Former Manager for $90 Million. *Los Angeles Times*, Calendar, part 6, p. 1, col. 6, Entertainment Desk. (Billy Joel's first lawsuit—against his manager—is well outlined in this article. Lawsuits brought by Billy Joel continued for the next sixteen years.)

Harrington, Richard (1987, May 13). Ire over King Day Reversal. *Washington Post*, Style, p. F7, On the Beat. (A very short article that emphasizes the length of time lawsuits take and the disruption they cause artists' careers.)

Kelleher, Kathleen (1992, July 7). Mozart No Pauper, N.Y. Economists Say. *Los Angeles Times*, Calendar, p. F1, col. 5, Entertainment Desk. (A fascinating economic analysis of Mozart's income translated into 1992 dollars by two economists.)

Knoedelseder, William K., Jr. (1986, May 7). MCA to Acquire Three Companies Partly Owned by Azoff. *Los Angeles Times*, Business, part 4, p. 1, col. 5, Financial Desk. (This journalist discloses details of a major record label purchasing a management firm.)

MacMinn, Aleene (1991, May 16). Morning Report: Pop/Rock. *Los Angeles Times*, Calendar, p. F2, col. 1; Entertainment Desk. (An account of one of Billy Joel's many lawsuits. This one describes his action against the accounting firm whom Joel accused of defrauding him of $30 million.)

Moore, Roger (1999, December 16). Boy Groups Rule—for Now—in Teen Music

Game. *Times Union* (*Albany, NY*), Preview, p. P14. (An article that describes the evolution of the group 'N Sync.)

Morris, Edward (1992, April 11). Black, Ham Take Spat to the Public. *Billboard*, Country, Artists and Music, Nashville Scene, p. 24. (Country artist and his former manager made several statements that demonstrated how personal relationships between managers and artists become name-calling games in the media.)

Newman, Melinda (1993, March 20). Joel Wins Another Round in Suit versus Ex-manager. *Billboard*, Artists and Music, p. 12. (A description of summary judgments that Billy Joel won in ongoing litigation.)

Newman, Melinda (1999, October 23). BMG Suing 'N Sync and Zomba. *Billboard*. (This article describes the beginning of a series of lawsuits and counter-suits involving the band 'N Sync.)

Newman, Melinda (1999, December 11). 'N Sync Case Settlement Talks Ordered. *Billboard*, Artists and Music. (An explanation of a judges ruling in the 'N Sync lawsuit.)

O'Connon, Karen (1991, August 3). Panelists Ponder Qualities of a "Perfect" Manager. *Billboard*, Talent, New Music Seminar Report, p. 26.

Pareles, Jon (1989, August 29). On-Again Off-Again Jefferson Airplane Is on Again. *New York Times*, p. C11, col. 3, Cultural Desk. (This article gives a thumbnail history of Jefferson Airplane, aka Jefferson Starship, aka Star-ship.)

Philips, Chuck (1994, September 28). Metallica Sues Label, Challenging 7-Year Contract Statute. *Los Angeles Times*, Business, p. D1, col. 2, Financial Desk. (The first major act to use the new California law that restricted the length of contracts to which artists could be held.)

Pollack, Marc (1999, October 13). The Battle of the Boy Bands Has Definitely Heated Up. *Hollywood Reporter*, Headline: 'N Sync Moves Draw $150 from Creator. (The man who takes credit for creating the band 'N Sync, Louis Pearlman, filed a lawsuit that began a string of lawsuits and countersuits.)

*Richardson v. Roland* (1996, July 15). Supreme Court of Georgia. 267 Ga. 34; 472 S. E. 2d 301; 1996 Ga. LEXIS 511; 96 Fulton County DR P2689. (A court case about the use of the group name "Collective Soul.")

Sandler, Adam (1998, December 1). Ex-manager Hits Jewel, Mom with $10-Million Lawsuit. *Variety*, News, p. 10. (A brief article about Jewel's former manager, who sued to force Jewel and her mother to honor the contract all parties had signed.)

Shprintz, Janet (1999, November 4). 'N Sync Sues Ex-manager. *Daily Variety*, News, p. 5. (An announcement of the lawsuit that the band 'N Sync filed against their manager.)

Sloane, Owen J. (1993, November 13). Beware Lawyers with Conflicts. *Billboard*, Commentary, p. 10. (An excellent expose of high-profile law firms that have conflicts of interests when negotiating deals for artists they repre-sent.)

Stark, Phyllis (1991, November 23). Managers' Royalty Rights Debated. *Billboard*, p. 83. (Prince sued his former manager in an effort to end an industry-wide practice of managers receiving perpetual publishing royalties for all songs created during the term of their management.)

*Toronto Star* (1991, December 23). Prince Fights $5-Million Lawsuit. Entertainment, p. C3. (An article about a lawsuit brought by Prince's former manager. The lawsuit alleged the song "Jughead" was a defamatory work by Prince about his manager.)

Trachtenberg, Jeffrey A. (1995, May 3). Lawyer for Billy Joel Discloses Payments. *Wall Street Journal*, p. B4, col. 3. (A brief report that discloses Sony Corporation of America's payments to settle a lawsuit between Billy Joel and his former attorney.)

Zimmerman, Kevin (1992, October 13). Grubman Returning Fire in Countersuit versus Joel. *Daily Variety*, News, p. 10. (A description of the countersuit Billy Joel's former attorney filed.)

## Organizations to Contact

The following bar associations are helpful in contacting attorneys whose practice includes entertainment law. They are located in the three major centers for music industry activities.

Association of the Bar of the City of New York
42 West 44th Street
New York, NY 10036
web: www.abcny.org/homepg.htm

Beverly Hills Bar Association, Entertainment Section
300 South Beverly Drive, Suite 201
P.O. Box 7277
Beverly Hills, CA 90212
Phone: (310) 553–6644
web: www.bhba.org/entertainment_law.htm

Nashville Bar Association
221 4th Avenue North
Nashville, TN 37219–2111
Phone: (615) 242–9272

## Web Sites

www.cybershowbiz.com/ncopm/index.html
National Conference of Personal Managers
This organization has a statement of ethics that members must accept; the statement is displayed on their web site.

# 10

# Freedom of Expression:
# Filth or Freedom?

Since music became a popular form of entertainment, the lyrics of songs and behavior of performers have quite often caused concern among the three *P*'s: parents, politicians, and preachers. The reaction of parents and clergy to rock music most often manifests itself as pressure on lawmakers and the industry—record labels and retailers—to place limits on creators of music. Earlier (chapter 3) we discussed how philosophers as far back as Plato expressed concern about the role of music in society. Nevertheless, we sometimes think conflict between society and the creators of its music is of fairly recent origin, perhaps going back only to the early days of Elvis Presley or Bill Haley.

However, the banning of music goes back hundreds of years, and involves even classical music. In 1858, for example, Verdi's *A Masked Ball* was banned in Milan. The opera is based on the assassination of King Gustavus III of Sweden, but after the work was linked, in some people's mind, to an attempt to assassinate Napoleon III, it was banned. Another Verdi opera, *La Traviata*, also ran into trouble because of "suggestive" lyrics. Thus the line, "He took the desired prize in the arms of love" was changed in order to protect the sensibilities of citizens of Naples and Rome (Nuzum, 2000). Indeed, in the early years of our own country the Puritans banned the use of musical instruments in worship services, saying they were from the devil. Years later, in 1912, the Massachusetts legislature made dancing the tango a misdemeanor, and Pope Pius X declared the dance a sin.

But it was the development of rock 'n' roll, with its fusion of rhythm and blues, or R&B (called "race music" in the pre–rock 'n' roll days), folk, and popular music that saw the beginning of a real fear of what music might be doing to the youth of America. It appears, however, that the real fear was not so much what music was doing to youths but what the music was saying and where it came from that bothered adults, particularly white Anglo-Saxon Protestants, or WASPs. After all, "R&B was sinful, 'race' music shunned by white people and God-fearing black folk alike. Gospel was reserved for the church and black singers didn't get near a country and western tune" (Deggans, 1999). And folk music, with its emphasis on social change, equality, and later, antiestablishment sentiments, was certainly not reminiscent of the tunes that got Americans through World War II. So when Bill Haley and the Comets fused the hard-driving, vaguely sexual elements of R&B with the sentimentality and boy-meets-girl trend of white music popular in the first-ever successful rock 'n' roll song, "Rock around the Clock," in 1955, the public, or at least the adult public, wasn't sure what to do with it.

Then there were the problems engendered by radio and the phonograph. Both devices are "color blind" in that the listener can't really tell the race or color of the singer simply by listening (remember, one of the things that attracted Elvis Presley to record executives was that he was "a white boy who sounded black"). So when DJs like Alan Freed, who coined the term "rock 'n' roll," began mixing white popular music with R&B on his radio programs, most adults didn't know what to think. The easiest thing to do was to rise up in protest to try to stop the music, or at least to try to keep their kids from listening.

Efforts to control or censor music have generally centered on a few areas: sex, violence, and pornographic or obscene lyrics. In Chapters 2 and 5 we discussed music with drug-related lyrics and the effects of music on listeners of satanic-oriented music. In this chapter, however, we want to examine what has actually been done to stop the music, or at least to channel it in a different direction, typically away from the youth who want to listen. The major question we as a society must ask ourselves is, Should we censor or control music that we—mainstream Americans—do not like? On the extreme right we find many persons and organizations who believe it is the government's job to repress certain forms of music for the general good of society. At the other extreme, First Amendment fundamentalists believe that an individual's right to freedom of expression should be protected and encouraged, regardless of how vulgar or bigoted those messages are.

Of course, not everyone sees a danger in the music. In fact, some people think the music is *reflecting* what is going on in society and thus acts as a warning to the general society. Rick Rubin, who has worked with the Beastie Boys and Red Hot Chili Peppers, said, "The arts reflect what is going on in our culture. The arts don't control the culture. . . . The reason that music is violent today . . . is that's what the world is like today" (quoted in Harrison, 1999). Said Jann Wenner, editor and publisher of *Rolling Stone* magazine: "Before the Los Angeles riots, the mainstream media was [sic] not documenting the level of rage in the black community, but rap music was. No music called anybody to riot, but that music told us the truth of what was going on out there" (quoted in Harrison, 1999).

In contrast, rapper Chuck D of the group Public Enemy said his music does have an impact on society. "We're living in a time of mass images and if a kid's reality is not being realized, fantasy and reality blur together. And that can lead to life imitating art" (quoted in Harrison, 1999). However, Dr. C. Delores Tucker, head of the National Political Congress of Black Women, disagrees: "Rappers say they are reflecting real life, but that is garbage. The majority of us go to church, work hard to raise our children. In fact many rappers were raised in churches" (quoted in Krum, 1995).

## PORNOGRAPHY, OBSCENITY, AND INDECENCY

Most of the controversy surrounding lyrics deals with the issues of pornography and obscenity. To make sure we are all reading off the same sheet of music, as it were, let's first note that although the First Amendment generally protects freedom of expression, the so-called "absolutist view" has never been held by a majority of the courts. Thus, the U.S. Supreme Court has held that some forms are outside that protection. Pornography, therefore, has First Amendment protections (and thus is legal), while obscenity has no such protection, and is illegal. Child pornography, however, falls into a whole different category and is also not protected. The philosophical debate about the effects of pornography, or the morality of pornography, or what if anything should be done about pornography remains a volatile issue beyond the scope of this book. Certainly this issue is so volatile partly because the courts have not been able to fashion a clear, concise definition of what either pornography or obscenity are.

However we define pornography, sexually explicit art is nothing new: "From Venus figurines with exaggerated breasts and buttocks fired in clay 27,000 years ago to today's CD called *Cyberorgasm*, there is ample evidence of the durability of pornography" (Gillmor, Barron, and Simon, 1998, p. 633). Even if material does not deal with sex, it can be declared obscene. Indeed, one of the first obscenity trials, *Regina v. Hicklin* (1868), dealt with whether anti-Church material could be harmful to minors. Thus, as far back as 1868 the court defined obscenity as material that tends "to deprave and corrupt those whose minds are open to such immoral influences, and into whose hands a material of this sort may fall" (pp. 360–361).

In addition, the effects of pornography are simply uncertain. Therefore, one must ask, If we aren't certain of any harmful effects of pornography, why regulate it? The 1970 report of the Presidential Commission on Obscenity and Pornography, also known as the Lockhart Commission, found no connection between pornography and inappropriate behavior and thus recommended that federal, state, and local laws dealing with adult pornography be repealed. However, in 1986, another presidential commission, the Meese Commission, found obscenity and pornography responsible for many of the problems society faced. The Meese Commission also called for a crackdown on the distribution of pornography and obscenity. As if to underscore the confusion, the commission used the two terms interchangeably, as if pornography and obscenity are the same thing.

Earlier, the U.S. Supreme Court, in *Roth v. United States* (1957), had noted: "Sex and obscenity are not synonymous. . . . The portrayal of sex, e.g., in art, literature and scientific works, is not itself sufficient reason to deny material the constitutional protection of freedom of speech and press" (*Roth*, p. 487). Thus for years the courts wrestled with trying to define obscenity and to distinguish between pornography and obscenity. After a number of decisions, the U.S. Supreme Court, in *Miller v. California* (1973), set out what is still the "definitive" three-part definition:

> The basic guidelines for the trier of fact must be: (a) whether "the average person, applying contemporary community standards," would find that the work, taken as a whole, appeals to the prurient interest, (b) whether the work depicts or describes, in a patently offensive way, sexual conduct specifically defined by the applicable state law; and (c) whether the work, taken as a whole, lacks serious literary, artistic, political, or scientific value.

It is possible, nonetheless, to give a few plain examples of what a state statute could define for regulation under part (b) of the standard announced in this opinion: "(a) Patently offensive representations or descriptions of ultimate sexual acts, normal or perverted, actual or simulated; (b) Patently offensive representations or descriptions of masturbation, excretory functions, and lewd exhibition of the genitals" (pp. 24–26). Thus for a work—record, album, CD cover, or the like—to be declared obscene, and therefore not under the protection of the First Amendment, it must meet the tests noted above. In fact, though, very few songs meet this high standard. As a result, though they may be pornographic, they are not illegal.

But what about minors? Do they fall into a different category and thus fall into a different area of protection? In *Ginsberg v. New York* (1968), the U.S. Supreme Court said they do, thus giving states and local communities the power to regulate music in the best interests of children.

Nevertheless, the U.S. Supreme Court itself has had trouble trying to figure out what is obscene. In a famous concurring opinion in *Jacobellis v. Ohio* (1964), Justice Potter Stewart wrote, "I shall not today attempt further to define the kinds of material I understand to be embraced within that shorthand description [of obscene material]; and perhaps I could never succeed in intelligibly doing so. But *I know it when I see it*" (1964). If a learned justice of the U.S. Supreme Court cannot determine what is obscene, how can a mere record store owner or recording artist figure it out?

A confounding issue, at least for the recording industry, is that the rules for material broadcast over radio and television differ from those governing print media. Here the standard is an even more elusive "indecent." Thus, a song perfectly acceptable for sale in a record store might not, under Federal Communications Commission guidelines, be suitable for airplay. This confusion is evident when one looks at two different sections of the U.S. Code. Regarding radio communication, the code states, "Nothing in this Act shall . . . give the Commission the power of censorship over the radio communications . . . [or to] interfere with the right of free speech by means of radio communication" (Censorship 47 U.S.C. 326, 1999).

On the surface this seems to be saying that the government will not censor the content on radio. However, another portion of the code, this one dealing with crimes and criminal procedure, states, "Whoever utters any obscene, indecent, or profane language by means of radio communication shall be fined under this title or imprisoned not more than two years, or both" (Broadcasting Obscene Language, 1999). Interestingly, although dealing with "obscene, indecent or profane language," this subsection is titled "Broadcasting Obscene Language," mentioning nothing of the "indecent" language addressed in the body of the section.

The Federal Communications Commission (FCC) is the government agency charged with regulating radio; and as we will see, it is also the agency that has taken a somewhat narrow view of what may, and may not, be broadcast. So how does the commission reconcile these two apparently divergent parts of the Communications Act of 1999? Another part of the Communications Act, Powers and Duties of Commission, 2000, has been held to provide that link: "The Commission, from time to time, as public convenience, interest, or necessity requires shall . . . generally encourage the larger and more effective use of radio in the public interest." So, on numerous occasions the FCC has declared that playing some music is not "in the public interest." Although the FCC may not tell a station outright that it cannot play some kinds of music, when it comes time for license renewal, the commission will take a long, hard look to see if the licensee is operating in the "public interest," which playing some kinds of music is not.

The U.S. Supreme Court has also followed this line of reasoning, and in *FCC v. Pacifica Foundation* (1978) the Court noted: "The prohibition against censorship unequivocally denies the Commission any power to edit proposed broadcasts in advance and to excise material considered inappropriate for the airwaves. The prohibition, however, has never been construed to deny the Commission the power to review the content of completed broadcasts in the performance of its regulatory duties" (p. 735). Thus, the FCC may not have the power to tell a radio station what music it cannot play, but it does have the power to mete *subsequent punishment* for airing material it deems "inappropriate."

In another case, *In Re WUHY-FM Eastern Educational Radio* (1970), the FCC fined radio station WUHY-FM $100 for broadcasting a Jerry Garcia taped interview in which "two of the most celebrated Anglo-Saxon four letter words were used with remarkable frequency by Garcia."

What is interesting here is that the commission clearly expanded on the U.S. Supreme Court's obscenity definitions: The Garcia interview could not under any circumstances be said to appeal to "prurient interest," nor did the interview deal with sex. Nevertheless, the FCC was establishing new guidelines and, in effect, challenging broadcasters to do something about it, if they dared.

The challenge was taken up in 1978 with the celebrated "Seven dirty words" case. In 1973, a New York City radio station owned by the Pacifica Foundation aired a twelve-minute George Carlin monologue in which the comedian talked about "the words you couldn't say on the public, ah, airwaves, um, the ones you definitely wouldn't say, ever" (*FCC v. Pacifica Foundation*, p. 729). Carlin then proceeded to use those seven words in every possible grammatical combination and variation.

The Court, in *Pacifica*, ruled the commission was within its rights to sanction the Pacifica station, and in summing up its decision, the Court used a barnyard analogy altogether appropriate to a decision on "barnyard language (and who said the Court doesn't have a sense of humor?): "As Mr. Justice Sutherland wrote, a 'nuisance may be merely a right thing in the wrong place,—like a pig in the parlor instead of the barnyard.' We simply hold that when the Commission finds that a pig has entered the parlor, the exercise of its regulatory power does not depend on proof that the pig is obscene" (p. 750).

It therefore appears that government has at least some right to control the music played on radio stations, and to control music that is "merely indecent," as opposed to obscene. But as we shall see, the application of these notions is far from settled.

## CONTROL BY RETAILERS

When people think of censorship, visions of suppression by the government typically come to mind. We must remember, however, that private industry also has power to control what kinds of music we hear.

At this point, we must make important distinctions between the government's power to censor and the power of business to censor. Let's start by taking a close look at the First Amendment to the U.S. Constitution, an often misunderstood part of our heritage and laws. The First Amendment says, "Congress shall make no law respecting an establishment of religion, or prohibiting the free exercise thereof; or abridging the freedom of speech, or of the press, or the right of the people peaceably to assemble, and to petition the Government for a redress of grievances."

Notice the amendment addresses Congress and, by extension, the federal government. The amendment says absolutely nothing about the relationship between the right of speech or press and private industry. The amendment does, therefore, absolutely nothing to protect an individual's right of speech from encroachment by another private citizen or by business or industry. In fact, the U.S. Supreme Court has held that an employer, for example, does have at least some right to control the speech of its employees.

Likewise, the Court has ruled that in some instances a commercial establishment may prohibit some kinds of speech, particularly that which is disruptive. Accordingly, stores such as Wal-Mart are, technically, not engaging in censorship when they decide to refuse to sell certain kinds of songs. Bookstores, record stores, and video rental stores make these kinds of decisions all the time. After all, a bookstore or a music store has only finite storage space and cannot possibly carry every song or book ever published. Stores carry merchandise they feel will sell. Conversely, if stores believe a certain album might offend large numbers of their customers, they will not carry the recording.

This is not to say, however, that efforts by stores to limit the distribution of songs the public may find offensive have not been without controversy. The two largest chains, K-Mart and Wal-Mart, both became involved in this controversial issue. Both K-Mart and Wal-Mart have for a number of years refused to sell records that contain explicit lyrics or are particularly violent.

In late 1997 the Wal-Mart chain, with more than 2,300 stores nationwide, and K-Mart, with more than 2,100 locations, pulled an album by the British rock act Prodigy because of lyrics contained in the song "Smack My Bitch Up." Although the album was released through WEA, the distribution entity of Warner Brothers, critics said the song glorified domestic violence. The song was also on the group's *The Fat of the Land* album, which sold more than 2 million copies in the United States. In 1997 Janice Rocco, at that time president of the Los Angeles chapter of the National Organization for Women, attacked the record, saying, "It sends a message to women and men who shop at their stores that these companies do not want to be a part of the problem in our culture that perpetuates violence against women" (quoted in Philips, 1997). However, the band's producer, Liam Howlett, said the song has nothing to do with abuse of women: " 'Smack My Bitch Up' is a phrase that means doing anything intensely, like being on stage—going for extreme manic energy" (quoted in Philips, 1997). Bob Merlis, senior vice president for corporate communication at Warner Music, said the whole controversy was manufactured, then covered, by the *Los Angeles Times* (Philips, 1997). Nevertheless, the group released the album with an alternative album cover that obscured the word "bitch" on the jacket.

An earlier controversy in 1996 pitted Wal-Mart against singer Sheryl Crow and her song "Love Is a Good Thing," which mentions children killing each other with guns from Wal-Mart. *Sheryl Crow*, the album containing the song, was pulled from Wal-Mart shelves, resulting in an estimated loss of some 400,000 copies of the CD (Tyson et al., 1998).

An interesting vignette similar to the Wal-Mart saga illustrates the difficulty in actually controlling the distribution of offensive material. In early January 2000 Wal-Mart began an on-line store offering thousands of items of merchandise, including books and videos. The store contracted with Books-a-Million as a third-party supplier of books and downloaded a database the company supplied. The database contained some unanticipated titles such as *The Best of Gay Adult Videos* and *The Couples Guide to the Best Erotic Videos*, certainly not the kind of fare Wal-Mart offers. Wal-Mart representative Melissa Berryhill apologized for the retail chain: "We did everything we could to ensure things like this wouldn't happen. In this case, some were overlooked, and we're working with all deliberate speed to get it taken care of and apologize to our customers" (quoted in Goldman, 2000).

## ACTIVIST PARENTS

If the government seemed unwilling or unable to control lyrics over the years, several groups of concerned citizens felt they had the means to do so themselves. Perhaps the most effective weapon in the public's arsenal has been the Parents Music Resource Center (PMRC), begun in 1985 by Tipper Gore, wife of then-senator Al Gore, Jr. The PMRC took aim at all forms of sex, violence, drug and alcohol abuse, and occult lyrics found in some rock music. After beginning to gain national publicity, the group held a series of meetings with Stan Gortikov, at that time president of RIAA. A 1985 letter from the group said, "It is our concern that some of the music which the recording industry sells today increasingly portrays explicit sex and violence, and glorifies the use of drugs and alcohol. It is indiscriminately available to persons of any age through record stores and the media" (Gore, 1987, p. 29).

Shortly after beginning discussions with RIAA, the Senate Commerce Committee on September 19, 1985—only five months after the PMRC was formed—held a hearing on the subject of rock lyrics. The hearing was attended not only by Tipper Gore and Susan Baker, wife of Treasury Secretary James Baker, but also by representatives of the National Parent Teacher Association (NPTA). In addition, Frank Zappa, John Denver, and Dee Snider of the band Twisted Sister also participated. From the very beginning John Danforth (R-Mo.), the chairman of the committee, said the committee did not intend to propose any legislation, but would simply hear what the two sides had to say. This comment prompted television critic Tom Shales to write, "It was stated repeatedly that the hearing was not convened to advocate legislation nor to formulate a governmental plan of action for dealing with the problem. Which is re-freshing in a way—a Senate hearing that admits from the outset that absolutely nothing will come of it" (Shales, 1985).

Publishers, the industry entities in direct contact with songwriters, were extremely concerned about potential censorship of lyrics. Although direct government action against the music industry seemed remote, the threat of an economic boycott was particularly worrisome to people. One such person, Ira Glasser, executive director of the American Civil Lib-erties Union (ACLU), stated emphatically: "If sufficiently deprived of such outlets, music publishers will surely conform, and the range of per-missible expression will narrow. That is exactly how blacklisting began in the 1950s, not through legislation or blunt government censorship, but through economic intimidation organized by private pressure groups" (Glasser, 1987).

Newspaper editorials later condemned the efforts of Congress to in-timidate, if not directly legislate, the recording industry. They also pointed out that a very small percentage of rock songs actually contain objectionable lyrics. In addition, it was noted that rock music can have a positive effect, not only on kids but also on the society as well. Industry representatives noted evidence to support the industry's positive effects in support of various humanitarian causes such as USA for Africa, Farm Aid, and Live Aid ("Rock Does Have a Conscience," 1986).

Despite the lack of direct government censorship and the failure of conservative groups to have the government impose such restrictions, the PMRC did force the recording industry to begin "voluntarily" plac-ing warning labels on records, including a "D/A" label for songs ad-vocating drug or alcohol abuse. In the highly charged Senate hearing, recording artists such as Dee Snider of Twisted Sister and Frank Zappa, founder of the Mothers of Invention, said the "voluntary" labeling amounted to censorship. Ironically, some of the most conservative, fam-ily oriented artists, such as Donny Osmond, also opposed the process of labeling records the same way movies are labeled. Osmond objected be-cause he believed a warning label would be considered "cool" by youths, and a lack of warning label would signal "milk toast music" in the minds of teenagers. He and other artists feared they would be pressured to add a song or two with lyrics requiring the label to avoid the "no-warning label" stigma.

In spite of pressure from many artists to resist PMRC suggestions, more than twenty record companies said they would abide by the voluntary labeling agreement. There was no enforcement mechanism, however, and each company was allowed to decide for itself if a song needed a warning label ("Warning: 'Love' for Sale," 1985). Although the PMRC is not nearly as active today as it was in the late 1980s, record companies still "voluntarily" put warning labels on their products.

Despite the notion that warning labels somehow lead to censorship, Americans use a lot of warning labels. We see them on food products, we see them on power tools, we see them on toys—we see them on a myriad of consumer goods. Even something as simple as putting a book on a certain shelf in a book store is a warning label of sorts.

One goal of the PMRC was to encourage record retailers to make song lyrics available so customers could see what they were buying. The goal follows a reasonable line of logic, since critics of any form of censorship generally defend their position by saying, "It's a parent's responsibility to monitor what recordings their children buy." If parents don't have the information—in this case, lyrics—to evaluate a recording, how can they possibly control what their children buy? Thus, advocates of the parental advisory warning labels do not view labeling as an attempt to censor music. They generally refer to it as a means of giving consumers more information, not as censorship, which is an attempt to restrict information.

Not everyone in the recording industry finds the PMRC idea of providing lyrics in record retail stores a bad idea. Wayne Halper, general manager for DreamWorks Records, Nashville, for example, would not be opposed to making lyrics available for parents to review. He noted, though, that it might make good marketing sense for certain genre, such as country, to let consumers see lyrics before they purchase a recording. "It's not a bad idea in terms of marketing," said Halper. "Maybe consumers would be happier when they get home, because they would never be surprised" (Halper, 1999).

In 1999, though, the Louisiana legislature considered a bill that would have required retailers to provide parents with a copy of the lyrics of any records that had a parental advisory warning label. The measure failed, however, when the legislators realized the measure would do more harm than good. Said Rep. Errol Romero of New Iberia, Louisiana: "I predict that 90 percent of high school students in Louisiana will have a copy of this in their hands if the state forces retailers to put this [the lyrics] in print" (quoted in Townsley, 1999). (New Iberia, by the way, was the town where, in 1989, the city council tried to pass a law making it illegal to display obscene material to anyone under seventeen who was not married.) Said Mike Cutshaw of the National Association of Recording Merchandisers: "The economic impact on the 1,600 Louisiana retailers would be drastic, many of which are mom-and-pop operations. It would be an incredible burden for Louisiana retailers to provide copies of all the lyrics of all the songs" (quoted in Townsley, 1999). A further problem would result if the copyright owner did not give permission for the lyrics to be reproduced, putting the store owners in violation of federal copyright laws. In addition, the measure did nothing about the lyrics broadcast on radio or television, nor did it address the problem of mail-order music from suppliers outside the state of Louisiana. These reasons are, of course, applicable to any scheme of labeling.

Although Wayne Halper acknowledged that some young listeners react inappropriately to music, he made clear that parents not labels, have the responsibility to monitor what their children listen to. Whose job is it to broker First Amendment rights? Not the label or creative community, according to Halper. "It all comes down to the parents doing a complete job of raising their children. My kids know that heavyweight wrestling is not real. They know the difference between reality and fantasy [in lyrics]" (Halper, 1999).

In all likelihood, most parents would admit they have little information to help make decisions about lyric content of records. For example, it is a fairly common practice for record labels to release two versions of singles from albums that contain profanity: "explicit" and "clean." Labels began releasing two versions not because they were concerned about young persons buying a recording with lyrics their parents might object to but to gain airplay. Simply put, radio stations will not broadcast songs with lyrics that go beyond permissible standards. The edited clean versions of songs played on radio present a potential problem for parents, however. If parents listen to a song on the radio and hear the clean version, they will probably give their child permission to buy the album. When their child returns home with the album, the same song that sounded benign on the radio might have lyrics that the parent disapproves of.

Another hypothesis to support the "more information" principal is that more detailed warning labels on music would enhance artistic freedom, rather than limit it. If consumers know what to expect, they will not be caught off guard or remain ignorant of the true content of a record or song. Thus, if a listener is offended by certain kinds of language, a warning label and/or lyric sheet would let the person know which songs to avoid because of offensive language. Indeed, in a sense, giving consumers more information might allow songwriters greater artistic freedom. If songwriters do not have to fear negative reaction by an unsuspecting customer, they could simply create what they want. Likewise, a label could say to a listener, "This album contains drug-related lyrics. If such portrayals offend you, then don't listen."

The latest regulatory efforts are aimed not at controlling the lyrics themselves but in using artists to send positive, anti-drug messages. According to Barry R. McCaffrey, director of the Office of National Drug Control Policy, such efforts are not aimed at writing anti-drug television shows and songs, for example, but in enlisting the help of entertainers and personalities to speak publicly against drug use (1999).

## "LOUIE, LOUIE"

Perhaps the strangest example of censorship and attempted censorship by private industry, the government, and individuals involves the song "Louie, Louie" as performed by the Kingsmen. Interestingly, the only truly intelligible part of the song is the instrumental opening, which by now is familiar to anyone who listens to rock music and anyone who has been to an *Animal House* type fraternity party. The actual lyrics are, for the most part, unintelligible. Perhaps it was the indistinct lyrics that were the reason an ostensibly simple song became the most investigated, censored, and misunderstood song of the rock era. "Louie, Louie" appears to be a song about a lovesick sailor who is confiding his woes to a bartender named Louie. There appear to be no references to sex or violence, and there are no dirty words in the song's lyrics. But that hasn't stopped people from looking for a hidden message, assuming that because the words are generally unintelligible, there must be one.

The song was written by Richard Berry in 1956, and was described by writer Ron Hayes in 1993 as, of all things, "a sea chanty cha-cha with a distinct rhythm and blues feel to it." After several versions were recorded by bands in the Northwest, the Kingsmen, a proto garage-grunge quintet, recorded it under conditions almost sure to guarantee that the lyrics were not understandable, as the Federal Bureau of Investigation (FBI) was later to say, "at any speed."

The definitive Kingsmen version was recorded in April 1963 in one hour at a studio in Portland, Oregon. The five members of the group were arranged in a circle, with a single microphone overhead. If one were to listen closely to the recording, one would hear drummer Lynn Easton utter an expletive as he mistakenly claps his sticks together at one point in the music. Guitarist Mike Mitchell misses several notes, and singer Jack Ely comes in too soon on the third verse. In addition to trying to sing in a Jamaican patois, he was wearing braces and had to stand on tip-toes to reach the microphone.

After the record was pressed, it languished until October 1963, when a DJ in Boston featured it as the "Worst Record of the Week." What he hadn't anticipated was that his listeners apparently liked the song and flooded record stores trying to find it. The song reached Number 2 on the *Billboard* chart in January 1964, missing the Number 1 spot by the popularity, of all things, of "Dominique" by Sister Luc-Gabrielle, the Singing Nun.

But what does this song have to do with the FBI? In March 1964 a woman brought the record to the FBI office in Indianapolis after a co-worker had given her a copy of it. She alleged it contained dirty lyrics and said they could be understood if the 45 rpm record were played at 33 rpm. For the next two-and-a-half years, the FBI collected various versions of the song, tried playing each at different speeds ranging from 16 rpm to 78 rpm, and generally brought the whole weight of the agency to bear in deciphering the lyrics. That is, they did everything except interview the lead singer, Ely. Their conclusion: The words were "unintelligible at any speed."

Ron Hayes commented, "It's a funny thing. Listen to the record with the dirty lyrics in hand and, hey, they sound dirty." One concerned citizen said, "If they can't state the lyrics clearly, they must be hiding something" (Driver, 1999). Because of the allegedly dirty lyrics, the governor of Indiana, Matthew Welsh, asked radio stations not to play the song because he considered it pornographic and said it made his ears "tingle" (Harrington, 1997). But the legislature passed a measure making "Louie, Louie" the official state rock song. The governor, however, vetoed the measure.

BMI, a performance rights licensing organization, estimates the song is still played on the radio about 200,000 times a year in the Untied States and has been "covered" (recorded by other artists) more than 1,200 times by university marching bands, heavy metal acts, easy listening artists, and innumerable rock 'n' rollers. One of the strangest incarnations is the John Belushi rendition of the Kingsmen's version in the movie *Animal House*.

## CENSORSHIP TIMELINE

Literally hundreds of songs have come under various forms of scrutiny, often resulting in limited distribution if not outright banning. Some of the older examples of censorship seem extreme by today's standards. However, as we pointed out earlier, music has always aroused passionate debate and concerns. What follows is just a small sample of incidents that involved two partisan viewpoints regarding music. One side, believing that society needed to be protected from certain types of music, fought for various forms of censorship. The other side, usually creative artists, fought for a free and open venue in which to express their ideas.

As you read this list, compiled by the authors, ask yourself, Is there merit to arguments in favor of censorship, or should we preserve the right to free expression regardless of what is being expressed?

## 1942

Abraham Jaffe is arrested and convicted of selling "certain obscene, lewd, lascivious and indecent phonograph records" (*New York v. Jaffe*, 1942, p. 105). The judge is concerned about the lyrics and the advertising used to sell the records, which feature "scantily attired women." He is even more outraged that the defendant has tried to argue, "The times had changed" and "society was different" (and, one must presume, more tolerant) than when the law under which he has been convicted was passed.

## 1943

The Rogers and Hammerstein musical *Oklahoma!* ushers in the era of musical comedy (Graybeal, 1999) and immediately runs into problems as some radio stations refuse to air the song "I'm Just a Girl Who Can't Say No."

## 1954

Rep. Ruth Thompson of Michigan introduces legislation that would forbid using the U.S. Postal Service to distribute records that are "obscene, lewd, lascivious or filthy." Violators would be fined up to $5,000 and be sentenced to five years in prison.

In October Memphis radio station WDIA bans the Midnighters' "Work with Me, Annie" and "Annie Had a Baby." The station also refuses to play the Drifters' "Honey Love."

## 1955

Young adults write more than 15,000 letters to Chicago radio stations complaining about the "dirty" lyrics the stations play. In response, WBBM promises the station will not play controversial or rhythm-and-blues music.

## 1956

ABC radio banned "Love for Sale" by Billie Holiday because of its prostitution theme.

"Transfusion" by Dot and Diamond is banned by all three major radio networks. The story in the song is told by a reckless driver who after a series of accidents asks for transfusions by singing such lines as "Pass the juice Bruce" and "Pass the claret Barrett." The song is listed as a "novelty," that is, as "comedy" song, but an NBC official says, "There's nothing funny about a blood transfusion" (Nuzum, 2000).

A line in the Cole Porter song "I Get a Kick Out of You" that mentions cocaine is changed by ABC to "I get perfume from Spain."

## 1957

After two performances on the *Ed Sullivan Show* generated so much negative publicity about the hip-swiveling singer, Elvis Presley was filmed only from the waist up for his final appearance. Elvis Presley, by the way, goes on to record more than one hundred Top 40 hits, including 18 that reach Number 1.

In March, Catholic schools in Chicago, at the instigation of Cardinal Stritch, ban rock music. The cardinal says the "tribal rhythms" lead to anti-social behavior and cause kids to "behave in a hedonistic manner" (Bronson, 1994).

## 1958

Jerry Lee Lewis proves that even a performer's lifestyle can offend people and lead to blacklisting. After Lewis marries his thirteen-year-old cousin, radio stations pull his records and concert venues cancel performances. Lewis, who could have provided a serious challenge to Elvis Presley's status as "the king," is never again a major factor in the music industry.

## 1959

Even songs without words are said to lead to inappropriate behavior, as seen when radio stations around the country banned the instrumental song "Rumble" by Link Wray, the "Father of the Power Chord" (Driver, 1999). "Rumble" is 1950s slang for a gang fight, and because the song is allegedly linked to gang violence, Dick Clark refuses to give the title of the song when he introduces Wray during a live performance on American Bandstand. If instrumental music can be said to have a soul, it is "Rumble": "Wray's guitar tone is positively menacing as he attacks his strings with feral agitation. Whoever it is he's gonna rumble with better run and hide in the hills" (Seigal, 1999).

## 1962

Several songs dealing with "The Twist" sweep the nation, but many adults are not amused. Bishop Burke in Buffalo, New York, says Catholic children are not to sing about, listen to, or dance to the new fad.

In February the Radio Trade Practices Committee says it wants the National Association of Broadcasters Code Committee to screen rock songs "due to the proliferation of songs dealing with raw sex and violence beamed directly and singularly at children and teenagers" (Bronson, 1994).

## 1963

Folk singer Bob Dylan refuses to appear on the *Ed Sullivan Show* after CBS officials tell him he will not be allowed to sing "Talking John Birch Society Blues."

## 1965

In June radio stations refuse to play the Rolling Stones hit "(I Can't Get No) Satisfaction." They complain about the sexually suggestive content. The Stones go on to have forty-one Top 40 songs, including eight that reach Number 1.

## 1966

During a March interview with the *(London) Evening Standard*, Beatle John Lennon opines that the Beatles are more "popular" than Jesus Christ. In response to the comment, numerous radio stations stop playing Beatles songs and some sponsor record burnings. Lennon later says he was not saying the group was "better" than Jesus, only more popular.

In June the Beatles release the infamous "butcher cover" for the *Yesterday and Today* album. The cover shows John, Paul, George, and Ringo wearing butcher smocks surrounded by pieces of raw meat and decapitated nude dolls. The ensuing outcry forces the cover to be withdrawn and a simple photograph of the group substituted. A spokesperson for Capitol Records explained, "The original cover, created in England, was intended as 'pop art' satire. However, a sampling of public opinion in the United States indicates that the cover design is subject to misinterpretation" (McAllister, 1999).

The song "Gloria" by Them, an Irish rock quartet, is banned by Chicago station WLS because of a suggestive lyric. But because the song is so popular, the station has a local group, Shadows of Knight, cut a new clean version, which reaches Number 10.

## 1967

The Rolling Stones run into trouble when they perform "Let's Spend the Night Together" in January on the *Ed Sullivan Show*. Mick Jagger is forced to change the lyrics to "Let's spend some time together," although his facial expressions during close-ups show his scorn for the change. Although the video of the performance clearly shows Jagger saying "some time," he later says he sang the original words (Bronson, 1994).

In September Ed Sullivan continues his tradition of headlining rock acts by booking the Doors. The group is supposed to sing "Light My Fire," but only if the line that mentions getting higher is deleted. Leader Jim Morrison agrees, but then he sings the line anyway.

## 1968

A radio station in El Paso, Texas, refuses to play songs by Bob Dylan. Station management says the songs may contain offensive lyrics, although the station continues to play recordings of other artists singing Dylan songs.

During the Democratic National Convention in Chicago, Mayor Richard Daley ordered stations not to play the song "Street Fighting Man" by the Rolling Stones because he said it would trigger riots. Stations played the record anyway. It is unlikely, though, that the ensuing riots were linked to the song.

In September 1968 Chicago radio stations, fearing another outbreak of violence like that which occurred during the Democratic National Convention, refuse to play the Rolling Stones' song "Street Fighting Man."

## 1969

In January, police in Newark, New Jersey, seize 30,000 copies of John Lennon and Yoko Ono's *Two Virgins* album, whose cover shows the couple nude. In Chicago, the vice squad raids a record store displaying the cover.

In April the group MC5 is forced to delete the song "Kick out the Jams" from the album of the same name because of an offensive first line.

In July "The Ballad of John and Yoko" is denied airplay by almost half of the Top 40 stations in the United States, despite the fact that it is the best-selling single in the country. The offensive line contains a reference to Christ.

## 1970

In Chapter 3, we discussed the relationship between music and the war in Vietnam. One of the songs mentioned was "Ohio" by the group Crosby, Stills, Nash and Young. The song dealt with the killing of four students at Kent State University by members of the Ohio National Guard. Although Governor James Rhodes orders radio stations in Ohio not to play the song, few comply. The song becomes something of an anthem for counterculture elements in society.

In October President Nixon tells radio executives that songs suggesting drug use should be banned.

## 1971

In Chapter 3, we discussed the drug associations in the Brewer and Shipley song "One Toke Over the Line." WNBC radio believed the lyrics were indeed "over the line" and banned the song.

## 1973

Drug-related lyrics in the Curtis Mayfield song "Pusherman" are deleted on the syndicated television program *Soul Train*.

## 1975

The Reverend Charles Boykin of Tallahassee, Florida, organizes a record burning, calling rock 'n' roll the "devil's music" (Bronson, 1994) and says that "984 out of every 1,000 unwed mothers are impregnated while rock music is playing" (Music Must-Know Info., 1999). During the demonstration $2,000 worth of records are destroyed.

## 1976

Immigration officials in the United States balk at issuing work visas to the British group the Sex Pistols for a concert tour in the United States. Officials say the group's music lacks "artistic value" (Nuzum, 2000). The group is eventually allowed into the country for a brief tour.

## 1977

The Sex Pistols prove that even banned records can reach the top of the charts. In early 1977 the group is dropped by EMI, and A&M later drops the group nine days after signing them. Virgin Records then signs the group and releases "God Save the Queen." However, British radio says the song is "treasonous" and refuses to give it airplay. The song then reaches Number 2 on the pop charts.

## 1981

Radio Stations in Provo and Salt Lake City, Utah, refuse to play the Olivia Newton-John hit "Physical" because the lyrics are deemed unsuitable for Mormons.

## 1986

Frank Zappa's *Jazz from Hell* receives a "Parental Advisory Warning" sticker from the RIAA, presumably because of the title, since the songs are entirely instrumental.

## 1987

Jello Biafra, leader of the Dead Kennedys, is accused of distributing pornographic material because of H. R. Giger cover art on the group's *Frankenchrist* CD. The prosecution began when an attorney's daughter gave a copy of the album to her brother for Christmas. The trial ended with a hung jury, although copies were seized and destroyed.

## 1989

Tom Leykis of KFI radio sponsors a record burning to protest Yusef Islam's (formerly known as Cat Stevens) support of the Ayatollah Khomeini's call for the execution of Salman Rushdie, author of *Satanic Verses*. Several other stations refuse to play Islam's songs.

The city council in New Iberia, Louisiana, passes an ordinance saying that music that fits the state's definition of obscenity must be removed from the view of unmarried people under seventeen. Penalties include a $500 fine and sixty days in jail.

## 1990

*As Nasty as They Wanna Be*, an album by 2 Live Crew, is declared obscene by a federal court. This represents the first time in the history of the music industry that a recording is deemed obscene by a federal court. Although there is expert testimony as to the social relevance and value of the record, the trial judge notes in *Skywalker Records v. Navarro* (1990), "The evident goal of this particular recording is to reproduce the sexual act through musical lyrics. It is an appeal directed to 'dirty' thoughts and the loins, not to the intellect and the mind."

After the district judge in Florida made the ruling, a store owner who sold the album was charged with distributing obscene material to children under eighteen. The store owner was arrested as part of a sting operation conducted by Dade County police. Actions against 2 Live Crew are also undertaken in Alabama, Texas, and Tennessee. Three members of the group, including Luther Campbell, the group's leader, are charged with obscenity following an adults-only club performance of material from the album. "Campbell amassed an intimidating array of enemies: law enforcement officials, senators, and right-wing zealots among them. They wanted his music banned. But, using the First Amendment to protect his ghetto verse, he survived all that, even thrived" (Korten, 1999).

A grand jury in Volusia County, Florida, bans two 2 Live Crew CDs and works by Ice-T and Eazy-E.

In April a grand jury in Florida declares that four rap albums, including Ice-T's *Freedom of Speech*, are obscene. As a result, area record stores pull the albums.

## 1992

A federal appeals court throws out the 2 Live Crew conviction, and sales reach into the millions. With the money he made, Campbell "spent $250,000 on a facility for the Optimist Club football and baseball programs in Liberty City. He created an alcohol-free teen club and on holidays, he loaded up a delivery truck and handed out turkeys, canned food, and gifts" (Korten, 1999).

Governor Pete Wilson of California demands the band Body Count, led by rapper Ice-T, be dropped from a concert because of their song "Cop Killer." The San Diego Police Officers Association wrote the group asking them not to perform the song, and promoters said they would not. However, Body Count closed their show with "Cop Killer," much to the chagrin of security officers at the concert.

There are reports that officials at Time Warner received death threats because of the album (a rather curious state of affairs: threats of violence against a record label that allegedly promoted violence), and perhaps because of the furor, Time Warner stopped distribution of "Cop Killer" through its affiliated label, Sire records.

Also in 1992, the Washington legislature tries to add "sound record-ings" to the state's laws concerning material "harmful to minors." The law is found to be unconstitutional.

## 1999

Shock-rocker Marilyn Manson cancels five concerts in the wake of the Columbine (Colorado) shootings. In a statement two days after the shoot-ings, Manson says: "People are trying to sort out what happened and to deal with their losses. It's not a great atmosphere to be out playing rock & roll shows, for us or the fans. The media has [*sic*] unfairly scapegoated the music industry and so-called Goth kids and has speculated—with no basis in truth—that artists like myself are in some way to blame. This tragedy was a product of ignorance, hatred and an access to guns" ("Manson Cancels," 1999).

In June K-Mart officials say the store will not stock Ministry's *Dark Side of the Moon* album because of "offensive" cover art.

Also in June, by a 2–1 margin Congress defeats proposed legislation that would ban the sale of violent music to minors.

In July officials at the Birmingham-Jefferson Convention Center reject a county commission call for a ban on violent and obscene concerts. However, some board members say they favor a concert rating system.

## CONCLUSION

Literally hundreds of artists and thousands of songs have aroused the ire of various persons and organizations. There are also hundreds of incidents one could relate in some way to struggles for and against music censorship. Likely we will continue to see disagreements in the market-place and in the courts about what is appropriate music for the public and what limits to freedom of expression society we should tolerate.

Music, going back hundreds, if not thousands, of years, has played a role in the social life of communities and nations. Yet, we must ask our-selves whether popular music has simply chronicled American society or has in fact influenced it. Indeed, music has often paralleled the issues and concerns of society in ways that are nearly impossible through any other medium, and thus music reflects the life and times of the com-munity.

Some artists have intentionally pushed the limits of artistic sensibility in their attempt to create an antisocial message. Artist G. G. Allin, for-merly of the band called the Toilet Rockers, frequently defecated on stage and then threw his feces at the audience. His concerts, so-called scato-logical performance art, were not always well received. Allin was ar-

Senator Orrin Hatch, R-Utah, and Senator Joseph Joseph Lieberman, D-Conn., during a Senate Commerce Committee hearing on ways to stop merchandising violence to children on Tuesday, May 4, 1999. Senator Hatch is holding a Marilyn Manson compact disc. (AP/Wide World Photos)

rested and charged with disorderly conduct in Milwaukee. A jury rejected his claim that he was merely exercising his First Amendment right to freedom of expression (Kleid, 1991).

Even the most ardent critics of rock music believe that laws should protect an artist's right to freedom of expression. Despite controversies surrounding music lyrics and artist lifestyles, Americans generally agree that the government must support free expression in the form of music. They also generally accept that music serves as much a social commentary role as do newspapers. Supporters and critics of rock music disagree, however, on where artistic expression stops and offensive words begin.

In its annual *State of the First Amendment* survey report, the Freedom Forum noted a paradox. According to Ken Paulson, director of the Forum, "Americans respect the First Amendment as an ideal but are ambivalent when it protects offensive ideas or troubling speech" (Shiffman, 2000). Almost 75 percent of persons surveyed felt song lyrics contribute to violence in real life. Slightly more than half of all individuals sampled felt the news media have *too much* freedom.

As Supreme Court Justice William O. Douglas concluded in *Yale Broadcasting* (414 U.S. 914): "The Government cannot, consistent with the First Amendment, require a broadcaster to censor its music any more than it can require a newspaper to censor the stories of its reporters. Under our system, the Government is not to decide what messages, spoken or in music, are of the proper 'social value' to reach the people" (918).

Every consumer decision requires making choices, and the more information we have, the more informed our choices will be. Consumers who make purchases based on informed choices are less likely to criticize the music they purchased. More important, fewer complaints about recordings will result in a lower likelihood that the government will step in to exercise direct control over music in this country. Music consumers and music creators alike may agree, at least, that government censorship is something they hope is never needed.

## TOPICS FOR DISCUSSION

1. Should the government ban or restrict music that proposes the overthrow of values the government is sworn to protect?

2. A group of parents picket Big Value discount store because the store sells CDs the parents find offensive. In response the store pulls the CDs from the shelves. Is the store engaging in censorship, or is it simply making a smart business decision?

3. You are the manager of the Big Value store mentioned above. You rethink your position and decide to start selling the offensive songs

again. A group of parents comes into your office and wants to know why you have done this. Justify your decision.

4. Who should determine if a song or performance has "artistic merit"? The songwriter? The performer? A government official? Members of the community?

## REFERENCES

### Interview

Halper, Wayne (1999, September 2). Halper is general manager of DreamWorks Records, Nashville.

### Books

Gillmor, D. M., J. A. Barron, and T. F. Simon (1998). *Mass Communication Law: Cases and Comment*. Belmont, CA: Wadsworth Publishing.

Gore, Tipper (1987). *Raising PG Kids in an X-Rated Society*. Nashville: Abingdon Press.

Lockhart Commission. (1970). *1970 Report on the Presidential Commission on Obscenity and Pornography*. New York: Bantam Books.

Meese Commission. (1986). *Final Report*. Washington, DC: U.S. Department of Justice.

### Legislative and Judicial Proceedings

Broadcasting Obscene Language, 18 U.S.C. 1464 (1999).

Censorship, 47 U.S.C. 326 (1999).

*FCC v. Pacifica Foundation*, 438 U.S. 726 (1978).

*Ginsberg v. New York*, 390 U.S. 629 (1968).

*In Re WUHY-FM Eastern Education Radio*, 24 F.C.C.2d 408 (1970).

*Jacobellis v. Ohio*, 378 U.S. 184 (1964).

*KFKB Broadcasting Ass'n, Inc., v. Federal Radio Commission*, 47 F.2d 670 (1931).

McCaffrey, B. R. (1999, October 21). The national youth anti-drug media campaign and entertainment industry outreach. Statement before the House Committee on Appropriations, Subcommittee on Treasury, Postal Service and General Government.

*Miller v. California*, 413 U.S. 15 (1973).

*New York v. Jaffe*, 35 N.Y.S.2d 104 (1942).

Powers and Duties of Commission, 47 U.S.C. 303(g) (1999).

*Regina v. Hicklin*, 3 L.R.-Q.B. 360 (1868).

*Roth v. United States*, 354 U.S. 476 (1957).

*Skywalker Records v. Navarro*, 739 F.Supp. 578 (S.D. Fla. 1990).

*Yale Broadcasting Co. v. Federal Communications Commission*, 478 F.2d (D.C. cir.) 594, 598–599 (1973); cert. den., 414 U.S. 914 (1973).

*Yale Broadcasting Co. v. Federal Communications Commission*, 414 U.S. 914 (1973) cert. den.

## Magazines, Journals, and Newspapers

Bronson, F. (1994, March 26). A Selected Chronology of Musical Controversy. *Billboard*, p. N36.

Deggans, E. (1999, November 17). The Voice of America. *St. Petersburg Times*, p. 3D.

Driver, M. (1999, September 23). Banned, Blamed, Hated and Shamed. *Seattle Weekly*, p. 29.

Glasser, I. (1987, December 5). Keeping the Censor Out of Rock. *New York Times*, p. 26.

Goldman, A. (2000, January 4). Wal-Mart Says Mix-up Put Sex Books on Web Site. *Los Angeles Times*, p. C1.

Graybeal, G. (1999, December 17). 20 Entertainment Milestones of the Century. *(Durham, N.C.) Herald-Sun*, p. D12.

Harrington, R. (1997, February 2). Famous Lost Words; How "Louie Louie's" Unintelligible Lyrics Won Millions of Hearts. *Washington Post*, p. G2.

Harrison, E. (1999, May 1). Hollywood: Ground Zero; the Entertainment Industry Looks Inward and Speaks Out on Its Products and Their Relationship to Real-Life Violence. *Los Angeles Times*, p. F1.

Hayes, R. (1993, November 28). 30-Year-Old Scandal Debunked: The "Dirty" Lyrics of "Louie, Louie." *(Minneapolis) Star Tribune*, p. F14.

Kleid, B. (1991, August 26). Morning Report: Pop/Rock. *Los Angeles Times*, p. F2.

Korten, T. (1999, June 3). Two Live Screwed. *Miami New Times*.

Krum, S. (1995, September 12). Now Hear This. *(London) Guardian*, p. T8.

Manson Cancels Final Five Dates. (1999, April 29). *Rolling Stone*.

McAllister, R. (1999, August 25). The Beatles Butchered a Cover. *(Richmond) Times Dispatch*, p. B1.

Music Must-Know Info. (1999, November 26). *Toronto Sun*, p. 9.

Philips, C. (1997, December 6). Wal-Mart, K-Mart Remove "Smack" Album. *Los Angeles Times*, p. D1.

Riemenschneider, C. (1999, June 4). Is It Only Rock 'n' Roll? Debate Continues over Role of Music in Columbine Shootings. *Tulsa World*.

Rock Does Have a Conscience. (1986, October 21). *Arkansas Democrat-Gazette*.

Seigal, B. (1999, November 19). The All-Time Top 20 Pissed List. *OC Weekly*, p. 38.

Shales, T. (1985, September 29). Commentary, *Los Angeles Times*, TV Times, p. 2.

Shiffman, John (2000, June 29). Poll Says People Mixed on First Amendment. *The Tennessean*, P. 1B.

Townsley, C. (1999, April 29). Panel Censors Measure to Print "Obscene" Lyrics. *(Baton Rouge) Advocate*, P. A9.

Tyson, J., Ward, A., Swindell, L., Stewart, P., Mitchell, E., Perkins, K. P., Ferman, D., and Gay, W. L. (1998, July 5). Freedom and the Fig Leaf. *Fort Worth Star Telegram*, Arts, p. 1.

Warning: "Love" for Sale. (1985, November 11). *Newsweek*, p. 39.

## Web Site

Nuzum, E. (2000, January 17). When did censorship begin? http://ericnuzum.com/banned/.

# 11

# Radio and Records:
# A Love-Hate Relationship

Record label executives like to blame radio whenever there is a sales slump in the recording industry. The problem, as they see it, is that radio has limited playlists and won't play the "great records" labels send them. Radio station music directors and program directors have a little different view of the problem. They blame the poor quality of songs and the lack of consistently good records from the labels. However, neither side can deny that it depends on the other for its existence.

As much as artists and labels hate to admit it, radio airplay sells records. In recording industry parlance, "spins equal sales" when it comes to mainstream record sales. Radio is the primary promotional tool used to create an awareness of a new recording. Research commissioned by one of the major label groups revealed that "four out of every five music purchases can be traced to radio airplay" (Phillips, 1996). Other forms of promotion, such as paid advertising in print or broadcast media, would be helpful, but their cost is prohibitive for a "product" that has a shelf-life as short as a record album. Companies hoping to promote sales of automobiles, beer, or hamburgers advertise their brand names and products for long periods of time. Recordings simply do not last long enough to justify an advertising campaign for each new recording by every different artist.

One might ask, Isn't radio airplay advertising? The answer is no, because theoretically the labels do not pay stations to spin their records on the air. Advertising, in contrast, is paid media support. The trade-offs are significant. Radio advertising is expensive, but the company buying advertisements knows when they will air. Record airplay is free, but the station, not the record label, decides which records to play and how often they are played.

The federal government created the FCC (Federal Communications

Commission) to regulate radio and television broadcasters. The legislature has also enacted laws that regulate the way radio stations do business. Those laws dictate the way record labels can try to influence radio stations' playlists.

## RADIO AIRPLAY AND RECORDS

The goal of the promotion staff at a record label is to create an awareness of, and demand for, each album and single the label hopes to sell. In an ideal world record promoters would simply call everyone on the planet and play the album for them. In turn, anyone who liked the album after hearing it would go to the store to buy it. Of course, it is not possible to play the album for millions of people over the telephone.

The next best way to create an awareness of a recording is to have radio stations broadcast it to the millions of listeners around the world. "People will not buy what they have not heard, and no matter what the alternative outlets (MTV and club DJs) claim, nothing blankets the universe like a radio signal" (Hall and Taylor, 1998). But here the matter becomes a little more complicated because radio stations in the United States are "formatted." That means they play a particular style of music. A station's format might include a mix of a few genres or subgenres of music. A genre describes a unique type of music. For example, country (formerly know as country and western), rock, classical, and jazz are considered uniquely different genres. Over the years, genres have tended to fragment into subgenres. Thus rock has numerous subgenre including acoustic rock, alternative rock, and heavy metal. Jazz evolved into classic jazz, smooth jazz, and New Age jazz. A radio station might broadcast one or more subgenres to create its own format.

Radio station formats have been in a state of continuous evolution since the beginning of radio. To determine which records various stations were playing each week, record "charts" were created. The charts reflect national airplay and sales of albums and singles; like other industry publications, charts also reflect numerous radio formats. For example, *Billboard*, one of the oldest and best known trade publications, and a leader in weekly charts, includes charts for adult contemporary, dance, Latin, contemporary christian, rap and many other categories of music.

The chart position of a record is extremely important because radio station programmers read the various charts. Some smaller stations use the charts as a guide in deciding what to program for broadcast. If a record does not appear on the charts, it is unlikely that it will be added to many station playlists, that is, to the lists of songs stations play. The number of times a station plays a record during a day—called "the rotation"—is often affected by chart activity. The process is somewhat of a paradox: Charts are affected by airplay, and airplay is affected by charts!

## CHARTS IN THE HIGH-TECH AGE

Record charts were based on subjective data until technological innovations permitted more scientific data to be used. Airplay is now monitored by Broadcast Data Systems (BDS), a company that collects and distributes summaries of airplay activity around the country. Recordings released by most labels have a "fingerprint" that allows BDS to detect and identify the recordings as they are broadcast. The fingerprint is actually a digital watermark that are embedded into each song. The digital tones act like a high frequency bar code and are imperceptible to the human ear.

Each time a song is broadcast, a BDS reception tower in the region detects information from the watermark and transmits the title, station, and time of detection to a centralized computer. The data are summarized and the total number of "spins" calculated. Publications such as *Billboard, Cashbox, Gavin,* and *Radio and Records* use BDS data each week to assemble their charts.

The other data needed to create a chart include number of sales of albums and singles. A company called SoundScan collects sales data in much the same way that BDS captures broadcast data. Retail stores that report to SoundScan capture and transmit data from each record's bar code for summaries. After all sales data arrive at SoundScan, any subscriber—chart publisher, label, or retailer—can access sales summaries for all albums of artists on participating labels.

Before the advent of BDS and SoundScan, charts were created by sales and airplay estimates. Most publications relied on information from a small number of influential stations, called "reporting stations." The reports were, unfortunately, subject to manipulation. Occasionally, it was discovered that a radio station reported having added a record to its playlist, but actually the record had never been played. Probably someone at such a station was paid by record promoters to submit a false report. If a few key reporting stations submitted false reports, a record with little or no airplay could appear on a chart.

Although data for sales and spins are less susceptible to deception than in the past, the need to get airplay remains critical. Because sales figures are influenced by airplay, convincing radio program directors to add a record to their playlists, in heavy rotation, is the key to selling large numbers of albums. Airplay typically increases sales; sales and airplay get a record charted; and chart position helps a record get more airplay. Because airplay can result in millions of dollars of profit for labels, record promoters are tempted to do anything possible to convince radio stations to play their records.

## RECORD PROMOTERS

There are two general types of record promoters: (1) salaried employees who work in the promotion department of a label and (2) independent promoters hired by labels on a per-project basis. Both types of promoters have the same goal: to convince radio stations to add a record. After a station begins to play the record, promoters try to motivate the station to move the song into heavy rotation. Successful record promoters are like persistent sales executives: They must work with the "gatekeepers" at radio stations on a weekly basis in order to get their records played.

The gatekeepers at radio stations have shifted over the years. Until 1960 DJs were in charge of deciding which records to spin. After 1960 program directors began to assume more control over what was played on the air by creating playlists. Today, on-air talent—DJs—are expected to broadcast only the songs listed on the playlist.

The first step in promoting a record is sending a copy of the single and information about the artist to the program director. The term "single" dates back to seven inch 45-rpm vinyl records that were a popular record configuration from about 1950 to 1965. In those early years of rock 'n' roll, labels sold large numbers of singles as well as albums. Gradually, though, consumers began to ignore 45's in favor of twelve-inch 33-rpm long-playing vinyl records. However, even though singles were no longer a strong commercial configuration, labels continued using them for promoting a particular song to radio. The promotional single has evolved from the seven inch vinyl 45 to the CD single configuration.

Today, after an album is recorded, label executives decide which songs—called "cuts"—from an album will be released to radio as singles. The promotion staff is often involved in this decision-making process because they will have to "sell" each single to radio. Some genres of music, such as jazz, blues, and americana, are promoted to radio as a complete album. Promoters of these genres hope that stations will select album cuts to program. In contrast, mainstream mass market–oriented music, such as pop, country, and urban, is worked to radio in the form of singles. Releasing singles helps a label control the evolution of an album and, thus, build momentum in a choreographed manner. Labels will, on occasion, actually ask a Top 40 radio station to stop playing a particular album cut in favor of the single being worked at the time.

When working with radio stations, promoters must remember the goal of radio is to sell advertising airtime. In order to sell airtime, stations must attract and retain listeners. Advertising rates correlate closely to listenership. Therefore, the more listeners stations have, the more money they can charge for a thirty-second radio commercial. In addition, the more listeners a station has, the easier it is to find advertisers.

In order to convince a program director to play his act's record, a promoter must demonstrate that listeners will want to hear it. The last thing radio stations wants is for listeners to change to a different station because they dislike the song being broadcast. Promoters present data that they hope will show that people who like the song are just like the radio station's listeners. Remember the BDS data and the charts that reflect spins and sales? Promoters cull through those data and present them to program directors in hopes of proving that other radio stations around the country with similar audiences are spinning the record. Successful promoters sift through large quantities of data and extract statistics that favor the single they are working to radio.

Each week promoters will call stations to update program directors on chart activity of their label's records. If stations in the Midwest are playing a song often, because of listener requests, then the song's promoter tells stations in other regions that they need to "get on this record." Of course, when the other stations begin to spin the single, the promoter will tell program directors in the Midwest that they need to move the record into higher (more frequent) rotation.

Promoters face a great deal of competition: Key stations receive calls from promoters working over a hundred records each week (Hall and Taylor, 1998, p. 183). In order to sway program directors' opinions, promoters must offer more than just data. Promoters can do a number of things to influence radio station gatekeepers:

- Offer to bring the artist to the station for an interview or, in rare instances, acoustic on-the-air live performances;
- Arrange promotional tie-ins with the station such as ticket and album giveaways, whenever the artist performs a concert in the area;
- Pay for "contests" in which listeners can win free trips to hear the artist in concert in other cities; and
- Take program directors and DJs to dinner and entertainment events.

It should be noted that some people feel that such actions constitute a subtle form of bribery and should not be allowed. However, government regulations do not prevent labels from making such offerings to radio station personnel. In 1979 the FCC approved an administrative ruling that allowed "social exchanges between friends" (Krasnowski, 1997).

Most record promoters interpreted that FCC ruling to mean that radio station employees could accept gifts as long as they did not cross the line of cash payments for airplay. Cash payments in exchange for playing a record constitute "payola" and are not permissible. The question many people are asking is, What's the difference between luxurious trips and payola?

## THE EARLY DAYS OF PAYOLA

As defined by *Webster's New World Dictionary*, payola is "the paying of bribes for commercial advantage, as to a disc jocky for promoting a song unfairly." Although since the 1880s money has changed hands for promoting songs in the music industry, the name used to describe it is a more recent phenomenon. According to Kerry Segrave, author of *Payola in the Music Industry* (1994), the term "payola" first appeared in *Variety* magazine in 1938. At that time, payola referred to payments publishers made to performers, particularly big band leaders, to perform their songs. The term gradually began to mean payments to DJs by record promoters. "Payola" became a household word when it was used to describe House subcommittee hearings in the late 1950s. The word "payola" is still used to describe unscrupulous methods of gaining airplay.

Between 1950 and 1958 radio emerged as the primary force behind the success or failure of a record. As radio stations sprang up around the country, DJs became the gatekeepers that record promoters tried to court. A DJ spinning records for one of the top stations in a large city could stimulate the sales of a record by talking favorably about it and playing it often. DJs had much more discretion in deciding which records to program during their shift than have present day on-air personalities. DJs could also help give a record momentum by inviting the artist to visit the studio to chat on the air. Unfortunately, where there is power, there is the temptation to abuse it: Some of the more powerful DJs asked for payments from record promoters to play their records.

Some DJs asked for a modest amount, such as $5 per spin. Others preferred an agreed-upon amount, usually $50 to $100, per week. In exchange for the weekly payments, the labels could expect to have all their records played on air. Industry trade publications criticized both record labels and radio for what they perceived as the common practice of payola. When asked about payola, label spokespersons hypothesized that a few greedy DJs asked for money, but their promotion staff members never gave in to the demands. Knee-jerk reactions from radio executives dodged responsibility. If payola was such a rare occurrence, why was everyone talking about it?

DJs became celebrities during this era of radio expansion. Some popular DJs made heretofore unheard of amounts of money. Howard Miller was an influential DJ at WBBK in Chicago who earned a reported $350,000 from all his on- and off-air activities in 1957 (*Time*, 1957). Not only was he a highly paid radio personality but he also hosted a television show and was in constant demand for personal appearances at "sock hops." In fact, he was so popular that he received 1,200 fan letters a week (Seagrave, 1994). Such success increased government investigators' suspicion that payola contributed to the bountiful incomes of DJs.

As thousands of DJs were dropping needles on records in November 1959, state and federal investigations into alleged payola in the music industry began to take shape. The investigation that sent shockwaves through the industry was the House Special Subcommittee on Legislative Oversight's ongoing scrutiny of all entertainment. The special subcommittee's first round of media attention surrounded hearings into television game shows like *The $64,000 Question*, which was found to be fixed. The subcommittee, propelled by the success of the game show investigation, went after payola with zealous conviction.

The House Special Subcommittee began its investigation of payola by gathering information from field investigations. The committee sent investigators to several different cities to take testimony from radio and label employees. After finding enough evidence to support formal hearings in Washington, the subcommittee began to call high-profile figures to testify. On April 29, 1960, the world's most famous DJ, Dick Clark, felt the heat of investigators' lights when he was called to give testimony. Although Dick Clark was able to use his charm and composure to deflect most questions, the congressional panel revealed that Clark had a proprietary interest in thirteen record labels and publishing companies (U.S. House of Representatives, 1960). Some members of the House panel tried to prove that Clark gave favorable treatment to records released on labels in which he had a financial interest. Clark's response to questions about his financial holdings outside radio was quite convincing: "I make a little bit of money, where am I going to invest it? I don't know anything about the hot dog business; I don't know anything about the steel business. The thing I know about is the music business. Why shouldn't I invest in the music business?" (Jackson, 1997, p. 157).

Even before the House Special Subcommittee could issue a statement about its findings, information was leaked to the press. In 1957 *Newsweek* exposed some of the subcommittee's findings in an article that cited the following abuses discovered during the investigation:

- Radio station employees accepted bribes from artists in exchange for live on-air appearances;

- Cash payments were made to DJs and other radio station employees for playing specific records;

- DJs and other station employees owned part of record labels and publishing companies whose records were played on the station; and

- Radio stations whose parent companies also owned a record label favored records released by the "kindred" label (*Newsweek*, 1957).

Although the shady activities described above were disturbing to most citizens, even more upsetting was the realization that such things weren't really against the law! Prosecutors hoping to punish persons who engaged in payola activities could rely only on state anti-bribery laws. Beyond prosecution on anti-bribery laws in a few states, the only sanctions that could be meted out were firing by the employer (radio station or record label) or revocation of a broadcaster's license by the FCC. Contrary to popular belief, at the time of the first payola hearings there were no laws that specifically made payola a crime.

The payola investigations had, up to that point, created as many questions as they had answered. It seemed as if "black-oriented"—rhythm and blues and rock 'n' roll—radio stations and labels were treated differently than mainstream pop radio and labels. The major labels, which were more pop-oriented than rhythm and blues or rock 'n' roll, did not seem to endure the close scrutiny endured by the independent labels, especially the successful R&B specialty labels. Was there a racial motivation behind the subcommittee investigations, or was it merely that throughout the investigations "big business" was treated better than small entrepreneurs?

The recording industry in the late 1950s was still racially divided. Some African American record promoters believed white politicians disliked rhythm and blues and "lawmakers figured that nobody could want to hear music that repulsive, so radio stations must be playing it only because they were paid to" (Barnes, 1993). It seemed that independent promoters who worked with black music were interrogated much more often and in greater depth than promotional staff employees of major labels.

Another question troubling some broadcasters was whether members of the subcommittee were merely attempting to create stronger public images to further their political careers or were really concerned about DJs being paid to spin a record? It should be noted that each member of the subcommittee was up for congressional re-election in the fall of the hearings and each was re-elected. As Dick Clark cynically observed, officials involved in the hearings grilled him in public and asked for his autograph in private. "And on yet another occasion, the wives and children of six of the congressmen on the panel attended Clark's Saturday night show in New York" (Jackson, 1997, p. 187). The most embarrassing event to taint the governmental image was the discovery that John Doefer, head of the FCC during the payola hearings, had vacationed on a broadcaster's yacht. As a result of his poor judgment, Doefer was asked to resign (Electronic Media, 1992).

## GOVERNMENTAL RESPONSE TO PAYOLA

After the dust settled from the House Special Subcommittee investigations, Congress passed the first payola law in 1960. If the hearings hadn't given the impression that lawmakers thought payola was a simple nuisance, the 1960 payola statute did. The law made payola a misdemeanor offense with a maximum fine of $10,000 and one year in prison. Section 507 of the Communications Act prohibits anyone from offering or accepting payments in exchange for programming requested music without the knowledge of the station management or owner. Section 317 of the act requires that stations inform listeners if the station has been paid to air any particular programming (*Entertainment Law Reporter*, 1988). As previously mentioned, the FCC weakened the law in 1979 by issuing an explanation of what constituted payola. The 1979 directive explained that "social exchanges between friends are not payola" in the eyes of the FCC (Dannen, 1990).

Amazing as it may sound, it is not illegal for a radio station to accept money or gifts for playing a label's records if the station informs its listeners of the arrangement! An announcement as simple as "Promotional support for this broadcast was paid for by XYZ Records" would be all that is necessary to take money from a label to spin the label's records. To further evade legal repercussions for payola, radio station personnel could accept gifts, as opposed to cash, from promoters.

Although payola laws did not seem to present a big threat to radio stations, a tremendous amount of self-policing occurred in the post-1960 radio broadcasting industry. Most decision-making power regarding which records are broadcast moved from DJs to program directors after 1960. The theory was that it is easier for station management to keep an eye on one program director than on a dozen disc jockeys. From the standpoint of record promoters, it is necessary to get cozy with only one program director instead of with several DJs.

While radio was attempting to polish its tarnished image, record labels mimicked the efforts. Labels attempted to distance themselves from the promotion process by hiring independent promoters to work records to radio. This logic raised a few eyebrows because the payola hearings had given lawmakers the impression that independent promoters were more likely to engage in payola than were major label in-house promotion staffers. Major labels felt that they would be insulated from any criticism if they used independent promoters. If allegations of wrongdoing were to surface, label heads could quickly declare their disapproval of an independent promoter's activities and vow not to hire that promoter for any future projects.

Major labels operated quietly behind independent promoters, spending millions to promote records, until a string of events lead to another industry-wide payola scandal. In 1984 the House Oversight and Investigations Subcommittee conducted an investigation into rumors about independent promoters' activities. After reviewing information from dozens of interviews with radio and label employees, RIAA representatives, and others, the subcommittee chair, John Dingell, decided that no public hearings would be forthcoming (Seagrave, 1994). Although the House decided against convening a formal hearing to investigate payola in the 1980s, media were reminded that payola remained a topic of discussion on Capitol Hill.

On February 24, 1986, *NBC Nightly News* broadcast the first of a two-part investigative report on independent promoters. The investigative reporters alleged that a handful of independent promoters had formed ties to organized crime figures and engaged in payola. The report alleged that well-known recording industry insiders Joseph Isgro and Fred DiSipio met with members of the Gambino Mafia family in 1986. Joe Isgro, a West Coast independent promoter, and DiSipio, an East Coast independent promoter, were prominent and successful "network" promoters (Knoedelseder, 1993). A loosely organized group of independent promoters from around the country who referred to themselves as "the network" was suddenly of interest to payola investigators and the media.

On February 27, 1986, a New York federal grand jury sent a subpoena to the RIAA asking for information about major labels' relationships with independent promoters. RIAA chairman Stan Gortikov quickly issued a statement that denied any knowlege of companies or individuals engaged in any illegal activity. His statement further defended the honor of major labels by lamenting, "Such broad and unspecific charges unfairly taint the innocent" (Dannen, 1990). As quickly as their trade association released the statement alluding to their innocence, the major labels issued a statement that they would sever ties with independent promoters (Goldstein, 1986). If they had no knowledge of wrongdoing, why did the major labels scramble to disassociate themselves from the independent promoters? Was it merely a public relations tactic, or did they know what the independent promoters were up to?

As major labels severed relationships with independent promoters, many promoters feared they would soon be out of business. Some independent promoters were understandably bitter and blamed a few dishonest promoters for the chaos. Promoter Cliff Gorov gave his perspective on the situation: "The record companies seem to be lumping us all together based on allegations against a very few. They know who the bad guys are, so I can't understand why they aren't differentiating among us" (Knoedelseder, 1986).

Joe Isgro, the independent promoter who was the focus of NBC's investigative report, quickly shifted from his defensive posture and went on the offensive. Isgro brought legal action against the RIAA and several major labels that had fired him and another independent promoter. He claimed that the major labels and the RIAA had conspired to push the independent promoters out of the business. Isgro's $25 million lawsuit against the RIAA and some of the major labels was dismissed in U.S. District Court in December 1988 (*Entertainment Law Reporter*, 1988). However, Isgro had already made out-of-court settlements with Capitol Records, Motown, Polygram, Chrysalis, RCA Records, Arista Records, and A&M Records. Once again the actions of the major labels raises suspicion. If Isgro's claim of conspiracy against his independent promotion company had no real merit, then why would the labels settle out of court? Were they worried that Isgro would go public with information that could be damaging to the labels?

While Joseph Isgro was waging his legal battle in Los Angeles against the major labels, another firestorm developed in northern California. In January 1988 a San Mateo, California, attorney, Dennis DiRiccio, was charged with helping Ralph and Valerie Tashjian evade paying income taxes by setting up a fraudulent partnership (Delugach, 1988). As investigators scrutinized the Tashjians' business records, they realized that Mr. Tashjian was an independent record promoter who had worked with Joe Isgro. As evidence fell into place, Tashjian was charged with tax evasion, providing false records to a grand jury, and making payola payments of cash and cocaine to radio executives (Delugach, 1988).

Tashjian pleaded guilty to one payola charge and to obstruction of justice. He was sentenced in December 1989 to sixty days in a halfway house and fined $100,000 by a U.S. District Court judge in Los Angeles. In exchange for his light punishment, Tashjian agreed to help prosecutors build a case against his former employer, Joe Isgro. Tashjian's detailed testimony about the process of payola and "drugola" (giving drugs rather than money for airplay) provided a shocking insight into the dark side of the recording industry (Rohter, 1990a).

On November 30, 1989, a few months after Tashjian negotiated his plea bargain in exchange for inside information, Joe Isgro was indicted on fifty-seven counts, including racketeering and payola, in U.S. District Court (Morris, 1995). Tashjian told the court that while working for Isgro, he provided money and cocaine to radio programmers to play records Isgro was promoting. Tashjian claimed to have been a middle-man between Isgro and radio executives (Rohter, 1990b). During the trial Isgro's former bodyguard, David Michael Smith, testified that he also made payola payments for Isgro. Four executives from radio stations stated in court that Ralph Tashjian gave them thousands of dollars in exchange for playing records for Isgro.

The Isgro trial was viewed as an important milestone in the pursuit of payola violations. It was so important that the U.S. Department of Justice and the Los Angeles Organized Crime Task Force worked together to prosecute Isgro. But much to the dismay of federal and state prosecutors, Judge James M. Ideman dismissed all charges against Isgro on September 4, 1990. To make matters worse for the prosecution, Ideman dismissed the charges "with prejudice" and criticized the manner in which prosecutors handled the case (Rohter, 1990b). Ideman believed that federal prosecutors had violated rules of evidence by withholding a key document from the defense lawyers and the grand jury.

After an extended appeals process, the U.S. Supreme Court ruled on March 22, 1993, that even though the prosecuting attorney's conduct was improper, the indictment should not have been dismissed (*United States v. Isgro et al.*, U.S. Sup. Ct., No. 92-1176). Following years of delays caused by the Justice Department, U.S. District Court judge Consuelo B. Marshall dismissed the case on March 25, 1996, because the prosecution had violated Isgro's right to a "speedy trial." After seven years and over $10 million in taxpayers' money, the case against Isgro was dead (Philips, 1996).

Where are the players in the case that had been called the "biggest payola trial in history" now? Two of the Justice Department prosecuting attorneys were fired for their mishandling of the case (Sandler, 1996). Tashjian presented his testimony against Isgro and served his modest penance. All charges against Valerie Tashjian were dropped. Ten years after first being indicted for payola and racketeering, Joseph Isgro became president of Private I Records, a label distributed by MCA/Universal label group (Mitchell, 1999). He remained under the scrutiny of the FBI, and on April 3, 2000, Joseph Isgro was arraigned on federal charges of loan-sharking and extortion. FBI agents continue to believe Isgro is "a soldier in New York's Gambino crime family" even though his offices are in Beverly Hills, California.

## PAYOLA AND THE NEW MILLENNIUM

Forty years after the first House Special Subcommittee hearings motivated Congress to enact laws regulating pay for play, not one person has served a jail term for payola. However, changes in the business environment of broadcasting during the 1990s had a pervasive effect on alleged payola activities. The Telecommunications Act, signed into law in 1996, deregulated the broadcasting industry. Owners of radio stations were no longer limited to a handful of radio stations. In the first six

Independent record promoter Joseph Isgro leaves U.S. District Court in Los Angeles after a federal judge, citing "outrageous conduct" by the Justice Department, dismissed all charges against Isgro. Isgro was being tried on fifty-seven counts of payola, racketeering, and other charges alleging he had made cash and cocaine payments to radio stations in California and Texas in return for airplay of specified songs. (AP/Wide World Photos)

months of 1996, more than two hundred radio stations changed hands each week (Phillips, 1996). Large companies bought independent radio stations, and consolidation swept through the broadcasting industry as the millennium came to a close.

One goal of multistation broadcasting companies was to achieve greater efficiencies in staffing and operations. Instead of paying employees to create playlists, radio groups began to outsource their programming needs to consultants. Another way radio stations enhanced their bottom lines was to develop income from revenue sources other than advertising. Because pay-for-play is not illegal if done according to FCC guidelines—the money must come to the station, rather than to individuals, and listeners must be informed that the broadcast is paid for by the label—radio station groups have begun to seek record labels' money openly.

Capitol Record's Nashville division upset many of its competitors in 1998 when it announced a plan to spend $500,000 for guaranteed "back announcing," when the DJ tells listeners the name of the song and the artist immediately after a song has been played on the air. Capitol called it their "endcap" program for radio. Record labels have known for years that back-announcing a record helps generate record sales. Using the same logic, CBS Radio created a special offer directed at country divisions of record labels called "Sudden Impact." The CBS packages were offered to labels for $14,700 to $19,600 depending on the frequency of the announcements (Taylor, 1998). Whereas some label executives felt that the back-announcing fees were nothing more than payola dressed in a business suit, others were glad that pay-for-play was finally out in the open.

Radio continues to evolve, and its future looks exciting. The FCC is listening to arguments for and against low-power radio stations, which could provide the opportunity for thousands of new niche-oriented stations to emerge in the early 2000s. Satellite car radios should hit the store shelves in 2001 and will likely undermine traditional radio stations' prime advertising times: morning drive time and afternoon drive time for commuters. Satellite radios will have dozens of channel options, much like cable television, without the interruption of commercials. The satellite radio station providers will make their revenue from monthly fees and the specialized radio necessary to receive the signals bounced off of satellites. Obviously, traditional broadcast radio stations will have to adjust to the new business environment.

The radio permutation that might provide the most competition to traditional broadcasting companies will come from webcast radio programs. Webcasts can merge elements of live concerts, music videos, and traditional radio in one exciting medium. The possibilities seem endless and are evolving quickly. Cynics might ask, however, "How will unscrupulous record promoters use their power and money to influence web radio in the future?" The House Telecommunications Subcommittee seems to ask the same question. A two-year oversight plan begun in 1999 includes a "new look into payola" (*Communications Daily*, 1999a).

## TOPICS FOR DISCUSSION

1. Do you think the federal government should create stronger laws to prohibit payola or any form of pay-for-play? Or should the government eliminate all existing laws and regulations in order to create an open market to gain airplay any way possible?

2. Do you agree with those who argue that payola investigations tended to target independent promoters? Do you find any validity in the theory that African American promoters were investigated more rigorously than their white counterparts?

3. What alternative forms of promotion, other than radio, do you think record companies can use today? Do you think that new ways to promote records will emerge in the future?

4. Charts utilize data from radio broadcasts and retail sales of records to determine rankings of songs and albums. Do you think that this is a fair system for ranking records? What are others ways charts could be created?

5. Record label executives accuse radio of not playing "good" songs. Radio programmers argue that labels are not producing "good" songs. Do you think that good music is not being broadcast on radio? If so, who do you think is most responsible: radio or record labels?

## REFERENCES AND RESOURCES

### Correspondence and Interviews

Anton, Douglas C. (1999, December 29). Anton is an entertainment attorney who practices on the East Coast. He is a former artist manager.

### Books

Cagle, Gerry (1989). *Payola!* New York Branden Publishing Co. (An in-depth look at payola before 1990.)

Dannen, Fredric (1990). *Hit Men: Power Brokers and Fast Money Inside the Music Business*. New York: Times Books, a division of Random House. (This book shocked the industry by revealing the relationship between organized crime figures and the record business. It also exposed the working relationships between label executives and independent promoters.)

Hall, Charles W., and Frederick J. Taylor (1996, 1998). *Marketing in the Music Industry*, 2nd edition. Needham Heights, MA: Simon & Schuster. (Chapter 12 presents an overview of how record companies solicit radio airplay.

Hall calls on his decades of experience as a label executive throughout this unique book.)

Haring, Bruce (1996). *Off the Charts: Ruthless Days and Reckless Nights Inside the Music Industry*. New York: Birch Lane Press/Carol Publishing Group. (A vivid portrayal of the warlike tactics used by record label executives. Haring, an entertainment journalist, interviewed over fifty music industry executives while preparing this exposé.)

Jackson, John A. (1997). *American Bandstand: Dick Clark and the Making of a Rock 'n' Roll Empire*. New York: Oxford University Press. (An interesting biography of Dick Clark that includes a discussion of payola hearings.)

Knoedelseder, William K., Jr. (1993). *Stiffed: A True Story of MCA, the Music Business, and the Mafia*. New York: HarperCollins. (A controversial book by a West Coast journalist that revealed the relationships between record promoters, major labels, radio stations, and Ronald Reagan.)

Rapaport, Diane Sward (1999). *How to Make and Sell Your Own Recording*, rev. 5th ed. Jerome, AZ: Jerome Headlands Press/Prentice Hall. (Rapaport explains the various ways an independent label or artist can promote a record.)

Seagrave, Kerry (1994). *Payola in the Music Business: A History, 1880–1991*. Jefferson, NC: McFarland and Company. (Seagrave's well-researched book chronicles the use of payola in the music industry from its inception.)

U.S. House of Representatives (1960). *Responsibilities in Broadcasting Licensees and Station Personnel, 1960*. Washington, D.C.: Government Printing Office. (This publication contains a fascinating diagram—an organizational chart—that shows thirteen labels and publishing companies in which Dick Clark had a proprietary interest during the House Special Subcommittee investigations into payola.)

## Magazines, Journals, and Newspapers

Barnes, Terry (1993, June 12). Dave Clark's Doorman. . . . *Billboard*, Rhythm and Blues, Spotlight, p. R16. (A brief overview of record promotion from the early days of rock 'n' roll.)

*Communications Daily* (1989, December 13). Record Promoter Ralph Tashijian. . . . (A brief report of sentencing for Tashijian's payola conviction.)

*Communications Daily* (1999a, February 12). Tauzin Cool to Debate on Open Access Consideration. Section: Today's News. (House Telecommunication Chairman Tauzin told reporters that his committee was taking another look at payola.)

*Communications Daily* (1999b, July 27). Latin Music Record Company Fonovisa. . . . (A very brief news item about an example of alleged corruption in the Latin music industry.)

Delugach, Al (1988, February 26). Promoter, Wife Are Indicted in Probe of Payola. *Los Angeles Times*, p. 1.

*Electronic Media* (1992, June 15). Ex-FCC Chief John Doerfer dead at 87. p. 6.

*Entertainment Law Reporter* (1988, August). Federal Communications Commission Issues "Warning" to Broadcasters Concerning "Payola." Section: Washington Monitor, vol. 10, no. 3. (A brief description of the FCC regulations concerning payola.)

*Entertainment Litigation Reporter* (1993, April 27). *United States v. Isgro et al.*, U.S. Sup. Ct., no. 92-1176. (The U.S. Supreme Court upheld the appeal's court decision to reinstate charges against independent record promoters.)

*Forbes* (1986, October 27). Richard Wagstaff Clark in "The Richest People in America, The Forbes Four Hundred, Under $200 Million," p. 229. (A brief biography of millionaire Dick Clark, who made the list of wealthiest people in the world.)

Gabe, Steven J. (1991). Use of RICO in Entertainment Suits. *Entertainment Law and Finance* 7 no. 7, p. 3. (An overview of how the Racketeer Influenced and Corrupt Organizations Act can be used against music industry activities such as payola.)

Goldstein, Patrick (1986, March 9). Pop Eye: CBS Severs Ties to Private I Label. *Los Angeles Times*, p. 82.

Goodale, Gloria, and Daniel B. Wood (2000, January 18). Static over Stealth TV Messages. *Christian Science Monitor*, USA, p. 1. (The authors analyze a new federal policy that rewards television show producers for incorporating anti-drug messages into their scripts. The practice is compared to payola in radio.)

Hilburn, Robert, and Chuck Philips (1997, October 12). What's Wrong with the Record Industry (and How to Fix It). *Los Angeles Times*, Sunday Calendar.

Hudis, Mark (1996, January 15). Pay-for-Play Goes Legit; Radio Infomercials. *Mediaweek* 6, no. 3, p. 14. (A company called Fair Air tried to circumvent payola laws by acting as a go-between for radio stations and record labels.)

James, Noah (1985, July 14). We Do What the Networks Want. *New York Times*, sec. 2, p. 21, col. 1, Arts and Leisure Desk. (A description of the empire that Dick Clark has built in television programming.)

Knoedelseder, William K., Jr. (1986, March 10). *Los Angeles Times*, Business, part 4, p. 1, col. 5, Financial Desk. (The author describes the reaction of independent record promoters to *NBC Nightly News'* expose of corrupt promoters.)

Krasnowski, Matt (1997, May 29). It's Not Your Father's Payola: Undue Influence in Radio Still Exists but It's All Legal. *Copley News Service*. (A revealing article about contests and gifts that promoters give radio stations, yet none of these activities are considered "payola.")

*Los Angeles Times* (1996, January 3). Bimbos' Nightclub in San Francisco Was Packed. . . . p. 1, Metro Desk. (A look at how EMI Music promoted a record by singer D'Angelo.)

Mitchell, Gail (1999, October 2). The Rhythm and the Blues. . . . *Billboard*, R&B. (A brief description of rap label Raw Deal Records' agreement to be distributed by Joe Isgro's label, Private I/Universal Records.)

Morris, Chris (1994, January 8). Judge's Ruling Hinders Fed's Case vs. Isgro. *Billboard*, Artists and Music, p. 12. (A federal judge refused to allow a key witness to testify for the prosecution.)

Morris, Chris (1995, January 28). Isgro Faces Possibility of New Trial. *Billboard*. (An update on the Isgro payola prosecution procedures.)

*Nashville Tennessean* (1999, March 21). Investigation Making Waves with Radio Station Airplay, p. E1. (An article that describes the FCC investigation into radio promotional deals between radio chains and labels.)

*Newsweek* (1957, April 1). Songs of Sixpence. *Newsweek*, p. 104. (Some testimony from the Senate hearings into payola were reported in this article.)

Patterson, Jim (1999, February 24). Are the Good Times Over for Country Music Business? *Associated Press Wire Service*. (Patterson presents statistics that show how sales have declined for country music. He also quotes top industry executive Joe Galante regarding the impact of radio on sales of country records.)

Philips, Chuck (1993, June 13). How Things Really Stack Up at the Capitol Records Tower. . . . *Los Angeles Times*, Calendar, p. 9, Calendar Desk. (Journalist Chuck Philips describes the staff changes at Capitol Records and an employee named Joe Isgro.)

Philips, Chuck (1996, March 26). Judge Dismisses Payola Charges against Record Promoter Isgro. *Los Angeles Times*, Business, p. D1, Financial Desk. (Philips describes the end of the Justice Department's seven-year prosecution of Joseph Isgro.)

Phillips, Beau (1996, July 27). Labels Need New Strategies for Radio. *Billboard*. (An excellent overview of techniques record promoters used at the time for gaining airplay.)

Rohter, Larry (1990a, August 25). At Payola Trial, Primer on Forms and Mechanics. *New York Times*, sec. 1, p. 11, col. 3, Cultural Desk. (A description of a major payola trial in U.S. District Court.)

Rohter, Larry (1990b, September 5). Payola Case Dismissed. *New York Times*, p. C15, col. 4, Cultural Desk. (A continuation of Rohter's previous article about the Joseph Isgro payola and racketeering trial.)

Sandler, Adam (1996, March 27). Isgro Charges Dismissed.

Taylor, Chuck (1998, May 9). Paid Play Changing Biz Landscape. *Billboard*, p. 1, Cover Story. (Taylor describes a new way of buying radio airplay that many label executives found disturbing. It draws attention to the power of radio programmers who supply playlists and programs to large numbers of radio stations throughout the country.)

*Time* (1957, April 29). What Makes Howard Spin? *Time* magazine, p. 50. (Howard Miller was one of the most successful DJs at the time this feature article was written.)

## Organizations to Contact

National Association of Broadcasters (NAB)
1771 N Street, NW
Washington, DC 20036
Phone: (202) 429-5300
web: www.nab.org
The National Association of Broadcasters (NAB) provides services and information to radio and television stations and employees. The NAB website provides some extremely helpful information such as statistics about radio stations in the United States.

## Web Sites

www.billboard.com/charts
Billboard Magazine Charts
Billboard creates charts that list the top albums and singles based on airplay and sales. This site also offers articles about artists and business
issues in the industry.

www.cmj.com
College Music Journal/CMJ
CMJ is directed toward college-aged readers. It has the first ever "Internet
Broadcast Chart" for web radio. CMJ sponsors the annual New Music
Seminar to showcase cutting edge alternative bands.

www.gavin.com
The Gavin Report
The "Gavin" also has charts, but they have some categories that other trade
publications do not have, such as americana, smooth jazz, and alternative
adult album formats.

www.rronline.com/homepm.asp
Radio and Records
Radio and Records (R&R) has current information about radio programming. Many radio executives use R&R as a "tip sheet" to alert them to
records that they should be playing.

# 12

# Turn Up the Volume: Music and Hearing Loss

*Note: This chapter is of particular interest to Richard Barnet, one of the coauthors of this book, because he suffers from noise-induced hearing loss. His hearing loss is most likely due to years of exposure to music—classical, rock, and jazz—as both a professional performer and an audience member.*

It has been estimated that over 30 million Americans work in environments that have hazardously high noise levels. Ten million people have had to adjust their lives because of noise-induced hearing loss (NIHL) (National Institute on Deafness and Other Communication Disorders, 1999). Most forms of hearing loss, unlike broken bones or other types of occupational injuries, are irreversible. Ironically, NIHL can usually be prevented if the victim takes simple and inexpensive measures. The music industry is not immune to NIHL. In fact, potential hearing loss as a result of a loud environment exists for music audiences as well as for persons who create the music. Hazardous noise levels can occur at concerts, in DJ or disco clubs, through personal cassette headphones, or in other music listening environments. In many respects consumers of recorded music are more likely to be victims of NIHL than are the performers who create the music.

Audiologists—medical practitioners who specialize in hearing disorders—feared that the evolution of amplified rock music would be accompanied by a generation of listeners with a higher incidence of NIHL than previous generations. Those fears have been confirmed by an observed increase in high frequency hearing loss among people who listened to rock music beginning in the 1960s and continue to listen to amplified music as mature adults (Jekel, 1996). This generation, labeled "baby boomers," might more accurately be described as "ear blasters," the first generation to experience widespread self-induced loss of hearing from music-listening habits.

A more recent generation, whose members went through high school and college in the 1980s, is nicknamed the "Walkman generation" by NIHL legal researcher and author Eric Daniel Johnson. Individuals in this group have experienced even greater levels of NIHL than their parents. Personal listening devices like the Sony Walkman were designed to give excellent reproduction of music in a portable device. The portability of cassette and CD listening devices permitted youths to wear headsets and hear music in school, at work, and while exercising. As a result, teenagers began to listen to their music for longer periods of time. Now researchers are asking, Does extended listening on portable cassette headphones cause hearing loss?

## THE NATURE OF SOUND

Sound is easy for most people to perceive physically, but it is difficult to explain in nonscientific terms. Sound is the movement of a fluid in the form of waves. A fluid can be either a gas or liquid, but in human listening environments, air is the vibrating fluid. A series of waves, called "vibrations," can be perceived either biochemically or eletroacoustically (Chasin, 1996). The rate at which the vibrations occur is "frequency." In music, frequency is referred to as "pitch." We usually describe frequency in qualitative terms such as high or low, but audiology professionals describe it in terms of hertz (Hz). Humans can hear as low as 20 Hz and as high as 20,000 Hz. Frequency is the first and most critical factor affecting hearing loss from music because higher frequencies tend to cause more damage to hearing than do lower frequencies.

It takes energy to make air move, so the level of energy causing a sound helps define the sound. The amplitude of a sound describes the degree to which vibrations displace molecules of the fluid they are moving. Musicians and audiences use the term "volume" to describe amplitude. Amplitude is the second critical factor affecting hearing loss. The greater the amplitude, or higher the volume, the more likely it is that one will experience damage to the hearing mechanism. Scientists measure amplitude on a scale using units called decibels. A decibel rating, commonly seen abbreviated as dB, generally ranges from zero to 140 dB in our environment.

The third element of sound that is crucial to the diagnosis and prevention of NIHL is the duration of sound. If we listened only to one frequency at a fixed volume for a measurable duration, the potential for hearing loss would be fairly easy to estimate. Unfortunately, in real-life situations these three elements vary almost constantly. Music is made up of a combination of many frequencies that occur in combination for

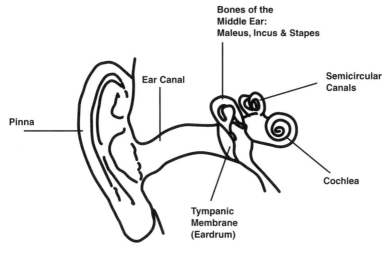

Figure 12.1. Diagram of the outer, middle and inner ear. (This diagram is for illustration purposes only and is not an exact representation of the human body. This information should not be used for diagnoses or treatment of any medical condition. If a medical condition exists, a licensed physician should be consulted.)

various lengths of time. That way, melody, harmony, rhythm, form, and texture can be used to create everything from simple songs to complex orchestral compositions.

## HOW HUMANS HEAR

Humans perceive sound vibrations through ears that, with the aid of an amazing three-stage mechanism, convert air pressure into electrical signals that travel to the brain through the nervous system. Each human ear functions as three distinctly different components: The outer ear, the middle ear, and the inner ear (see Figure 12.1). The outer ear consists of the pinna, the skin, and cartilage flaps we refer to as ears. The pinna capture the vibrating air of sounds and funnel it into a tube called the ear canal. Note that both the pinna and ear canal are exposed to the air. The outer ear ends at the tympanic membrane, or as it is commonly known, the eardrum.

The inner ear is an air-filled cavity, with a mucous-coated lining, that transmits vibrations from the air-filled outer ear to the fluid-filled inner ear. Sound waves flow through the ear canal and strike the thin eardrum. The eardrum resonates inward, but two delicate muscles of the middle ear tighten to restrict excessively strong (i.e., loud) sound vibrations if necessary. These two muscles serve to protect the inner ear from too much sound. Like most muscles, however, they cannot remain flexed very long. If the loud sound persists for too long, the muscles become fatigued, relax, and allow excessive levels of sound into the inner ear (Kavaler, 1978, p. 12). This is an important factor in prevention of NIHL: The damage that loud sounds do is relative to the length of time the ears are exposed to the sounds.

Three tiny bones in the middle ear—the hammer, anvil and stirrup—transmit vibrations from the eardrum to the inner ear. The process of translating vibrating air to corresponding vibrations of a liquid, as found in the inner ear, is not a simple process. Anyone who has ever been under water and tried to hear people talking on the surface knows that sound is lost when communicating from air to water. To be precise, about 99 percent of a sound's energy is lost through an air-to-water barrier (Chasin, 1996, p. 11). One can, therefore, appreciate the complexity of the middle ear: It must protect the inner ear from sudden bursts of loud sounds yet accurately translate sounds as subtle as articulated speech into vibrations of a liquid medium.

If the inner ear were a fabricated listening device, it would probably receive numerous design awards for the clever way in which it transforms motion into electrical impulses. The inner ear contains three sections: the semicircular canals, the vestibule, and the cochlea. The first two sections, the semicircular canals and the vestibule, help humans maintain balance and equilibrium (Bess and Humes, 1990). Infections of, or damage to, these two parts of the ear can cause a person to have vertigo and trouble with balance.

The cochlea, a coiled array of tissues about the size of a pencil eraser, contains the delicate hairlike receptor cells that are the essence of hearing. Its coiled shape makes it resemble a snail crawling vertically up a wall. Inside the cochlea is a long, thin membrane on which the organ of Corti, the sensory mechanism of hearing, is located (Bess and Humes, 1990). The organ of Corti contains thousands of hairlike sensory receptor cells, or "hair cells." At the end of each of these hair cells is a nerve ending that translates vibrations into electronic nerve impulses and transmits the impulses to the brain through the auditory nerve.

Like a piano or organ keyboard, the hair cells are arranged in order from the highest perceived frequency to the lowest. Each hair cell is activated by a different frequency and, in that way, allows us to distinguish lower sounds from higher sounds. The hair cells also determine the amplitude, or loudness, of the sounds entering the ear. The information for many frequencies, all at different amplitudes, is transmitted to the brain, where it is interpreted. Only the brain can interpret the massive amount of aural data coming from the cochlea and make subjective judgments such as whether the sounds are pleasant or irritating.

## SOUNDS THAT DAMAGE HEARING

As one might assume, precise measurement of sound levels that might contribute to hearing loss is a complex scientific process. Fortunately, scientists have developed ways of estimating sound levels and their potential dangers. An increasing amount of research into NIHL has focused on noisy environments and ways to prevent damage from extended exposure to music. Although amplified music has been the subject of much of the research, a fairly substantial number of scientific investigations have been conducted using classical music environments.

Because many delicate hair cells and corresponding nerve endings are necessary to distinguish different frequencies, humans' ability to hear is fragile. Nerve cells can suffer damage after being exposed to loud sounds for extended periods of time. Like other nerve cells in the body, those of the ear cannot be restored after they have been destroyed. Hearing loss from loud sounds, such as music, is usually permanent and irreversible (American Academy of Otolaryngology—Head and Neck Surgery, 1997).

Two common maladies can result from exposure to loud sounds: tinnitus and permanent hearing loss. Tinnitus, a ringing in the ears, is not well understood by medical practitioners. It is annoying to persons who suffer from it, and it often accompanies permanent hearing loss. Tinnitus can be attributed to a sudden short-term, extremely loud sound, such as a firecracker too close to one's ears, or exposure to moderately loud sounds for a long time. Short-term tinnitus is often observed in persons who have been exposed to the loud music of rock concerts. Because tinnitus is also often associated with a more debilitating hearing loss, the condition should be considered a warning sign. Whenever tinnitus persists for longer than a few hours, the individual should seek medical help to test for permanent damage.

The second type of damage one might experience after extended exposure to loud sounds is permanent hearing loss. Damage to inner-ear nerve cells reduces one's ability to perceive certain frequencies. The nerves that are stimulated by frequencies from 3,000 Hz to 6,000 Hz are the ones most often damaged by extended exposure to loud music. Hearing loss attributable to noise exposure characteristically damages perception at the 4,000 Hz (abbreviated 4 kHz) level the most. A loss in that frequency range is so characteristic of NIHL that it is referred to as a "4 k notch." The notch extends upward to 6 kHz and downward to 3 kHz for NIHL victims. On a graph of hearing level in decibels compared to a range of frequencies, the line drawn for someone with NIHL looks like one with a V-shaped notch cut into it around the 4 kHz range.

Audiologists test a person's hearing and graph the results on two

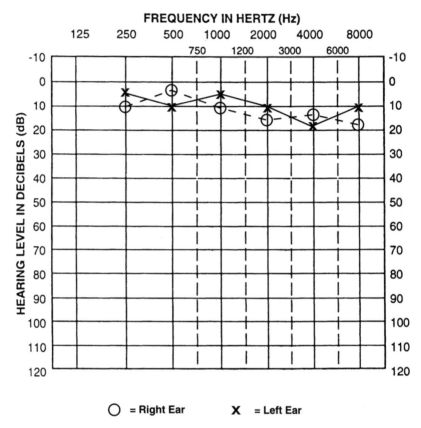

Figure 12.2. An audiogram for a person with normal hearing.

planes: frequency and level of perception in decibels. This testing and graphing methodology is called an "audiogram." Figure 12.2 is an audiogram of someone with normal hearing. Figure 12.3 is the audiogram of someone who has suffered hearing loss represented by a 4 k notch. Although humans can hear frequencies ranging from 20 Hz to 20,000 Hz, those frequencies critical to understanding speech of others range from 300 Hz to 4,000 Hz. Frequencies critical to speech recognition are in the NIHL notch range. Consonant sounds are usually more difficult for persons with NIHL to hear than are vowel sounds (Lollar, 1997). Therefore, persons who suffer from NIHL have difficulty recognizing exactly what other people are saying, even though they can "hear" all frequencies well, except those that affect consonants in speech. Persons with the 4 k notch are particularly frustrated when they are in crowds because clearly audible frequencies overwhelm their ability to discern notched frequencies. They hear many voices but cannot understand any of them.

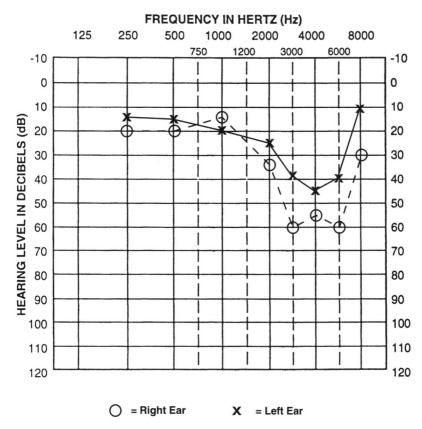

Figure 12.3. An audiogram for a person with noise-induced hearing loss due to music. Note the characteristic 4 k notch.

## DAMAGE TO HEARING

One out of every ten persons in the United States suffers from hearing loss or deafness (Maugh, 1998). Of those 28 million hearing-impaired people, a large number could have prevented their disability. It is likely that many of the young adults who suffer from NIHL sustained their hearing loss from listening to music at rock concerts, in loud clubs, or through personal listening devices such as the Sony Walkman. "Utilizing current knowledge about ear protection, NIHL is entirely preventable except in cases of accidental exposure" (Brookhouser, 1994).

When is music too loud? The federal government has gradually developed laws and regulatory procedures to help prevent hearing loss in workplace environments. In 1972 Congress enacted the Noise Control Act (42 U.S.C. @ 4901 [a] [1] [1988]). To help ensure that every American worker would be free of harmful noise levels at work, the federal government directed the Environmental Protection Agency to create data with which to assess workplace noise levels. In October 1974 the Occupational Safety and Health Administration (OSHA) began a review of the occupational noise exposure standards in place at the time.

The complexity of this issue is reflected in the length of time it took OSHA to accomplish its task. It wasn't until April 7, 1983—almost ten years—that the *Occupational Noise Exposure; Hearing Conservation Amendment; Final Rule*, known as the Hearing Conservation Act, finally went into effect (Occupational Safety and Health Administration, 1983). The act describes permissible exposure levels for employees. In general terms, it defines the maximum decibels a worker should be exposed to in an eight-hour day. Because amplitude typically varies in the workplace, OSHA adopted a system for estimating the average sound level. This system uses the expression dBA to indicated an estimated sound level based on its A-weighted system. For example, according to OSHA guidelines contained in the act, a person should not be exposed to 90 dBA longer than eight hours. If the noise level is measured at 95 dBA, the worker should not be exposed to it longer than four hours. Sound levels of 110 dBA—the level of some rock concerts—should not be endured for longer than thirty minutes.

Noise levels of 85 dBA and below are considered safe for human hearing. Levels above that may damage hearing. The following safe sound levels were developed and published by OSHA (29 CFR 1910.95, Table G-16):

| Sound Level | Allowable Time per Day |
| --- | --- |
| 90 dBA | 8 hours |
| 92 dBA | 6 hours |
| 95 dBA | 4 hours |
| 100 dBA | 2 hours |
| 110 dBA | 30 minutes |
| 115 dBA | 15 minutes |

It is noteworthy that the OSHA safe sound level guidelines are directed at employees and employers only. The Hearing Conservation Act does not pertain to leisure listening environments. Although employees working around loud music might have legal grounds for OSHA intervention, audience members at concerts are not protected by the act. Ironically, OSHA guidelines regulate the length of time factory workers should be exposed to the sounds emitted by factory equipment, but they do not restrict the amount of time that audience members are allowed to listen to music even though rock concerts reach levels at or above 120 dB (League for the Hard of Hearing, 1999).

## LISTENING TO LIVE MUSIC

Concerts that depend on amplified music in large venues such as arenas present potentially hazardous sound levels. Japanese researchers found examples of temporary hearing loss and tinnitus in audience members when they conducted hearing tests just prior to and after a rock concert. They also found a case of a nineteen-year-old boy who suffered from permanent hearing impairment in both ears after a loud rock concert (Tomioka, 1982). A British organization, the Royal National Institute for Deaf People, identified concerts that registered 150 dB, well beyond the safe listening threshold. Obviously, concerts with sound levels that high could damage audience members' hearing.

Concerts that present amplified music in large spaces are dangerous because the amount of power necessary to fill the room with an accurate representation of the music being created on stage varies by location. Clusters of loud speakers used at rock concerts must be arranged in an array that disperses the amplified sound to large portions of the audience seating area. Therefore, individuals sitting closest to the speaker cluster will receive more sound energy than those sitting farther away. When speakers are stacked on the floor or stage, there is more potential for overexposure to loud sounds because audience members often rush toward the stage in hopes of being close to the performers. Persons who stand in close proximity to speaker stacks for an hour or more during excessively loud concerts will, in all likelihood, suffer damage to their hearing.

Smaller venues, such as dance clubs, discos, or music bars probably give audience members the illusion that they need not fear NIHL because the amplifiers and speaker systems are much smaller than arena shows. That false sense of security has prompted several scientific investigations into small-venue sound levels. All studies of small dance-oriented clubs reviewed by this author revealed measurement of music at levels well above the safe 85 dB threshold (Murray, 1999; Babisch and Ising, 1994; Gunderson, Moline, and Catalano, 1997). More ominous is the realization that patrons of dance clubs often remain there for several hours, much longer than the duration of the typical rock concert. A trend toward "after hours" clubs—ones that stay open long after others close—increases the likelihood of club patrons' spending long periods of time in these loud environments.

Because OSHA noise standards apply only to employees in their work environments, new legislation is needed to address hearing loss attributable to leisure music listening. In 1991 the House of Representatives

created the Select Committee on Children, Youth and Families to investigate NIHL in children (O'Neill, 1991). Although researchers and audiologists explained that teenagers experience NIHL at twice the rate of
other age groups, no legislation was ever drafted. Attorney Eric Daniel
Johnson noted that the federal government has done little to prevent
high nonoccupational-related sound levels. Therefore, Johnson proposed
legislation aimed at preventing NIHL in nonworkplace environments
(Johnson, 1993). He proposed two approaches to the problem: posting of
warning signs at concerts and establishing maximum decibel levels.

Federal legislation requiring posted warnings and decibel ceilings
would require designating a responsible party for compliance and establishing mechanisms for enforcement. Discussions concerning who should
be held responsible for sound levels at concerts have amounted to finger-
pointing in the past. Concert promoters argue that the sound engineer
is the expert who controls sound levels; sound engineers explain that
they merely respond to the wishes of the band members when it comes
to volume; and band members are certain that audience members dictate
the sound levels by shouting "louder" until the volume meets their
approval. Compared to industrial employment settings, where the
employer is the obvious responsible party, concert settings make responsibility for sound levels difficult to determine.

Regulatory legislation would also require a system for enforcement of
the sound-level limitations. Police officers could easily check to ensure
that warning signs are clearly posted, but should we really expect police
officers to be qualified in the use of sophisticated sound pressure level
meters necessary to calculate A-weighted decibel levels at concerts? Who
should bear the added expense of training officers and purchasing sound
measurement equipment? In cities that have numerous performance venues, would police be diverted from more urgent needs to enforce concert
sound levels?

An opposing viewpoint is "let the consumer beware." One might argue that concert goers who decide to stand in front of a painfully loud
sound system for two hours deserve what they get. However, ordinary
concert attenders—youths between the ages of fourteen and seventeen—
may not be well equipped to fully understand the potential hazards of
loud music. Not allowing minors to enter into contractual agreements
without parental consent is a concept based on the assumption that minors may not be mature enough to understand and evaluate promises
made in a contract. As minors mature and reach college age, though,
some may begin to drink alcoholic beverages while listening to music at
clubs and concerts. Alcohol diminishes one's ability to understand things
like warning notices. In addition, persons who have consumed more
than moderate amounts of alcohol may not feel pain that could warn
them of impending hearing damage. The additive effect of immaturity

and alcohol yields a group of individuals who may need more protection from the dangers of loud music than is currently being provided.

In lieu of any federal laws regulating sound levels at concerts, local governments have created noise ordinances to address the problem. Noise level ordinances in California and New York were tested in the courts. Concert promoters, siding with artists, argued that noise ordinances were overly restrictive and violated artists' freedom of expression guaranteed by the First Amendment (Hochman, 1989). Municipal governments argued that the noise levels at concert venues often amounted to disturbing the peace because they affected persons outside the immediate concert area. The U.S. Supreme Court eventually affirmed local governments' right to restrict sound levels. It should be noted, though, that local ordinances were not intended to protect the fragile hearing of concert attenders; they were simply dealing with nuisance sound in the vicinity of concerts.

The "big bass" car stereo phenomenon began in California in the early 1980s and quickly spread to the South, Midwest, and East Coast. Because booming bass frequencies characteristic of highly amplified car systems are not as directional as higher frequencies, low-pitched sounds emanating from these powerful stereo systems invade the aural space on all sides of the vehicle. Noise ordinances affecting car stereos grew as quickly as their amplifiers. California, the first state to pass a noise ordinance restricting car stereos, enacted a law that went into effect on January 1, 1990 (Bishop, 1990). The law makes it illegal to operate a car emitting sounds that can be heard fifty feet away. Although many municipalities have enacted legislation modeled on the California law, none have addressed the damage being done to drivers and passengers of autos with booming stereos.

## PERFORMERS AND LOUD MUSIC

If sound levels for audience members at rock performances can cause hearing loss, then one must wonder what impact loud music has on the performers, who are bombarded by loud music each time they perform. Performers on the concert stage are facing in a different direction than audience members. Because of that, sound engineers have a separate system, the "monitor system," to give the performers an on-stage mix of the concert. The blend of sounds going to the audience, the "house system," is usually very different than what each musician hears on the stage. The monitor system allows each musician to hear different volumes and different proportions of the other musicians at each of their locations.

The standard manner in which musicians hear the monitor mix is through triangular speakers that sit on the floor in front of the performers. These speaker enclosures, or "wedges," are aimed toward the ears of the musicians. If amplification levels are high for a particular wedge, the musician closest to it will be susceptible to hearing loss. A sad phenomenon on stage is volume creep during a concert: If the vocalist asks for more of himself in the monitor, for example, the guitarist might ask for more guitar in his own wedge to overcome the sound of too much vocal. As each person insists on more of himself in the monitors, the on-stage volume can become excessively loud.

In addition to the monitor mix coming through the wedges, other loud sounds are present on the stage. The drum kit played by the drummer contains several percussion instruments that generate some high frequencies at extremely high decibels. The cymbals are particularly dangerous to hearing, especially that of the person playing them. Guitar players often have an amplifier and speaker cabinet on stage directly behind them. The high-frequency, high-decibel output of the guitar cabinet is another potential problem for the ears of everyone in close proximity, especially the guitarist themselves.

Pete Townshend, legendary guitarist for The Who, lives with constant tinnitus and a significant hearing loss from years of playing concerts with his guitar amp cranked to high levels. The band had to hire a second guitarist for their 1989 concert tour so that Townshend could play an acoustic guitar, without much amplification, to protect what hearing he had left. Townshend is not alone: There are many rock musicians who suffer from NIHL. The House Ear Institute, a Los Angeles clinic and research foundation dedicated to solving hearing problems, started an educational program specifically for rock musicians because of their concern for the growing number of professional musicians with hearing loss. A spokesperson for the House Ear Institute's educational outreach program told reporters that "hearing loss for those who make their living in music is getting worse as instruments and pop styles have pushed decibel levels higher and higher" (Streeter, 1999).

Whereas few people are surprised to learn that rock music has the potential to harm musicians' hearing ability, most are shocked when told that symphony orchestra musicians are also susceptible to NIHL. Measurement of sound levels in different locations in the orchestra has indicated that some areas, such as in front of the trumpets, exceed permitted noise levels (Jansson and Karlsson, 1983; Royster, Royster, and Killion, 1991; Kwiatkowski, Schacke, Fuchs, and Silber, 1986). A study of musicians in the Chicago Symphony Orchestra revealed that 52 percent of the performers had "notched audiograms consistent with noise-induced hearing damage" (Royster, Royster, and Killion, 1991). Because unamplified orchestral music gives the illusion of being safer than amplified rock music, classical musicians may actually be at higher risk of NIHL. Educational programs directed at musicians have tended to focus on rock music; as a result, classical musicians are less aware of the potential dangers of their work.

Even participants in school music programs should be aware of potentially hazardous sound levels when performing in bands and orchestras. School officials in Lakewood, Colorado, created a policy that required students to wear earplugs while performing in band. The earplug rule was implemented in 1987, after a music teacher successfully sued the school district because of hearing loss (Crook and Caulfield, 1987). More disturbing data, provided by Judith Montgomery and Sharon Fujikawa, were drawn from studies in the Fountain Valley, California, school district (Montgomery and Fujikawa, 1992; Friend, 1989). The research compared students who studied music to students who did not take part in band or orchestra. Twenty-six percent of high school senior musicians had a hearing loss compared to only 13 percent of nonmusicians.

## PROTECTION FOR PERFORMERS

In order to prevent NIHL in musicians, a two-step program is necessary. First, musicians must be educated about the nature of hearing loss, especially in real-life professional settings for performers. Some organizations have been created to elevate awareness of NIHL in musicians, but not enough musicians, particularly those in nonrock genres and amateur performers, are benefiting from their information (see the list of organizations at the end of this chapter). Next, hearing protection devices should be strongly encouraged whenever sound levels exceed 85 dB in the working environment for musicians. A hearing protection device is something that attenuates (reduces) sound levels so that individuals wearing the devices can be exposed to the potentially harmful sound for longer periods of time than if they were unprotected. Protective devices that are effective in industrial environments are not practical for musicians, however. For example, large bulky "ear-muff" hearing protectors work well in a noisy factory or at a target range, but they are too cumbersome for a singer, guitarist, or violinist, especially in concert settings. Earplugs that fit into the beginning of the ear canal are a more practical solution for musicians.

Performers, who must hear subtle nuances of the music they are playing, have not been satisfied with the types of earplugs that are commonly used in industrial settings (Chasin, 1996; Santucci, 1990). Inexpensive over-the-counter earplugs, like the compressed foam types, do not work well for musicians because they reduce higher frequencies more aggressively than they do middle and lower frequencies. Performers describe the sounds they hear through these earplugs as dull and inarticulate. When using compressed foam earplugs, musicians usually overcome the apparent "dullness" of their own performance by playing louder or by overamplifying upper frequencies. Obviously, either adjustment, in response to the change in sound caused by their protective earplugs, is unacceptable to other performers or the audience.

Fortunately, there are earplugs designed specifically for musicians. Earplugs manufactured by Etymotic Research were the first earplugs to become widely accepted by musicians. Using an acronym from the company name and the attenuation level, the company created the popular ER-15 earplug. This hearing protection device attenuates music and other sounds 15 dB over a very wide frequency spectrum rather than merely in the upper frequencies, as did its predecessors. Other models, such as the ER-25, were developed for higher attenuation levels.

Hearing protection device manufacturers have continued to make design improvements in earplugs. Current models include custom-molded inserts with sophisticated mechanisms that are both aesthetically pleasing and fully functional for performers. Musicians who resist purchasing this newer type of earplug may do so out of ignorance: They have tried older solid devices that don't sound natural. Others may be concerned about the cost of this type of protective device. The obvious response is, "How much would a musician who suffers from NIHL pay to regain their hearing?"

Professional musicians who perform loud amplified music in concerts and clubs also have an alternative to on-stage monitors. Newly developed in-ear monitors easily replace wedge monitors and protect musicians' ears from receiving excessively high levels of sound. The in-ear monitors are a hybrid of hearing protection earplugs and hearing aids. They prevent loud ambient sounds from entering the inner ear but allow the wearer to hear all necessary frequencies in proportion to on-stage performance sound quality.

## PERSONAL LISTENING DEVICES

Sony Corporation introduced the Walkman personal listening device in 1979 (Sony, 2000). Although it was a tremendous success in the marketplace, the Walkman-style portable cassette player has precipitated a great deal of debate over its potential for causing hearing loss. The major concern has been for youths who tend to wear the lightweight earphones for long periods of time at high volume. As the cassette Walkman is being replaced by the compact disc–based Walkman, potential for higher frequencies at greater volumes is of extreme concern to many audiologists.

Several studies attempted to measure the range of volumes at which young people listen to music on portable headphone cassette players. Most of the studies revealed that teenagers turn the volume up to levels

People who wear personal listening devices such as the one shown here should be aware of the potential for noise-induced hearing loss that can occur. Use of the automatic volume limiter is highly recommended in order to prevent volumes from exceeding 89 decibels. (Photograph © Jerry R. Atnip)

as high as 112 dB (League for Hard of Hearing, 1999b). The question of actual hearing damage caused by Walkman-type headphone listening was addressed in numerous studies with varied results. However, a study conducted in 1996 demonstrated significant differences between the hearing ability of people who listen to music on cassette player headphones and those who do not (Meyer-Bisch, 1996). Two years later researchers who conducted a large-scale study involving 1,724 subjects concluded that personal cassette players, even in moderate use, can lead to hearing loss similar to that caused by industrial noise trauma (LePage and Murray, 1998).

The greatest potential for dangerously high volumes occurs in noisy environments such as at work, in traffic, or at athletic events. One study that compared listening levels indicated that test subjects' headphone volumes were greatly elevated in noisy environments (Airo, Olkinuora, and Pekkarinen, 1999). One simple test should guide the use of personal listening devices: If you cannot hear those around you who are speaking at a normal volume, then your music is too loud.

## INDUSTRY RESPONSE TO HEARING LOSS

Some manufacturers, including Sony, have added a switch, an "automatic volume limiter," to their portable listening devices. The limiter is designed to keep the sound level from exceeding 85 dB. The limiter switch is especially helpful when listening to music for extended periods of time, such as during long trips. Unfortunately, many owners of the Walkman-type players do not employ the limiter. Should manufacturers be required to make the limiter active 100 percent of the time? Because OSHA regulations do not apply to leisure listening—only to workplace noise—there are no laws motivating such a move by manufacturers at this time. Should the federal government enact laws that require automatic volume limiters on all personal stereo devices?

Although some manufacturers voluntarily print in the directions for use information about the potential dangers of headphone listening devices, customers probably do not read the warnings. How many people really read all the printed material that accompanies electronic devices? Perhaps warnings should be prominently and permanently displayed on both the player and the headphones. That way, users would be constantly reminded of the potential danger to their hearing from listening at high volumes.

Retailers and manufacturers of automobile sound systems feign concern about consumers' hearing loss while encouraging increased noise levels. An organization called the International Auto Sound Challenge Association (IASCA) coordinates competitive events for car and truck stereo systems. Competitions held in Jackson, Tennessee, in 1999 and sponsored by New Wave Electronics, a retail store, and Kenwood Electronics, a manufacturer of car stereo equipment, included IASCA-sanctioned "dB Drag Racing SPL" competitions. Please note that the winner is determined by the loudest stereo system as measured by sound pressure level (SPL) and no auto racing is involved. The winner, Danny Brittain of Harrison, Arkansas, took top honors with 171.5 dB (Sias, 1999). A glance through the IASCA board of directors reveals a long list of persons affiliated with retail stores and manufacturers of car stereo equipment.

When queried about the potential for damage to contestants' hearing, an IASCA spokesperson provided the following response: "Any time you are around a loud noise, it is always best to protect yourself in one way or another. When a competitor sits in his vehicle and cranks up for SPL testing, it is always suggested (and sometimes required) that he wear hearing protection. IASCA endorses ear-muff [sic] style protection, much like gun enthusiasts use at the shooting range. These cover the ears and provide adequate muffling to protect your hearing. Nobody wants to go deaf from good music, but if you've got a kickin' system, there's no reason not to let the rest of the town know it" (IASCA, 2000). Although ear-muff style hearing protectors are effective for preventing hearing loss in loud environments, one has to question if owners of "kickin' systems" really wear them while traveling in their cars. When was the last time you saw the driver of a car with a booming sound system wearing hearing protectors?

The live entertainment industry may begin paying more attention to sound levels if the pattern of successful lawsuits by people suffering from NIHL continues. A man who attended a U2 concert was able to demonstrate in court that the Irish band's loud volumes were the cause of his NIHL. Although the 1997 decision to award the plaintiff $35,000 for his hearing loss was handed down in a French court, it established a model for NIHL sufferers to follow on this side of the Atlantic (Gieske, 1997). Another lawsuit, one that may have a precedent-setting effect on the entire music industry, was filed by Peter Jeffrey, a Princeton University music professor, in 1999 (Morrison, 1999). Jeffrey attended a Smashing Pumpkins concert for approximately twenty minutes in search of his son. In the short time he was in the venue, the professor alleges he suffered a hearing loss in spite of the earplugs he was wearing. What makes this an unusual case is the list of defendants: The Smashing Pumpkins, Virgin Records (the band's label), the manufacturer of the earplugs, and the city of New Haven, Connecticut, where the concert was held. This case could help determine in the courts who is ultimately responsible for NIHL from concerts.

Rock bands often feel that they are in a Catch-22. If they lower the volume of their performance, they may be labeled "wimps" and lose audience members. If they crank the volume in order to generate excitement in the audience, they risk causing hearing loss in audience members. Motley Crue, a loud heavy metal band that has been sued more than once by fans alleging hearing damage from their performances, may have a solution to this paradoxical situation: They began selling earplugs at their concerts in 1994 (Vercammen, 1994). Their novel idea serves several purposes. First, it alerts audience members to the need for hearing protection, making it more difficult for someone to win a hearing loss lawsuit against the band. Second, it genuinely helps prevent hearing loss while the band plays at high decibel levels. Third, the earplugs sell for $3 a pair—a substantial markup that generates additional income for Motley Crue.

Former Beatle Paul McCartney sparked a bit of controversy when he took a stand against NIHL research that uses animals as subjects. McCartney spoke out against experiments at the University of California,

San Francisco, that used monkeys. The researchers exposed six monkeys to high-frequency high-decibel music after administering anesthesia to the monkeys. The sound levels were similar to those experienced by rock concert audiences and were intended to investigate the nature of NIHL. McCartney told reporters, "It's a gross intrusion into the rights of harmless creatures. Isn't it about time that we as a society started to show some respect to innocent animals?" (Eldredge, 1998). Ironically, the music of the Beatles and Wings, bands in which McCartney performed, may have subjected innocent teenagers to the same sound levels used on the monkeys in the experiments.

Concert attenders, personal listening device users, boom bass auto owners, and musicians need to understand that hearing loss is preventable. Once it occurs, though, it is irreversible and permanent. Warnings about potential causes of hearing loss are being offered by manufacturers, health care practitioners, and nonprofit organizations. Unfortunately, these warnings are falling on deaf ears.

## TOPICS FOR DISCUSSION

1. Why do you think many young people ignore the warnings on personal stereo listening devices and play music at high levels? Do you think they would continue to do so if they were aware of the potential for hearing loss?

2. Should the federal government create laws to regulate how loud music at concerts can be, or should the level of sound be left to the discretion of audience members?

3. Why do you think symphony orchestra musicians do not use hearing protection? Do you think they assume that unamplified classical music does not have the potential for damaging one's hearing?

4. Do you think manufacturers of powerful car stereo equipment are irresponsible in making equipment that is potentially hazardous to hearing? Should consumers who purchase amplified sound systems be warned about the potential harm these systems can cause one's hearing?

5. Who should be held responsible for NIHL in people who frequent dance clubs: the club owner, the DJ who plays music, or the person who installed the sound system? Should employees and customers be warned about the potential for NIHL in small venues? Should dance club employees be required to have their hearing checked periodically?

## REFERENCES AND RESOURCES

### Legal Cases and Laws

Occupational Safety and Health Administration (OSHA) (1983). Occupational Noise Exposure; Hearing Conservation Amendment. *Fed. Regist.* 48 (46), 9738-9783.

### Books and Pamphlets

American Academy of Otolaryngology—Head and Neck Surgery (1997). *Noise, Ears and Hearing Protection.* Alexandria, VA: American Academy of Oto-laryngology—Head and Neck Surgery. (A pamphlet that explains the various forms of ear and hearing protection.)

Axelsson, Alf, and Hans M. Borchgrevink, eds., with Roger P. Hamernik (1996). *Scientific Basis of Noise-Induced Hearing Loss.* New York: Thieme Medical Publications. (A collection of thirty-six papers presented at the Fifth International Symposium on Effects of Noise on Hearing in Sweden, May 1994).

Babisch, W., and H. Ising (1994). Music Listening Habits in Adolescents. *Z. Larmbekampf,* 1994, 41/4 (91–97). (A major study of dance club and disco listening habits of 10,000 teenagers.)

Bess, Fred H., and Larry E. Humes (1990). *Audiology: The Fundamentals.* Baltimore, MD: Williams and Wilkins. (As the name implies, this book presents the nature of sound and hearing in humans.)

Chasin, Marshall (1996). *Musicians and the Prevention of Hearing Loss.* San Diego, CA: Singular Publishing Group. (This is the most authoritative source for information about the effects of loud music on performers' hearing. It discusses clinical assessment of hearing loss and prevention techniques.)

Kavaler, Lucy (1978). *The Dangers of Noise.* New York: Thomas Y. Crowell. (Although this is intended for young readers, it presents an excellent overview of how noise can harm one's hearing.)

League for the Hard of Hearing (1999a). *Noise: Double Trouble.* New York: League for the Hard of Hearing. (A brief, but fact-filled, booklet about how to know when noise is too loud and what to do to protect your hearing.)

League for the Hard of Hearing (1999b). *Noise and Music Fact Sheet.* New York: League for the Hard of Hearing. (The league has synthesized some of the most pertinent research regarding NIHL related to music in this short summary. It can be accessed through the league's website.)

League for the Hard of Hearing (1999c). *Personal Stereo Systems and Hearing Fact Sheet.* New York: League for the Hard of Hearing. (This fact sheet offers some excellent advice on steps one can take to prevent hearing loss from use of personal listening devices. It can be accessed through the league's website.)

Lipscomb, David M., ed. (1988). *Hearing Conservation in Industry, Schools and the Military.* Boston, MA: Little, Brown and Company. (A collection of articles by some of the top audiologists, speech pathologists, and acoustical engineers in the country. This work contains thorough explanations of governmental regulations concerning noise levels in the workplace.)

National Institute on Deafness and Other Communication Disorders (1999). *Noise-Induced Hearing Loss*, NIDCD Fact Sheet. (An easily understood overview of damage to hearing from loud noise and music.)

## Magazines, Journals, and Newspapers

Airo, Erkko, Pekka Olkinuora, and Jussi Pekkarinen (1999). Listening to Music with Earphones: A Noise Exposure Assessment. *Hearnet*, the website of H.E.A.R., www.hearnet.com. (A brief summary of research sponsored by the Finnish Consumer Council.)

Bishop, Katherine (1990, January 17). Laws Aim to Turn Off Ear-Splitting "Boom" Cars. *New York Times*, p. A16, col. 2, National Desk. (A description of noise ordinances that affect car stereos.)

Brookhouser, P. E. (1994). Prevention of Noise-Induced Hearing Loss. *Preventative Medicine* 23, no. 5 (September 1994): 665–669. (A study that concluded NIHL could be prevented, but the general public is not using protection that is readily available.)

Crook, David, and Deborah Caulfield (1987, December 10). Morning Report: Music. *Los Angeles Times*, Calendar, part 6, p. 2, col. 2. (A public school band teacher filed a lawsuit because he alleged his hearing loss was attributable to the band room acoustics.)

Drucker, Trudy (1989). What's That I Hear? Far Too Much. *New York Times*, sec. 12NJ, p. 34, col. 2; New Jersey Weekly Desk. (Drucker discusses the Supreme Court decision to uphold New York's right to regulate volume levels at concerts.)

Eldredge, Richard L. (1998). Charismatic Canine "Air Bud" Dug Up One of the City's.... *Atlanta Journal and Constitution*, Features, p. 2D. (This contains a quotation from Paul McCartney about NIHL research involving monkeys.)

Fine, Marshall (1989, June 30). Pete Townshend and the Who. *Gannett News Service*. (Townshend suffered serious hearing loss from years of playing lead guitar in the Who.)

Friend, Tim (1989, November 13). A Downside to School Band Practice. *USA Today*. (A study by Judith Montgomery in Fountain Valley, California, indicated that school band programs might contribute to hearing loss in students.)

Gieske, Tony (1997). Legal Briefs. *The Hollywood Reporter*. (This article gives a very brief overview of the U2 lawsuit that awarded $35,000 to a man who attended a concert where he suffered NIHL.)

Gower, Timothy (1998, June 21). Checkups: Feel the Burn, Don't Hear It. *New York Times*, sec. 15, p. 3, col. 1, Women's Health. (A story about one woman's fight against loud music in health clubs.)

Gunderson, E., J. Moline, and P. Catalano (1997). Risks of Developing Noise-Induced Hearing Loss in Employees of Urban Music Clubs. *American Journal of Industrial Medicine* 31, no. 1 (1997): 75–79. (A study of nonmusicians who work in clubs that have loud music.)

Hearnet (2000, January 28). Small Band Hearing Damage. H.E.A.R.: www. hearnet.com/text/articlesmallband.html. (This Hearnet article explains how low-watt amplifiers in small venues can cause hearing loss.)

Hochman, Steve (1989, March 6). Putting a Lid on Loud Music? *Los Angeles Times,* part 6, p. 1.

House, John (August 8, 1996). Sound Advice for Better Hearing. *Business Wire,* Medical/Health. (The House Ear Institute, established by Dr. John House over fifty years ago, is one of the foremost clinics and research centers for hearing loss. This brief press release gives practical advice for how to prevent damage to one's hearing.)

Ising, H., J. Hanel, M. Pilgramm, M. Babisch, and A. Lindthammer (1994). Risk of Hearing Loss Caused by Listening to Music Via Headphones. Berlin, Germany: Umweltbundsambt, Institut fur Wasser, *HNO* 42, no. 12 (1994): 764–768.

Jansson, E., and K. Karlsson (1983). Sound Levels Recorded within the Symphony Orchestra and Risk Criteria for Hearing Loss. *Scandinavian Audiology* 12, no. 3 (1983): 215–221. (Investigators measured sound levels in various sections of the orchestra.)

Jekel, J. F. (1996). Rainbow Reviews VII: Recent Publications of the National Center for Health Statistics. *Journal of Clinical Epidemiology* 49, no. 7 (1996): 765–768. (A review of research literature pertaining to hearing loss from music.)

Johnson, Eric Daniel (1993). Sounds of Silence for the Walkman Generation: Rock Concerts and Noise-Induced Hearing Loss. *Indiana Law Journal* 68, no. 1011 (summer 1993). (An extremely comprehensive look at legal issues surrounding noise-induced hearing loss.)

Kwiatkowski, A., G. Schacke, A. Fuchs, and Ph. Silber (1986). Sound Pressure Level Measured in the Orchestra Pit of an Opera House. *Zentralbl Aarbeitsmed Arbeitssch Prophyl Ergonomie* 36, no. 3 (1986): 58–64. (A study that concludes sound levels in orchestra pits cannot be controlled.)

LePage, Eric L., and Narelle M. Murray (1998). Latent Cochlear Damage in Personal Stereo Users: A Study Based on Click-Evoked Otoacoustic Emissions. *Medical Journal of Australia* 169 (1998): 588–592. (An abstract of research into hearing damage caused by personal listening devices.)

Lollar, Michael (1997, October 9). Turn On, Turn Up: Rock-and-Walkman Generations Face Earlier Hearing Loss. *The Commercial Appeal (Memphis, TN),* Appeal, p. C1. (A disturbing article about hearing loss from use of personal listening devices and from other sources of loud music.)

Maugh II, Thomas H. (1998, February 26). Science File: An Exploration of Issues and Trends Affecting Science, Medicine and the Environment. *Los Angeles Times,* p. B2.

McBride, D., et al. (1992). Noise and the Classical Musician. *Birmingham Medical Journal,* 305, no. 6868 (1992): 1561–1563. (A study of sound levels generated by different orchestral instruments.)

Meyer-Bisch, C. (1996). Epidemiological Evaluation of Hearing Damage Related to Strongly Amplified Music (Personal Cassette Players, Discotheques, Rock Concerts): A High-Definition Audiometric Survey on 1,364 Subjects. *Audiology* 35 (1996): 121–142.

Montgomery, Judith, and Sharon Fujikawa (1992). Hearing Thresholds of Students in the Second, Eighth and Twelfth Grades. *Language, Speech and Hearing Services SCHS* 23, no. 61, 62.

Mori, T. (1985). Effects of Recorded Music on Hearing Loss among Young Workers in a Shipyard. *International Arch. of Occupational Health* 56, no. 2 (1985): 91–97. (An interesting study of shipyard workers who listened to recorded music versus those who did not.)

Morrison, Richard (1999). And Now, the Prime Minister of Australia. *The Times (London)*, Features. (This article describes a lawsuit by a Princeton professor against the Smashing Pumpkins.)

Murray, Ian (1999, August 3). Clubbers Risk Losing the Sound of Silence. *The Times (London)*, Home News. (An alarming article that predicts premature hearing loss in people who frequent dance clubs.)

Newman, Melinda (1999, September 18). Beck Bids V2 Fond Adieu. . . . *Billboard*, The Beat. (Dan Beck resigned as president of V2 Records because of his hearing loss. Beck started a scholarship fund for students with hearing loss.)

O'Neill, Catherine (1991, July 30). Turn Down the Volume. *Washington Post*, Health, p. Z14. (A description of the House Select Committee on Children, Youth and Families hearings about NIHL.)

O'Neill, Ann W. (1998, January 11). The Court Files/Ann W. O'Neill; No Foundation to Cosmetics Lawsuit. . . . *Los Angeles Times*, Metro, p. B1, Metro Desk. (A news brief about a sound engineer's lawsuit against funk musician George Clinton.)

Palin, S. L. (1994). Does Classical Music Damage the Hearing of Musicians? A Review of Literature. *Occupational Medicine* 44, no. 3 (1994): 130–136. (The author reviewed studies from over 150 years of research.)

*PR Newswire* (1999, March 11). Music to Our Ears Often Leads to Hearing Loss in Musicians. (A news release that describes the Smashing Pumpkins lawsuit over damage to their hearing from loud sound levels.)

Royster, J. D., L. H. Royster, and M. C. Killion (1991). Sound Exposures and Hearing Thresholds of Symphony Orchestra Musicians. *Journal of the Acoustical Society of America* 89, no. 6 (June 1991): 2793–2803. (A study of hearing loss in Chicago Symphony Orchestra performers.)

Santucci, Michael (1990). Musicians Can Protect Their Hearing. *Medical Problems of Performing Artists* 5 (1990): 136–138. (An easily readable article that explains how to measure sound levels in performance environments and types of hearing protection for musicians.)

Sias, Melody (1999). Boffo Sound All Around. . . . *The Commercial Appeal (Memphis)*, Appeal, p. C1. (This journalist describes the bass boom car stereo craze and competitions.)

Sony Corporation (2000). Milestones in Product Development, www.world. sony.com/History/sonyhistory.html. (Sony Corporation offers extensive historical information at this website. The Walkman headphone stereo is identified under the milestones section.)

Streeter, Kurt (1999, January 31). Sound Advice May Be Falling on Deaf Ears. *Los Angeles Times*, Metro, p. B3. (An article about the House Ear Institute educational programs for musicians.)

Tomioka, S. (1982). Two Cases of Bilateral Hearing Loss Due to Exposure to Rock-and-Roll Music. *Otolaryngology (Tokyo, Japan)* 54, no. 12 (1982): (1005–1011). (This article gives an account of two teenagers who suffered serious hearing loss after attending a rock concert.)

Turunen-Rise, I., G. Flottorp, and O. Trete (1991). A Study of the Possibility of Acquiring Noise-Induced Hearing Loss by the Use of Personal Cassette Players (Walkman). *Scandinavian Audiological Supplement* 20, no. 34 (1991): 133–144. (A study of potential danger from Walkman type listening devices.)

Vercammen, Paul (1994, October 11). Ear Protection Available Now to Loud Concert–Goers. *Showbiz Today*, CNN transcript 644–5. (A news show transcript that describes lawsuits by fans who have been harmed by loud music at rock concerts.)

Verna, Paul (1995, January 7). A&M Fosters Hearing Safety. . . . *Billboard*, Pro Audio, p. 96. (A&M recording studios worked with California's OSHA officials to develop a model program for protecting the hearing of employees.)

Virginia Merrill Bloedel Hearing Research Center and the Department of Otolaryngology–Head and Neck Surgery, University of Washington School of Medicine (1998). Noise-Induced Hearing Loss in Young Adults: The role of Personal Listening Devices and Other Sources of Leisure Noise. *Laryngoscope* 108, no. 12 (December 1998): 1832–1839. (A study that was inconclusive regarding the use of Walkman-type listening devices and hearing safety.)

Yonke, David (1986, April 11). High Volume. . . . *State Journal-Register (Springfield Illinois)*, Entertainment, p. 19. (The author provides an excellent overview of hearing loss and details how earplugs are being used by bands like Korn.)

## Organizations to Contact

American Academy of Audiology
8201 Greensboro Drive, Suite 300
McLean, VA 22102
Phone: 1–800-AAA-2336
web: www.audiology.org
This organization is a good source for locating a qualified audiologist for hearing testing.

American Tinnitus Association
P.O. Box 5
Portland, OR 97207
Phone: 1–800–634–8978
web: www.ata.org
This organization will provide information regarding diagnosis and treatment of tinnitus.

Hearing Education and Awareness for Rockers (H.E.A.R.)
50 Oak Street, Room 101

San Francisco, CA 94102
Phone: 1–415–432-EARS
e-mail: hear@hearnet.com
web: www.hearnet.com
This organization provides musicians with information, hearing protection
   devices, and seminars about hearing loss. It also presents concerts to
   raise funds for the organization.

House Ear Institute
2100 West Third Street
Los Angeles, CA 90057
Phone: (213) 483–9930
web: www.hei.org
The House Institute and the House Clinic were established in 1946 by
   Howard P. House, M.D. The institute is staffed by 120 researchers dedicated to the advancement of otologic research. The accompanying clinic
   diagnoses and treats all forms of hearing loss.

League for the Hard of Hearing
71 West 23rd Street
New York, NY 10010
The league offers many programs and publications that assist individuals
   with hearing loss or deafness cope with their challenges.

National Information Center on Deafness
Gallaudet University
800 Florida Avenue, NE
Washington, DC 20002–3695
Gallaudet University serves deaf students and individuals wishing to work
   with the deaf. It has the largest collection of resources about hearing loss
   and deafness available anywhere. The National Information Center on
   Deafness is located on the campus of Gallaudet University.

### Web Sites

www.iasca.com
International Auto Sound Challenge Association (IASCA)
The IASCA is an organization that sanctions competition among owners
   of car stereos.

www.osha.gov/
Occupational Safety and Health Administration (OSHA)
OSHA provides a wealth of information about hearing conservation in this
   web site. It has links to research articles about measurement of sound
   levels in workplace environments.

# Index

## About the Authors

RICHARD D. BARNET is a Professor in the Department of the Recording Industry at Middle Tennessee State University. He has worked in various positions in the music industry, including artist management, booking, concert promotion, television, and live show music production, performance, and conducting. He is a former officer of the Music and Entertainment Industry Educator's Association and a gubernatorial appointee to the Tennessee Film, Entertainment, and Music Advisory Council as well as a member of the National Academy of Recording Arts and Sciences.

LARRY L. BURRISS is a Professor of Journalism at Middle Tennessee State University. He served as Director of the School of Journalism and was the first director of its graduate program. Burriss has published extensively on First Amendment issues and has won numerous awards, including the Tennessee Associated Press Radio award, for his written and broadcast commentaries.

780
BAR

Barnet, Richard D.,
1949-

Controversies of the
music industry.

$45.00

| | | DATE | | |
|---|---|---|---|---|
| | | | | |
| | | | | |
| | | | | |
| | | | | |
| | | | | |
| | | | | |
| | | | | |
| | | | | |
| | | | | |
| | | | | |
| | | | | |